WOMEN
A Feminist List edited by

Editorial Advisory Group

Phillida Bunckle, *Victoria University, Wellington, New Zealand;* Miriam
David, *Polytechnic of the South Bank;* Leonore Davidoff, *University of
Essex;* Janet Finch, *University of Lancaster;* Jalna Hanmer, *University of
Bradford;* Beverley Kingston, *University of New South Wales, Australia;*
Hilary Land, *University of Bristol;* Diana Leonard, *University of London
Institute of Education;* Suan Londsdale, *Polytechnic of the South Bank;*
Jean O'Barr, *Duke University, North Caroline, USA;* Arlene Tigar
McLaren, *Simon Fraser University, British Columbia, Canada;* Jill Roe,
Macquarie University, Australia; Hilary Rose, *University of Bradford;*
Susan Sellars, *Centre D'Etudes Feminines, Universite de Paris;* Pat
Thane, *Goldsmiths' College, University of London;* Clare Ungerson,
University of Kent at Canterbury; Judy Walkowitz, *Rutgers University,
New Jersey, USA.*

The last 20 years have seen an explosion of publishing by, about and for
women. This new list is designed to make a particular contribution to
this continuing process by commissioning and publishing books which
consolidate and advance feminist research and debate in key areas in a
form suitable for students, academics and researchers but also accessible
to a broader general readership.

As far as possible, books will adopt an international perspective
incorporating comparative material from a range of countries where
this is illuminating. Above all they will be interdisciplinary, aiming to
put women's studies and feminist discussion firmly on the agenda in
subject-areas as disparate as law, literature, art and social policy.

WOMEN IN SOCIETY
A Feminist List edited by
Jo Campling

Published

Christy Adair **Women and Dance: sylphs and sirens**
Sheila Allen and Carol Wolkowitz **Homeworking: myths and realities**
Niamh Baker **Happily Ever After? Women's fiction in post-war Britain**
Ros Ballaster, Margaret Beetham, Elizabeth Frazer and Sandra Hebron **Women's Worlds: ideology, femininity and the woman's magazine**
Jenny Beale **Women in Ireland: voices of change**
Jennifer Breen **In Her Own Write: Twentieth-century women's fiction**
Valerie Bryson **Feminist Political Theory: an introduction**
Ruth Carter and Gill Kirkup **Women in Engineering**
Joan Chandler **Women without Husbands: an exploration of the margins of marriage**
Angela Coyle and Jane Skinner **Women and Work: positive action for change**
Gillian Dalley **Ideologies of Caring: rethinking community and collectivism**
Leonore Davidoff and Belinda Westover (editors) **Our Work, Our Lives, Our Words: women's history and women's work**
Emily Driver and Audrey Droisen (*editors*) **Child Sexual Abuse: a feminist reader**
Elizabeth Ettorre **Women and Substance Use**
Lesley Ferris **Acting Women: Images of women in theatre**
Diana Gittins **The Family in Question: changing households and familiar ideologies**
Eileen Green, Diana Woodward and Sandra Hebron **Women's Leisure, What Leisure?**
Tuula Gordon **Feminist Mothers**
Frances Heidensohn **Women and Crime**
Ursula King **Women and Spirituality: voices of protest and promise**
Muthoni Likimani (*Introductory Essay by Jean O'Barr*) **Passbook Number F.47927: women and Mau Mau in Keyna**
Jo Little, Linda Peake and Pat Richardson (*editors*) **Women in Cities: gender and the urban environment**
Susan Lonsdale **Women and Disability**
Sharon Macdonald, Pat Holden and Shirley Ardener (*editors*) **Images of Women in Peace and War: cross-cultural and historical perspectives**
Mavis Maclean **Surviving Divorce: women's resources after separation**
Shelley Pennington and Belinda Westover **A Hidden Workforce: homeworkers in England, 1850–1985**
Vicky Randall **Women and Politics: an international perspective** (2nd edn)
Diane Richardson **Women, Motherhood and Childrearing**
Rosemary Ridd and Helen Callaway (*editors*) **Caught up in p. + Conflict: women's response to political strife**
Susan Sellers **Language and Sexual Difference: feminist writing in France**
Patricia Spallone **Beyond Conception: the new politics of reproduction**
Taking Liberties **Collective Learning the Hard Way: women's oppression and men's education**
Clare Ungerson (*editor*) **Women and Social Policy: a reader**
Kitty Warnock **Land Before Honour: Palestinian women in the Occupied Territories**
Annie Woodhouse **Fantastic Women: sex, gender and transvestism**

Forthcoming

Eileen Aird and Judy Lown **Education for Autonomy: processes of change in women's education**
Maria Brenton **Women and Old Age**
Joan Busfield **Women and Mental Health**
Tuula Gordon **Single Women**
Frances Gray **Women and Laughter**
Annie Hudson **Troublesome Girls: adolescence, femininity and the state**
Ruth Lister **Women and Citizenship**

Acting Women

Images of Women in Theatre

Lesley Ferris

MACMILLAN

First published 1990 by
THE MACMILLAN PRESS LTD
Houndmills, Basingstoke, Hampshire RG21 2XS
and London
Companies and representatives
throughout the world

ISBN 0–333–43290–8 hardcover
ISBN 0–333–42391–6 paperback

A catalogue record for this book is available
from the British Library.

Printed in Hong Kong

Reprinted 1992

Series Standing Order
If you would like to receive future titles in this series as they are
published, you can make use of our standing order facility. To place a
standing order please contact your bookseller or, in case of difficulty,
write to us at the address below with your name and address and the
name of the series. Please state with which title you wish to begin your
standing order. (If you live outside the United Kingdom we may not
have the rights for your area, in which case we will forward your order
to the publisher concerned.)

Customer Services Department, Macmillan Distribution Ltd
Houndmills, Basingstoke, Hampshire RG21 2XS, England

This book is dedicated to my daughters,

Amie Cordelia and Phoebe Rosalind

'Men and women perform. Figures of men and women dance, walk, sing, and talk in front of me. They are lit, while I'm in darkness; they are mobile, while I'm still. I focus on them, and their images enter my brain.

I'm a little girl, and therefore especially interested in the women. Mommy, I want to say, Mommy, why is she wearing so few clothes/ why is she laughing at that man/why is she kissing him/why is he killing her. Mommy, will I be like that when I grow up. But I don't ask. Sitting in darkness, I peer at the lit moving images.'

Martha Roth, 1983

'Finally, women. Reflect on the whole history of women: do they not have to be first of all and above all else actresses? . . . finally, love them – let yourself be "hypnotized by them"! What is always the end result? That they "put on something" even when they take off everything.

Woman is so artistic.'

Friedrich Nietzsche, *The Gay Science*, 1881

Contents

Preface

Every book has another story behind it; an old story, hidden and buried in time, untold because of apparent unimportance. But now I make the connection. At thirteen I am cast in a boy's role in a school play. There aren't enough boys who want to act, so I audition and get the part. It is the best part in the play. Ten years later in a graduate theatre arts department I discuss my career plans with a professor. When I tell him I intend to be a theatre director, he sternly shakes his head and advises me that costume design or children's theatre would be better for me, since I am a woman. Now I make the connection.

This book developed in more recent years from a course I devised and taught called 'Women and Performance'. Many people helped, encouraged and facilitated my work and research, and deserve my thanks and gratitude, for without such assistance the book would never have reached fruition.

My thanks to my parents, William and Mary Ferris, who spent endless hours driving me to play rehearsals many years ago and who have supported and aided my research in America. Thanks are also due

— to my students, who have in many ways been the source of motivation by asking so many questions;

— to those members of staff in the School of Drama and the BA Performance Arts course at Middlesex Polytechnic who supported my work and made possible my sabbatical leave;

— to Janet Goodridge, for her knowledge and expert advice in relation to women and dance;

— to Martha Roth, for her vigilant spirit of inquiry and outrage at injustice;

— to the Center for Advanced Feminist Studies at the University of Minnesota and At The Foot of the Mountain Theatre Company, who co-sponsored my talk on 'Acting Women';

— to Rena Fraticelli, whose expert advice and experience in theatre was greatly appreciated;
— to Dick Barker who inspired me with his own vision of Homer's Greece;
— to Rachel Morgan, whose helpful suggestions as librarian at Ivy House, Middlesex Polytechnic, saved me many unnecessary hours of book hunting;
— to Maggie Gee and Philomena Muinzer, who from their different perspectives offered expert suggestions, editorial criticism and support;
— to Ziona Orr, Daniela Toneatto, Franca Busso, Vera Putelli, Rosa Rius-Gomez, and Ester Turro, who provided an essential foundation of childcare which made it possible for me to write and research;
— to Jo Campling's humour, good will and editorial alertness, who having witnessed a 'member of the public' buying a ticket for the first Women in Society book launch, ended by commissioning her to write this book;
— and last, but hardly least, to my husband, Brian Rotman, whose in-house energy and editorial intelligence were invaluable.

LESLEY FERRIS

Prologue

Nine years ago, after the birth of my first daughter, I felt impelled to write a script for three women. A particular image haunted me, an image that fused the theatrical practice of auditioning with the old social prejudice that women are essentially deceivers, dissemblers, playactors. The image took concrete theatrical shape: a woman enters a darkened stage, a whistle blows, the spotlight flashes on, before the unseen judges she auditions with episodes, events, personal moments from her life. Startling questions unfolded in performance about the links between theatre and women. If you are a woman, where is the boundary between playacting and the 'self'? Don't society and culture condition women to internalise a means for survival which centres on auditioning, dressing up, wearing costume? If there appear to be connections between the stage and women, how did this come to pass when women were forbidden to perform for centuries?

This book delves into many of those unanswered questions of nine years ago and focuses on the revelation that beyond the literary analysis of texts it is *performance* that offers a key to understanding the social construction of gender as well as the ambiguous position of women in theatre. The three-dimensional, here-and-now quality of live performance creates problems for historians because of the very impermanence and fleeting transitoriness of the supercharged experiential moments known to its participants. I wanted to re-imagine those moments when men were the sole purveyors of theatre, and to re-view those early, precarious instants when the first women acted. I wanted to re-think the historians' favoured position of judging and evaluating theatre history from the text. Part of such an inquiry involves questioning and challenging conventional historical viewpoints which for the most part have only considered the role of women in theatre peripherally or ignored it altogether. As Lisa Jardine (1983) points out in her book, *Still Harping on Daughters*,

> Every schoolchild knows that there were no women actors on the Elizabethan stage; the female parts were taken by young male actors. But every schoolchild also learns that this fact is of little consequence for the twentieth-century reader of Shakespeare's plays. Because the taking of female parts by boys was universal and commonplace, we are told, it was accepted as 'verisimilitude' by the Elizabethan audience, who simply disregarded it, as we would disregard the creaking of stage scenery and accept the backcloth forest as 'real' for the duration of the play.(p. 9)

The Shakespearean canon itself is a major example of academics' privileging of the written text over its imagined performance, where generations of literary critics argue vagaries of punctuated form from one folio to the next. Significantly, recent feminist criticism has initiated a vital discussion centred on the leap from the page to the stage, where the circuit of actors and spectators takes precedence over the analysis of the written word. This book extends and pursues such debate with a two-fold purpose informing the first half of my study: to examine the theatrical convention of men playing women's roles and to scrutinise the social, cultural and theatrical changes that occurred when women were subsequently allowed to play their own roles.

Part I of the book, 'Theatre History and the Sign of the Female', surveys a range of historical material which significantly reveals that the absence of women in theatre created the notion of woman as a sign, a symbolic object manipulated and controlled artistically by male playwrights and male actors. When women begin to act for the first time another discovery reveals itself: far from being credited with artistic invention, skill or talent, actresses merely *play themselves*, a patriarchal premise that conveniently and skilfully removes women from any possibility of cultural creativity.

My starting point in Chapter 1, 'The power of women, the gender enigma in Renaissance England', is unquestionably the English Renaissance, because here, in its theatre productions, definitions of gender were both enforced and questioned and certainly 'played' upon variously, not only in dramatic texts where sexual disguise both regulated and effected machinations of plot, but in the theatrical and social convention of all-male casts. The changing position of women during this period has recently engendered much literary and historical debate. As Phyllis Rackin (1987) has pointed out, contemporary writers often arrive at contradictory and opposite conclusions in spite of the fact that they have studied similar material.[1] So although the historical evidence evades a definitive interpretation, both the abundance of material and the intensity of much of its sentiment reflect a major social and cultural conflict – a provocative dissonance between competing ideologies which centre on an obsessional fascination with cross-dressing. This charged topic involved opponents and supporters across a wide spectrum from anonymous pamphlet writers, playwrights and clergymen, to the monarchy itself.

In Chapter 2, 'The Greeks, cross-dressing and the wily phallus', the roots of one-sided theatrical cross-dressing are examined in the exclusively male theatre of classical Greece, where the source of much comic invention relies on men dressing as women. In particular I explore Aristophanes' script, *The Women Celebrating the Thesmophoria*, which relies on men-dressing-as-women throughout its narrative structure while simultaneously providing its female characters with a theatrical grievance: that playwrights aesthetically misrepresent women on stage. This script simultaneously demonstrates the creation of the theatrical sign 'woman' and exemplifies the way in which male playwrights rely on list-making to define women.

The following chapter, 'Historical precedents: woman unmasked', briefly surveys the position of women in theatre from the Romans through medieval theatrical practice, and focuses on the subsequent development of the professional actress in Italian comedy. *Commedia del'arte*, an improvised theatrical form relying on archetypal masked characters for its comic impetus, provides a fascinating clue to the patriarchal assumptions of theatrical creativity; for in this theatrical practice, which both permitted and encouraged women to perform, all female characters were unmasked.

Chapter 4, 'Goethe, Goldoni, and woman-hating', looks at three bastions of male theatrical power which either maintained or re-instituted all-male casting: the boys' companies of England, Jesuit drama on the continent, and the religious ban on women actresses enforced in the papal states of Rome. The chapter offers a particularly relevant document for scrutiny, Goethe's essay, 'Women's parts played by men in the Roman theatre', while simultaneously exploring the Goldoni text which prompted the essay, *La Locandiera*.

The fifth chapter, 'Masques and masking', investigates the royal performances of pre-revolutionary England, when English queens began to perform for the first time, and the post-revolutionary innovation of the Restoration actress. This chapter concludes an argument I begin in Chapter 3 and continue in Chapter 4: that the notion of the female 'self' permeates all discussion about women performing and that it is an assumption that virtually and conveniently removes women from the source of cultural creativity.

In Part II of the book, 'Archetypal Images of Women in Theatre', I take up the question of the legacy of male-generated Western theatre by examining some of the major female images, born, like Athena, fully developed from their 'fathers'' heads to play out again and again their fictional existences on the stages of Europe and America. The first of these is considered in Chapter 6, 'The penitent whore'. The chapter examines the early theatrical representations of the prostitute and her link with the Catholic Church. In the nineteenth century this image became a secular one with the popularity of the novel/play *La Dame aux Camélias* by Alexandre Dumas fils.

In Chapter 7, 'The speechless heroine', I explore the patriarchal ideal of the silent woman through Ben Jonson's play *Epicoene, The Silent Woman* and Colley Cibber's *The Careless Husband*, and by considering the impact of the Romantic ballerina in the nineteenth century.

Chapter 8 scrutinises a female image which threatens the security of the patriarchy, 'The wilful woman'. Here Clytaemnestra, the Duchess of Malfi, Miss Julie, and Medea are united by their sexual transgressions: they have acted autonomously by choosing their own sexual partners. The public stage provides a didactic platform in which the punishments for this crime can be enacted.

The next chapter looks at a particularly American image, 'The golden girl', which developed out of the penchant for child performers during the California gold rush. I explore David Belasco's *The Girl from the Golden West* and the career of the American comedienne Lotta Crabtree as the major source for this image.

Just as my starting point was the evaluation of men playing women's roles in both the English Renaissance and classical Greek comedy, my ending in the final chapter, 'Women acting men' moves full circle to examine women playing male roles both on the stage in theatrical costume and off the stage in social disguise. In distinguishing the gross lack of symmetry between men-acting-women and women-acting-men, an imbalance where women seek freedom through male dress and men achieve aesthetic creativity through acting women, I locate the perpetuation of patriarchal image-making in the cross-dressed actor or actress.

Where can all this historical revision lead us? How can we, as women in theatre, intervene successfully in this art form whose very impetus and invention arise from an entirely masculine pursuit of aesthetic representation? I am reminded of a conversation I had a few years ago with Martha Boesing, the artistic director for many years of the At the Foot of the Mountain Theatre collective in Minneapolis. When I told her that the first actresses were not considered as artistic creators but merely as playing themselves, she stared at me with troubled wonder. 'Where, then,' she asked, 'does that leave us? Our entire impulse toward theatrical creativity was a painful, tortuous path toward revealing the "self" in performance.' And, of course, in those early days of the women's theatre movement which stressed improvisation, ensemble work, and devised projects, that very self-initiated interrogation so common among women theatre practitioners was an essential intervention in the masculinised *mise-en-scéne* of theatre history. Those women directors, writers, performers of twenty years ago grappled with a concept which forms the very basis of women working in theatre: the asymmetrical disclosure of actively defining the possibilities of a female *self* versus the limiting strictures of a male-defined female 'self' safely removed from aesthetic creativity. 'Where does that leave us?' It leaves us with an important step towards intervening in the dominant male discourse of *who we are*.

Part 1

Theatrical History and the Sign of the Female

1

The power of women on stage: the gender enigma in Renaissance England

The Women are all welcome; for the men,
They will be welcome: our care's not for them.
'Tis we, poore women, that must stand the brunt
Of this dayes tryall: we are all accused.
How wee shall cleere our selves, there lyes the doubt.
The men, I know, will laugh, when they shall heare
Vs rayl'd at, and abused; and say, 'Tis well,
We all deserue as much. Let um laugh on,
Lend but your kind assistance; you shall see
We will not be ore-come with Infamie,
And slanders that we neuer merited.
Be but you patient, I dare boldly say,
(If euer women pleased) weele please to day.
    (Prologue, *Swetnam the Woman-Hater Arraigned by Women*, 1620)

Shakespeare and contemporaries: double cross-dressing

Brought up on the plays of Shakespeare as our main staple of Renaissance drama, we are accustomed to seeing women disguised as men. On the Renaissance stage, however, costume created a complicated, multi-faceted doubling of vision: men playing women playing men. When Viola in *Twelfth Night*, after a shipwreck, decides to don the apparel of a page and serve the local duke, Orsino, (s)he says:

Conceal me what I am, and be my aid
For such disguise as haply shall become
The form of my intent. I'll serve this duke:
Thou shall present me as a eunuch to him.
    (I.ii.51–3)

3

With an adolescent boy actor in the role of Viola, her urgent request to 'conceal me what I am' plays on the theatrical convention of cross-dressing, as the boy is already 'concealed' in his role of the girl Viola. And it is this theatrical boy-girl Viola who asks to be presented as a eunuch to Duke Orsino.

In *As You Like It*, Rosalind, daughter of the banished duke, is forced after her father into exile and for protection dresses as a young man. She explains to her cousin, Celia:

> Were it no better,
> Because that I am more than common tall,
> That I did suit me all points like a man? . . .
> We'll have a swashing and martial outside,
> As many other mannish cowards have
> That do outface it with their semblances.
>   (I.iii.118–25)

Here again we see an example of theatrical playfulness with Rosalind's mocking attitude to those 'mannish cowards' who think they can fool the world with mere appearance (the swords, boots, doublet of conventional masculinity), while the boy-actor-as-Rosalind-as-man confounds everyone in the Forest of Arden with 'her' male costume. Such double cross-dressing adds dramatic tension and ironic wit to these plays as well as other plays of Shakespeare where women disguise as men, such as *The Merchant of Venice, Two Gentlemen of Verona* and *Cymbeline*.

The notion of disguise and clothing as a code for one's gender generated immense social, philosophical and existential concern in late Elizabethan and Jacobean society. In Shakespeare these concerns operate directly through his device of female characters dressed as men, who through such disguise gain access to previously unavailable, yet prestigious, male power. However, playwrights contemporary with Shakespeare extend the possibilities for gender disguise by having their male characters appear as women.

For example, in Beaumont and Fletcher's *Love's Cure, or the Martial Maid* (1625?), Clara and Lucio, sister and brother, are separated as infants. Their mother raises Lucio as a girl to protect him from his father's enemies; he wears long skirts, practises needlecraft with aesthetic agility, and feels most comfortable in the kitchen overseeing the preparation of meals. Conversely, his sister Clara, raised by their father, exhibits a propensity for male pursuits:

she rides horses, wears doublet and hose, excels in sword-fighting. Their unconventional lifestyles clearly establish that their costumes manifest their preferred gender, a preference which the plot soon reverses. Exiled and then pardoned, their father returns home with his masculine daughter. Reunited with his wife and son, and reinstated as family patriarch, the first concern he expresses to his spouse is to reinstitute his children's 'natural' gender:

> Now our mutuall care must be
> Imploy'd to help wrong'd nature, to recover
> Her right in either of them, lost by costume:
> To you I give my Clara, and receive
> My Lucio to my charge: and we'll contend
> With loving industry, who soonest can
> Turne this man woman, or this woman man.
> (I.iii.176–82)

In *Love's Cure*, Beaumont and Fletcher seem to toy with the idea of a socially constructed gender: how else could Lucio cook happily in the kitchen and Clara swear like a trooper on the battlefield? But 'wrong'd nature' follows the consequence of a wronged father; just as the father reclaims and recovers his family and title, so 'nature' redeems itself through 'love's cure'. Thus, Lucio forgoes his female dress when he falls in love with a woman; Clara drops her sword in the middle of a fight when suddenly she becomes enraptured by her male combatant.

An earlier, more homosexually charged, dramatic examination of gender role-playing can be found in John Lyly's *Gallathea* (c. 1587) in which two girls disguised as male pages fall in love, each believing the other a boy. They are desolate and heartbroken at the revelation of their true sexual identity when the possibility of a traditional marriage evaporates. However, in a sex-change *deus ex machina* manoeuvre, Lyly and the goddess Venus intervene, changing one female page into a boy.

In *Love's Cure* and *Gallathea* the issue of gender is raised only to be more deeply buried in an idealising harmonisation, unrelated to anything outside the illusions of theatre. In strong contrast to this, Thomas Middleton and Thomas Dekker, in their play *The Roaring Girl* (1611?), base their central character, Moll Cutpurse, on an actual woman, the notorious Mary Frith, who dressed as a man not for deliberate concealment or conniving intrigue, but simply because she chose to. The play thematically exploits the saying 'the clothes make the man' by suggesting that in this case 'the clothes make the woman'. The introduction to the play, written by Middleton, extends the wardrobe metaphor to playwriting itself:

> The fashion of play-making I can properly compare to nothing so naturally as the alteration in apparel; for in the time of the great crop-doublet, your huge bombastic plays, quilted with mighty words to lean purpose, was only then in fashion: and as the doublet fell, neater inventions began to be set up. Now, in the time of spruceness, our plays follow the niceness of our garments, single plots, quaint conceits, lecherous jests, dressed up in hanging sleeves . . . for *Venus, being a woman, passes through the play in doublet and breeches; a brave disguise and a safe one, if the statute untie not her codpiece point.* (lines 1–15, my italics)

The point raised in Middleton's preface transcends the level of text and character to engage with the issue of Renaissance theatrical convention: only men performed. Middleton compares playwriting to fashion, to 'alteration in apparel' – a metaphor which resonates in a script that features a woman who blatantly violates social convention and 'nature' by dressing in male clothing. The narrative plays with its own ironic stimulus of Moll Cutpurse's passage through the play in 'doublet and breeches'; yet at the same time Middleton's preface reminds us that her mode of dress forbids the audience to untie 'her codpiece point'. Such a mental stripping of Moll's male clothing would not reveal a woman but an adolescent boy.

Middleton and Dekker's preoccupation with the gender enigma in this play seems to draw swords with a least one modern scholar interpreting and analysing the script. Andor Gomme, a recent editor and commentator on *The Roaring Girl* footnotes the line 'if the statute untie not her codpiece point', as follows:

> Though there was much legislation regulating the dress of particular trades and classes, none is known which proscribed women from wearing men's clothes. Presumably, therefore, the phrase is proleptic: 'provided no law is made to prevent her going dressed as a man'. (p. 3)

Gomme's interpretation of the line makes no reference to the fact that men played all the women's roles in all Renaissance productions of the play. Moll Frith may dress as a man in real life, but *this* theatrical Moll Frith, – if you untie her codpiece point, – *is* a man. While Gomme rummages historical archives for dress regulations, Middleton delights in the variety of form which the theatrical convention of all-male casting allows (not to mention the fact that 'statute' could possibly be a typographical misspelling of 'statue', which then completely negates Gomme's research).

We find another instance of the gender enigma in the epilogue spoken by Moll Frith. According to Gomme, one particular passage has generated much discussion among theatrical scholars as to what these lines actually mean:

> . . . if what both [actors and writer] have done
> Cannot full pay your expectation,
> The Roaring Girl herself, some few days hence,
> Shall on this stage give larger recompense.
> (33–6)

Could it mean that Moll, herself, would appear on the London stage or that the actor who played Moll would simply play in another role of a different play? Historical evidence cited by Gomme describes how in 1605, a few years before Middleton and Dekker's play, the *Consistory of London Correction Book* recorded that Mary Frith, the real Moll Cutpurse, had confessed to the Court that, 'being at a play about three-quarters of a year since at the Fortune in mans apparel', she had spoken a variety of 'immodest and lascivious speaches . . . and also sat upon the stage in the public viewe of all the people there present in mans apparel and played upon her lute and sange a song' (p. xiii). While Gomme and the numerous scholars before him attempt to interpret the meaning of this passage, they apparently bypass the significance of the event itself: that Mary Frith, herself a woman in male dress, had performed on a 'male only' London stage. The significance of this event recorded in 1605 is not lost on the playwrights, who use it in their epilogue as a tantalising trailer, a sort of post-performance advertisement which promises that subsequent productions of his play will feature 'the real thing' – that is, a woman.

Both *Love's Cure* and *The Roaring Girl* demonstrate the interest in the early seventeenth century in issues linking theatrical performance and gender. In particular, the use of clothing to signify gender became a matter of urgent public dispute, when not only a fictional woman, like Clara in *Love's Cure*, but a *real* woman, Mary Frith, dressed as a man. As Moll Cutpurse and her extemporaneous performance demonstrate, the juxtaposition of real events with their fictionalised theatrical versions created a frisson of excitement from the clash between 'reality' and mimesis.

The pamphlet war: misogyny in print

In 1620 an anonymous pamphlet was published with the title, *Hic Mulier: or The Man-Woman: being a Medicine to Cure the Coltish Disease of the Staggers in the Masculine-Feminines of our Times.* The angry author of this work strikes out at the masculine woman as a 'monstrous deformitie . . . not halfe man, halfe woman; halfe fish, halfe flesh; halfe beast, halfe Monster: but all Odyous, all Divell' (in Shepherd, 1981, p. 84). Furthermore, the pamphleteer sees this monster-woman as usurping masculine characteristics by specifically wearing male clothes. She becomes

> man-like . . . in every condition: man in body by attyre, man in behaviour by rude complement, man in nature by aptnesse to anger, man in action by pursuing revenge, man in wearing weapons, man in using weapons. And in briefe, so much man in all things, that they are neither men, nor women but just good for nothing. (quoted in Woodbridge, 1984, p. 146)

The vituperative tone of this pamphlet undoubtedly expresses the measure of the threat posed by the practice of female cross-dressing. The woodcut on the title page of the pamphlet depicts one woman being fitted with a man's plumed hat while another waits solemnly in a barber's chair to have her hair cut. The pamphlet describes in spiteful detail, through a descriptive sequence, the specific characteristic of the transformation from woman to man using the significant metaphor of changes in language and grammar:

> For since the daies of *Adam* women were neuer so Masculine; Masculine in their genders and whole generations, from the Mother, to the youngest daughter, Masculine in Number, from one to multitudes; Masculine in Case, euen from the head to foot; Masculine in Moode, from bold speech, to impudent action; and Masculine in Tense: for (without redresse) they were, are, and will bestill most Masculine, most man-kinde, and most monstrous. (quoted in Woodbridge, 1984, p. 144)

The author of the pamphlet clearly sees the real women behind their deceitful attempts to create a masculine façade as eternal, unchanging entities, fixed by uncompromising nature. In the eighteen pages of the *Hic Mulier* essay, the author uses the words 'deforme(d)' or 'deformitie(s)' twenty-one times (Woodbridge, p. 145). The message of the essay never escapes from the conventional dichotomy of female stereotyping. Women are 'natural' (tender, weak, modest, supportive of mankind, soft, gentle and charming) and with feminine perversity also the opposite: unnatural, aggressive, masculine, monstrous, deformed.

Within a week of its promulgation the *Hic Mulier* essay received an angry but well considered answer. The second anonymous pamphlet clearly took its title from its bellicose predecessor: *Haec-Vir; or, The Womanish Man: Being an Answere to the late Booke intituled Hic-Mulier. Exprest in a briefe Dialogue betweene the Womanish Man, and Hic-Mulier the Man-Woman.* Whereas the original pamphlet attacks women for wearing masculine clothing, its response attacks men for their current fashion of foppishness, arguing that since men had abrogated their masculinity by wearing feminine dress, women simply had to 're-dress' the balance with male clothing which would maintain the gender distinctions. The pamphlet begins with Hic-Mulier, a female transvestite, and Haec-Vir, an effeminate male courtier, in a comic interchange in which each speaker mistakes the other's gender as their own, a similar *faux pas* made by Lyly's female pages in *Gallathea*. Throughout the encounter, the female speaker proclaims a variety of proto-revolutionary sentiments. To the male courtier's attack on her violation of custom she proclaims that '*Custome* is an Idiot', and later she asserts that 'We are as free-borne as Men, haue as free election, and as free spirits, we are compounded of like parts, and may with like liberty make benefit of our Creations' (Woodbridge, p. 147). But such powerful pronouncements are partially negated by a predictable ending which parallels the fate of Clara and Lucio in *Love's Cure*: the male courtier proposes that not only should they exchange clothes and behaviour, but also the Latin pronominal prefixes to their names so that order and harmony can be restored.

The attack on the male-clothed women found in the *Hic Mulier* essay corresponds to similar reprimands issued by the Church of England and King James I. During 1619 and 1620 a variety of sermons preached in London focused on the outlandish nature of women's dress. John Williams delivered *A Sermon of Apparell* at the court of King James. This fire and brimstone tirade provides the fascinating evidence that women were wearing their male dress inside the patriarchal church itself:

> What flesh and blood hath his thoughts so staunch, but must be distracted in his Church-deuotions, at the *prodigious* apparition of our *women*? . . . For a woman therefore to come vnto Church . . . halfe male, and halfe female . . . lifting vp towards his throne *two plaister'd eies* and a *polled head* . . . In *Sattin* (I warrant you) in stead of sackeclothe . . . standing most manly vpon her *points*, by wagging a *Feather* to defie the *World*, and carrying a *dagger*, . . . to enter God's house, as if it were a Play-house . . . what deuotion in the world but must start aside? (quoted in Woodbridge, 1984, p. 143)

Williams' enthusiastic religious barrage attacks women dressed as men while simultaneously providing tantalising evidence that Mary Frith was certainly not the only woman who entered a playhouse dressed in male attire. The sermon must have discomfited a large portion of his audience by the paradox of his attack: while assaulting the mannish-women, his remonstrations took place in the presence of the main object of ridicule in the *Haec-Vir* pamphlet, King James himself. King James I and his male courtiers were criticised for their extravagant 'feminine' fashion. King James was notorious for both his misogyny and his homosexual court, which overtly operated on the basis of sexual favouritism. The foppish male courtier in the *Haec-Vir* pamphlet is obviously modelled on the male members of King James's court. But rather than acknowledge anything amiss within his own exclusive social sphere, King James pressed for action against women. In January 1620 the King requested that the Bishop of London require his clergy to begin an attack on the Hic-Muliers of the King's domain – those aggressive females who wore 'brode brimd hats, pointed doublets, theyre haire cut short or shorne, and some of them stillettaes or poinards' (Woodbridge, p. 143).

The Swetnam controversy: performance over text

Many issues concerning women, besides questions about their short hair, masculine doublets, and poinards, elicited considerable polemical argument during the Jacobean period. A look at play titles after 1603 – the year of Elizabeth's death – up to the closing of the theatres in 1642, reveals the startling obsession playwrights had with the female: the word 'woman' or 'women' in a title is very frequent, not to mention 'maid', 'lass', 'widow', 'witch', 'girl', 'whore'. Examples range from Beaumont and Fletcher's *The Woman Hater*, Thomas Heywood's *A Woman Killed With Kindness* and *The Wise Woman of Hogsdon*, Philip Massinger's *The Woman's Plot* and *Very Woman*, Nathan Field's *The Woman is a Weathercock*, Thomas Middleton's *Women Beware Women* and *More Dissemblers Besides Women*, John Fletcher's *The Woman's Prize, or the Tamer Tamed*, Ben Jonson's *Epicoene, or the Silent Woman*, to Richard Brome's *The City Wit, or The Woman Wears the Breeches*.

Possibly one of the period's more controversial plays with 'woman' in the title, acted in 1618 or 1619 at the Red Bull, was *Swetnam the Woman-hater Arraigned by Women*. The play itself is a culmination of what has been called the Swetnam controversy. In 1615 Joseph Swetnam initiated a war of words when he published his pamphlet *The Araignment of Lewde, idle, froward, and vnconstant women: Or the vanitie of them, choose you whether*. His essay, an uncompromisingly hateful, mysogynistic and vituperative attack on women, went through at least ten reprints before 1637 and was reprinted in at least another six editions before 1880 (Woodbridge, p. 81). Here is a sample of his insistent, harping tone:

> Many women are in shape angels but in qualities devils, painted coffins with rotten bones . . . Although women are beautiful, showing pity, yet their hearts are black, swelling with mischief, not much unlike unto old trees whose outward leaves are fair and green and yet the body rotten. (quoted in Shepherd, 1985, p. 53)

Swetnam's work was not an isolated campaign; pamphlets and essays on the nature of women abounded. Indeed, much of the Swetnam essay clearly plagiarises other earlier works of a similar contentious vein. But what is historically significant about Swetnam's work is that it provoked three rebuttals, written by women, and an anonymously authored play. The first, published in 1617 by Rachel Speght, is called *A Movzell for Melastromvs, The cynicall Bayter of, and foule mouthed Barker against Evahs Sex; or, an Apologeticall Answere to that Irreligious and Illiterate*

Pamphlet made by Io. Sw. and by him Intituled 'The Arraignment of Women'. The next two rejoinders to Swetnam are by women who have clearly chosen pseudonyms for their work: *Ester hath hang'd Haman; or, An Answere To a lewd Pamphlet, entituled, The Arraignment of Women. With the arraignment of lewd, idle, froward, and vnconstant men, and Hvsbands* by Ester Sowernam (her last name presenting an ironic converse to 'Swe(e)tnam'); and Constantia Munda's *The Worming of a mad Dogge; or, A Soppe for Cerbevs the Iaylor of Hell*. All three women (remarkably enough in the face of such hatred) produce intelligent, well-argued attacks on Swetnam which display solid, educational backgrounds and the ability to use all the devices of rhetorical argument, so central to Renaissance discussion and thought.[1]

The unusual aspect of this whole controversy is that instead of remaining a purely literary exercise confined to the printed page, the debate was made material and three-dimensional through performance on a public stage. Although the author of *Swetnam the Woman-Hater Arraigned by Women* remains anonymous, clearly the writer demonstrates knowledge of both Swetnam's essay and those of the three women writers. In fact, so much of the unattributed material in the play finds a source in the pamphlets of the three women that it is tempting to speculate that a woman could have possibly written the script.[2] A brief summary of the plot will reveal how performance transformed literary and political rhetoric into a vibrant, compelling tragic-comedy.

Swetnam himself becomes a character in the play. He has been run out of England by a group of women angered by the anti-feminist essay he has just written. He takes great pride in the stir his document created and revels in his infamy:

> Oh, but for one that writ against me, *Swash*,
> Ide had a glorious Conquest in that Ile.
> How my Bookes tooke effect! how greedily
> The credulous people swallowed downe my hookes!
> How rife debate sprang betwixt man and wife!
> The little Infant that could hardly speake,
> Would call his Mother Whore. O, it was rare!
> (I.ii.43–9)

Swetnam's exile takes him to Sicily with his clown-like companion, Swash. There he opens a fencing school where, under the alias of

Misogynos, he plans to tutor young men in sword play and masculine pursuits. At the same time, the King of Sicily has just found his unmarried daughter in an apparently compromising position with the man she loves. The enraged King arrests them both, assuming his daughter culpable of a crime he believes all women share: lack of chastity. While planning a trial for the erring couple, the King invokes a law which requires death for the primary offender in this crime of sexual transgression and banishment for the secondary offender. The couple learn the harsh terms of the trial and, with romantic predictability, each lover admits guilt to save the other's life. Swetnam's subplot merges with the main story when he is brought into the trial by the King to act as an advocate for the man. While he serves in this legal position he spouts epithets from the original Swetnam pamphlet:

> What Tyrannies, Oppressions, Massacres,
> Women stand guiltie of: and which is more,
> What Cities haue beene sackt and ruinate,
> Kingdomes suburted, Lands depopulated,
> Monarchies ended! and all these by women.
> (III.iii.203–7)

The judgement which the all-male jury passes condemns the King's daughter to death, with Swetnam/Misogynos claiming a glorious victory for both himself and the male contingent.

An innovative twist of the plot discloses the appearance of a lost, presumably dead, son of the King of Sicily. When the son, Lorenzo, returns to his father's kingdom and sees the mortal difficulty his sister is in, he disguises himself in woman's dress as an Amazon and acts as defender of the women against Swetnam. After the original trial and the male victory, Lorenzo, still disguised as an Amazon, and his mother, the Queen, trap Misogynos and put him on trial before their own all-woman tribunal. This scene has a particular vindictive poignancy in light of the daughter's impending execution and the reported lover's suicide.

Perhaps more importantly, the scene of Misogynos on trial is a reversal of masculine retribution. The previous court trial effectively tried the whole of womankind under the guise of a single sexual crime committed by two innocent lovers, with Misogynos and the all-male jury cheering the outcome: death to the daughter of the King. Now Misogynos finds himself on trial and exposed as weak, cowardly, lying. When confronted by a court of women who coolly accuse him of slandering them, his bravura, polemical performance for the all-male jury collapses into a faint-hearted timidity:

LORETTA: Thou are here indicted by these names, that thou,
            Contrary to nature, and the peace of this Land,
            Hast wickedly and maliciously slandred,
            Maligned, and opprobriously defamed the ciuill
              societie
            Of the whole Sex of women: therefore speake,
            Guiltie, or not guiltie?

MISOGYNOS: Not guiltie . . .

OMNES: Not guiltie?

MISOGYNOS: No, not guiltie.

AURELIA: Darest thou denie a truth so manifest?
            Didst thou not lately both by word, and deed,
            Publish a Pamphlet in disgrace of vs,
            And of all women-kind?

MISOGYNOS: No, no, no, not I.

                                            (V.ii.259–69)

The epilogue of the play shows Misogynos, led by women, bound, gagged, recanting to the audience for his slanderous misdeeds. Happily the young lovers are discovered alive and well, allowing the daughter to be restored to her repentent, contrite father who arranges her marriage. The King's lost son, Lorenzo, takes off his Amazon disguise and rejoins his family.

Swetnam the Woman-Hater provides a fascinating example of the multi-dimensional debate about the nature of women which figured so prominently in late Elizabethan and Jacobean discourse. It begins by looking at the plight of a single persecuted woman, the King's daughter, and then moves to the condemnation of women in general. But this misogynistic development of plot meets an obstacle, not by a single character, but by a *collective* female voice: a group of women who put a misogynist on trial. In fact, Swetnam/ Misogynos, as Linda Woodbridge has pointed out (p. 318), is perhaps the best comic character example of a long line of stage misogynists. The playwright seems to realise the potential of such a character by requiring him to deliver a direct address to the audience in the epilogue to beg forgiveness and promise repentence. He stands out as an outrageously laughable figure whose line in women-hating seems to be on automatic pilot: he just cannot put an end to those anti-feminist jokes. The Jacobean audience, many well versed in the Swetnam controversy with first-hand knowledge of the original pamphlet, must have enjoyed the joke against Swetnam's unstoppable bombast. Swetnam as author in a pamphleteering debate was earnest, serious and threatening; but when Swetnam/Misogynos took the stage as a character he clearly became buffoon-like and ridiculous. Could anybody in the audience take his self-regarding nature, his uncompromising woman-hatred seriously? On the other hand, a sinister outcome of the comic charade of the Swetnam/Misogynos rhetoric condemns a woman to death. It is this acute mixture of comedy with serious issues that makes the stage misogynist fascinating. In one respect he is likeable simply because he is so ridiculous. Linda Woodbridge articulates this alarming appeal of the Swetnam/Misogynos character:

> It is hard to dislike these sprightly fellows; one is tempted to admire them, if only for their persistence and their good natured cussedness. Most are granted enough human touches to make us want to forgive them . . . [But] behind the smiling faces of all literary misogynists . . . is a kind of evil, a deprivation of feeling, an antihuman principle. Women in the play go to court seeking justice and find a laughing opponent. It is an image of the frustration of women's movements throughout history. Seeking human justice, we confront the inhuman face of the Jester. (Woodbridge, 1984, pp. 318–19)

The playwright offers the audience another unusual element: an unconventional use of cross-dressing. Unlike the majority of scripts from the period that employ cross-dressing to disguise female characters as men or boys, a single male character, Lorenzo, dresses as a woman in *Swetnam the Woman-Hater*. When male characters do dress as women, as with Lucio in *Love's Cure*, the disguise is balanced by a woman dressing as a man, but here Lorenzo goes solo, with no female character dressed as a man to complement him. Moreover, in contrast to the treatment given to Lucio, Lorenzo's dress does not provoke condemnation or degradation. His disguise gives him the opportunity to defend his sister in court, and although he loses the case, he argues eloquently and forcefully for the rights of women. The writer does not present him as a figure of fun but juxtaposes his power and dignity against the ridiculous male-clad figure of Misogynos. This comparison is particularly powerful in the courtroom scene, where the writer pits Misogynos, champion of masculinity, feeble head of a fencing school for male courtiers, against Lorenzo, the prince returning victorious from war, renowned for his military prowess and skill. While Misogynos relentlessly thrusts forward his anti-women rhetoric, Lorenzo performs the ultimate act of support and corroboration for women: he wears their clothes.

While we have seen examples in the plays of Shakespeare in which female characters who dress as men gain access to a position of power not usually available to them as women, in this singular piece Lorenzo as a women has a parallel but inverted experience: rather than becoming empowered, 'she' becomes a sex object when Misogynos lusts after 'her'. Through this clever narrative situation, the playwright exposes the hypocrisy of Misogynos, who advises men to avoid women at all costs, yet privately to his servant claims to have 'fallen in love'. For Misogynos, however, 'love' is just a cross-dressing of lust where he sends a conventional love letter to Lorenzo as his first step towards a lecherous seduction. Thus it is that Lorenzo learns at first hand the workings of a sexual politics based on assumptions of masculine superiority.

Armed women and the battle of the sexes

The image of the Amazon as the armed woman, utilised by the anonymous writer of *Swetnam the Woman-Hater*, was a popular literary device which received wide currency at the end of the sixteenth century. In 1590 Spenser used this image in *The Faerie Queen*. In this epic story Britomart, the chaste, indomitable warrior-maid, rescues her lover Artegall from the evil Amazon Radigund. Artegall's imprisonment involves dressing in women's clothes, which Spenser presents as a demeaning humiliation forced on all male prisoners. On a conventional, allegorical reading of Spenser's poem, Justice (Artegall) is saved by Chastity (Britomart) from Lust (Radigund). But such a reading would miss Britomart's connection to the Virgin Queen, Elizabeth I, and to other virgin warriors whose powerful chastity is metaphorically linked to the impenetrable masculine armour they wear.

An obvious forerunner to Spenser's Britomart is Athena, the Greek goddess, daughter of Zeus, who leapt from her father's skull fully grown and clad in armour. While other women warriors such as the Amazons posed an unacceptable threat to Greek perceptions of masculinity, Athena did not. Time and time again the male Greek poets employ her to retrieve the mythic males of Homeric Greece from perilous predicaments and restore them to positions of unflinching valour. Perseus becomes her protégé, whom she helps behead the Gorgon Medusa. And Odysseus, the wily hero of the Trojan war, whom she helps return home to Ithaca, is her most-favoured of mortal men. Athena represents and embodies the law and culture of the city of Athens.

Athena and Britomart, both chastely armoured, advance the 'important myth about order's victory over disorder' (Warner 1985, p. 103). Britomart defeats the Amazon Radigund and releases Artegall from captivity; Athena supports Theseus and Heracles in their battle with the Amazons. As virgin warriors these mythical women not only stand for law-abiding chastity, but they give their virtuous consent to the destruction of another kind of warrior woman – a female who represents an armoured threat to the status quo: the Amazon. These frightening warrior women govern themselves without male authority by choosing to live in an exclusively female community. As a result, to the Greeks they represented the ultimate in social disorder: the female aping of masculinity (made grotesquely concrete by the classical belief that Amazons sliced off one breast in order to draw a bow more efficiently). Such mythical distortion of the female body becomes one of the main arguments against women dressing as men centuries later in the Jacobean period, where women are characterised as 'deformities', 'monsters', and 'good for nothing' in the *Hic Mulier* pamphlet.

Fighting women, armoured females, were therefore embraced by classical Greece and Renaissance England as long as they remained mythical figures whose allegorical apparel could be made to uphold the social order. In these mythical instances male dress gives symbolic women, such as Athena and Britomart, superhuman power. Indeed, male dress for women in Shakespeare is a pathway to power. Viola has access to the local court, Portia is elevated to a doctor of laws, and even Rosalind, through 'male' friendship with Orlando, becomes privy to her lover's secrets. These women achieve a higher social status and access to language and discourse unavailable to them as women dressed as women.

To be dressed in women's clothing, however, visually signifies a less fortunate position. For Artegall it is aligned with his imprisonment, his loss of power, his submission. For Lucio in *Love's Cure* it is emblematic of the scorn and the derision he receives from his servants. And for Pentheus in Euripides' *The Bacchae*, women's dress is his route to a horrific death, in which his frenzied mother mistakenly tears his head from his body. This power through clothing can be seen in the nineteenth-century English pantomime where the dame – a male actor dressed as an old, ugly woman – forms the play's centre of ridicule and fun. In contrast, the principal boy – a young female actor dressed as the romantic male lead – assumes the traditional heroic figure. The theatrical profession itself embodied such disparity: *adolescent* boys played women's roles while they trained for the male parts which were in most cases larger and more challenging. Dramatic clothing thus provides an immediate and unchallengeable sign of one's presence and power in the world.

Against such a background of defensively armoured artistic myth, Lorenzo's act of transvestism – dressing as an Amazon in *Swetnam the Woman-Hater* – stands out as an astonishing attempt to rewrite cultural assumptions about gender and clothing. He has entered the arena of a battle between two types of armoured women: the Britomarts/Athenas and the Amazons and he opposes both of them. Unlike Britomart and Athena, whose armoured virgin purity validates patriarchal strength, Lorenzo does not subscribe to Misogynos' male view of women in the play but specifically opposes it in a courtroom trial. Unlike the feared aggressiveness of the latter, he does not epitomize social and cultural disorder. Indeed, his Amazonian costume brings harmony and order to a narrative that has been riven apart by the woman-hater, Misogynos. Lorenzo's importance and uniqueness lie in the fact that he is a male character who *chooses* women's clothing, in contrast to the adolescent male actors required to wear women's clothing by theatre convention. In fact, he seems to take on both aspects of Spenser's female characters in the *Faerie Queen* by combining elements of the warrior-woman Britomart and the

Amazon Radigund in a single corrective character. In 1590 these two armoured women fight a fierce battle within the text of Spenser's poem; thirty years later the battle has shifted. Not only has it moved from printed page to theatrical production, but now it has produced a single armoured woman (who acts like a chorus of her literary predecessors) battling against an external enemy in the shape of a Swetnam-producing society. Therefore, in many ways *Swetnam the Woman-Hater* represents a feminist high point in the public debate over gender which took place in the late Jacobean period.

Argument and discussion over the nature of women appears as one of the great recurrent themes of Western drama, as will become clear in the following pages. The controversy over women is an issue fundamental to the very nature of theatre, for the mimetic art of acting has produced the greatest of imaginative leaps required by the spectator: the theatrical illusion involved in witnessing men playing women. 'Femininity', as feminist theory has soundly argued, exists as a cultural and social construction; central to that construction, as far as the illusionistic art of theatre is concerned, remains the fact that women had absolutely no part in their own dramatic image-making. Theatrical production provided, as we shall see in a variety of different ways, a visual and verbal performance of man's imagined women.

2

Cross-dressing, the Greeks, and the wily phallus

What poet would dare, in depicting the delight caused by a beauteous apparition, to distinguish between the woman and her garb? Where is the man who, in street, theatre or public park, has not taken an utterly disinterested pleasure in a skilfully composed attire, and gone away with a mental picture in which this latter is inseparably mingled with the beauty of its owner – *thus making of the woman and her garb an indivisible whole*? (Charles Baudelaire, *The Painter of Modern Life*, 1863, my italics)

The coupling of comedy and costume

The dramaturgical fascination with cross-dressing which culminates in pre-revolutionary England has its roots in theatrical conventions which go back to classical Greece. In particular, the comedies of Aristophanes use the charade of gender costume – specifically the dress of women – as a wild comic device. Examples of the histrionics of cross-dressing include the *Ecclesiazousae* (*The Women's Assembly*), *Lysistrata*, and, most importantly, *Thesmophoriazousae* (*The Women Celebrating the Thesmophoria*). In the first two of these plays women intrude into the public, male-controlled arenas of Athens, namely the Agora and the Acropolis; in the third play, however, the battle of the invading sex has shifted its ground: here the issue is not so much the intrusion of women into male domains as the way in which women themselves become represented theatrically.

In order to see the potential of cross-dressing for Aristophanes' comedy, one must appreciate that costume and mask were essential ingredients to Greek drama, both comedy and tragedy. In the huge amphitheatres which formed the sites of the theatre productions, often holding up to 10,000 spectators, the mask and dress of the actor was a broad sign with which to identify the play's character. Much of this identificatory coding came from the iconography of the classical deities, so that Athena would appear with helmet and a breast plate with the Medusa head; Heracles flourished his club and lion-skin, and so forth. Over a period of centuries the Greek theatre developed conventional representations of stock characters – slave, old man, lecher, young unmarried woman. A woman's 'type' was often signalled in the mask by her form of hairstyle: hair parted down the middle, for example, denoted a 'pure young woman' (Prosperi, 1982, p. 29).

In Greek comedy the physical attributes of the characters were exaggerated and made more grotesque both in the mask and in the actor's body. The Dionysiac element of comedy, considered to be the source of all theatrical revel-making, publicly licensed the privilege of exposing those body parts normally hidden by conventional dress. The comic actor wore tights over heavy padding and a tight tunic cut abnormally short in order to reveal an artificial leather phallus. Needless to say, the mere appearance of an exaggerated phallus as part of the comic actor's costume – from the evidence of the few existing comedies we have – engendered endless sight gags. And, of course, the phallus, the ultimate sign for gender definition, though openly displayed and made fun of, still demonstrates to the audience a blatant source of power: in Aristophanes' case, comic power which generated the laughter and celebrated the interconnection of its male participants. For example, in Aristophanes' play *Peace*, when the leading character flies up to heaven on the back of a dung beetle, he uses his phallus as a kind of ancient gear shift, a joy-stick that pushes him into free flight. Or in *The Frogs*, where Aeschylus and Euripides debate literature in front of a set of adjudicatory scales, Euripides, who wants to throw weight to his argument, begins searching himself for something 'strong and big' to toss on to the scales. In *The Wasps*, a character throws his phallus to a flute girl to use as a hand-rope to pull herself on to the stage; and so on '*ad hilarium*'.

Gender conspiracy and the Pygmalion syndrome

In Aristophanes' play the *Thesmophoriaszousae*, the comic role of the phallus is dramatically upstaged by the comedy of men dressed as women. This play, which was performed in 411 BC, focuses on the Festival of Thesmophoria celebrated every October by the women of Athens, a three-day event at which various religious rites were performed to mark the autumn sowing. Significant, from the point of view of the present essay, is the fact that the ritual was *secret* and excluded the men. The festival takes place on the Acropolis, but this time, unlike events in *Lysistrata* where the women illegally appropriate the male domain, it is granted to them for their exclusive ceremonial use. Euripides, the well-known and controversial tragic dramatist and one of the characters in the play, discovers that the women of this festival have been plotting revenge for his slanderous portrayal of them in his tragedies. As part of their festive rituals the women have a meeting where they discuss the injury Euripides has inflicted on them. Euripides' crime against the women is that of aesthetic mis-representation; they object to the way he depicts women in his plays:

> FIRST WOMAN: Give him a stage and a theatre full of people, and does he ever fail to come out with his slanders? Calling us intriguers, strumpets, tipplers, deceivers, gossips, rotten to the core and a curse to mankind. And naturally the men all come home after the play and give us that nasty suspicious look, and start hunting in all the cupboards for concealed lovers. (p. 113)

Unknown to the women, a male intruder in female dress has infiltrated their secret ceremony. Euripides has planted an old man, his kinsman Mnesilochus, briefed to defend the playwright's name against the women and to convince them that the 'wrongly accused' dramatist does not deserve punishment. In an extended comic monologue Mnesilochus, guying as a woman, counters the women's attack on Euripides's portrayal of wilful, erotic heroines who openly beguile and entice men by defending him on the grounds that, far from being indiscreet, the tragic playwright has practised moderation and restraint by not revealing women's other secrets which are much worse:

> MNESILOCHUS: There are thousands of little things he *doesn't* know

about, aren't there? . . . what about that trick of chewing a bit of garlic in the morning, when you've had a bit of fun? Dad comes home from duty on the Wall, takes one sniff and says, 'Well, she's not been up to mischief this time, anyway.' You see? Euripides has never mentioned that. If he wants to go off the deep end about Phaedra, let him get on with it, I say. He's never said a word about the woman who spread her skirt out wide, to show her husband how nice it looked in the light. Her boyfriend was underneath . . . Why pick on Euripides? He's done nothing worse than we have. (pp. 115–17)

Outraged by such unabashed treachery to their sex, the leader of the women (who, one should not forget, is, like the rest of the cast, a man) turns aside to the audience and says, 'Nothing can be worse than a shameless woman – except another woman' (p. 117). What is interesting in this single line is its quality of intrigue and conspiracy with the audience – an audience who, it is assumed, will agree whole-heartedly with such sentiment. Indeed, the entire play conspires with its audience against the women it has dramatically stereotyped; first, by allowing the audience to take part in the secret rituals of the women's festival; secondly, by allowing a man disguised as a woman easily to enter the festival, and to subvert with equal ease the women's purpose in relation to Euripides; and lastly, by allowing the audience to witness the 'creation' of a stereotypical woman twice over.

As we have already seen, the first 'creation' occurs early on when Euripides dresses and disguises Mnesilochus as a woman; it is one of the key comic scenes of the play, and Aristophanes spends much time and detail in building his counterfeit woman. Euripides first strips Mnesilochus down to his tunic, shaves his beard and moustache, and singes off the pubic hair with a torch. Such depilation of the genitals was commonplace among women to maintain the Greek standard of female beauty. The actual dressing of the counterfeit involves donning a yellow gown, a girdle, a wig, a hair-net, a head-dress, a shawl, and shoes. Euripides surveys his creation with delight and says to him:

> Well, you certainly look like a woman now. But when you speak, mind *you put on a real feminine voice.* (p. 109, my italics)

One of the principal sight gags running throughout the play is Mnesilochus' womanly disguise, and the final bit of his costume is the fabricated voice of a woman.

Mnesilochus is not the only man who dresses as a woman. There are three other instances. The first is the character Agathon, a tragic poet whom the audience encounters 'clean-shaven and bewigged, wearing female attire and seated at a dressing-table' (p. 103). Agathon, observed by both Euripides and Mnesilochus, sings 'arpeggios in a fruity falsetto' and then launches into song, taking the part of the chorus leader and the chorus of maidens alternately. When Mnesilochus recovers from the first shock of Agathon's performance, he queries the poet's androgynous appearance, which includes an array of women's objects oddly juxtaposed with male artefacts:

> MNESILOCHUS: Tell me, why this perturbation of nature? A lute, a yellow-gown? A lyre and a hair-net, a woman's girdle and a wrestler's oil flask? A sword and a hand-mirror? (p. 105)

It is this early scene of androgyny which initiates and sets the terms for the sexual warfare in Aristophanes' play: a dramatically garbed conflict of theatrical form – what Froma Zeitlin (1981, p. 170) describes as a battle of aesthetics in which theatre as a mimetic art encounters reality. We have already seen one such manifestation when the 'real' women of the play object to Euripides' representation of them on the stage, arguing that the male audience for Euripides' dramas make direct links between the tragically distorted female characters and their own wives: suspecting wives of adultery after seeing adulteresses on stage.

This scene with Agathon, the tragic poet dressed as a woman, calls into question the earnest intentions of tragedy. If tragedy is the theatrical genre which unlike comedy imitates serious action, then Aristophanes lampoons this concept of tragedy by mocking poets who in order to effect genuine mimesis think they must become the characters they create. This, then, is the *real* explanation of Agathon's erratic and inconsistent androgyny:

> AGATHON: I wear my clothes to suit my inspiration. A dramatic writer has to merge his whole personality into what he is describing. If he is describing a woman's actions, he has to participate in her experience, body and soul . . . If he's writing about a man, he's got all the bits and pieces already, as it were; but what nature hasn't provided, *art can imitate.* (p. 105, my italics)

The play's second instance of a man dressed as a woman is Cleisthenes, described in the character list as a 'notorious effeminate'. Even in this homosexual culture, men with womanly qualities are ridiculed and derided. It is Cleisthenes, dressing as a woman through personal choice and not through Agathon's so-called artistic necessity, who runs into the women's assembly and tells the women of Euripides' counter-plot. Although Euripides considers asking Cleisthenes for help, and does ask Agathon to act as his defender in front of his female accusers, the play reveals both men to be unsuitable candidates. They are both too close to women, too 'feminine' to be of any real use. Cleisthenes declares himself a kindred spirit of the women with his lines: 'I come as a friend . . . I adore you all – you do resemble me so very closely . . . and I always try to protect your interests' (p. 118). It takes a 'real' man, the kinsman Mnesilochus, whose hairy masculinity must be forcibly burnt away, to save Euripides.

The third instance of the man-dressed-as-woman occurs when Euripides disguises himself in a last-ditch attempt to save Mnesilochus from imprisonment. Once again, the audience witnesses an active creation of a conventional woman on the stage. Mnesilochus is guarded by a Scythian who has bound him to a plank – still in his women's weeds – and propped him up centre stage. When the Scythian guard has fallen asleep, Euripides enters, 'carrying a lyre and the mask and costume of an old woman. He approaches the Chorus conspiratorially' (p. 142) and promises the women that in return for Mnesilochus' release he will never say anything bad about them again. This plea quickly transforms into blackmail when he threatens to tell their husbands even worse things about them. The leader of the chorus quickly agrees with Euripides' deal, but leaves him to tackle the sleeping Scythian. Euripides is prepared for this event; the stage directions read: 'He puts on the disguise, and calls out in an old woman's voice' (p. 143). Waking the guard, Euripides saves Mnesilochus by acting as a procuress for a flute-girl conveniently brought on for the occasion. The ruse works: Euripides releases his kinsman Mnesilochus and they both run offstage united in women's costume.

The play begins with a tragic poet in women's dress, and it ends in the same way. But the distance travelled between Agathon's vision of artistic inspiration and Euripides' obligatory drag to save his kinsman is great. Euripides' disguise has two aspects: in one sense it redresses the adverse effect his tragedies have had on his female accusers by forcing the poet to enter the realm of women by wearing their clothes. Here the great tragic poet and creator of women's roles must himself enter Aristophanes' narrative *as a woman* in order to resolve his comic predicament, after unsuccessfully sending his kinsman Mnesilochus, in women's dress, to do his work for him and right his dramatic wrongs. This theatrical penance-by-proxy parallels Euripides' occupation as a playwright: other men, actors, have performed Euripides' bidding by playing female characters in his plays. Aristophanes comically twists this servitude so that the poet himself, not a proxy, must act out the consequences of his own misrepresentation of women by becoming one. But in a second sense Euripides' disguise restores the women to the very position to which they object. And it does so by having Euripides the procuress exploit and betray 'her' own sex by selling a girl's sexuality.[1]

Phallus as costume: costume as woman

We have seen with Aristophanic eyes how easy it is to become a woman. Some men, like Agathon, do it for reasons of artistic creation; others, like Cleisthenes, for personal choice; whilst Mnesilochus and Euripides become 'female' to save each other from the retribution of 'real' women. By becoming precisely what they despise, women, the poet and his kinsman negate and escape the assertions of female power.

Although in one sense men, as well as women, are dramatically defined through their costume, there is a major difference which Aristophanes' script demonstrates: women are reduced to signs – signs that are created and controlled by male playwrights and male actors. In contrast, men in comedy display openly their sign of gender – the phallus – and they present this aggrandised sign as a companion, a plaything, an instrument of power, pleasure and delight, an appendage which binds men to men. In the Greek comedies the phallus plays an ultimately versatile, symbolic role with a range of changing shapes from stiff erection to a floppy (but ever useful) piece of rope. Additionally, the phallus shows an ability to conspire with its owner in matters of urgency or deceit. Nowhere does this wily characteristic become more evident and hilariously concrete than in the *Thesmophoriazousae*, when the phallus plays hide and seek with the women as they undress the disguised Mnesilochus to discover his true but evasive gender. First, the kinsman desperately clutches his lower parts to avoid detection. The comic ingenuousness of Mnesilochus' roving phallus, which seems to have a life all of its own, is worth encountering in full:

FIRST WOMAN: (*pointing triumphantly*) There you are, you see? No tits like ours at all.
MNESILOCHUS: That's because I'm barren. (*pathetically*) I never had a child.
FIRST WOMAN: A moment ago you were the mother of nine. (*Despite Mnesilochus' feverish clutching, Cleisthenes now manages to fling open the lower half of the robe. In desperation, Mnesilochus bends down as if to do up his shoe.*)
CLEISTHENES: Stand up straight! (*Mnesilochus does so, adopting a statuesque feminine pose. There is no sign of what one might expect to see, and Mnesilochus' face bears a complacent smirk.*) What have you done with it?
FIRST WOMAN: (*lifting the robe from behind, and screaming*): Oooh! He's pushed it through to the back. (*She hastily lets the robe fall again.*) A beauty, too – such a pretty colour. (*The Chorus shriek and titter at the revelation.*)
CLEISTHENES: (*lifting the robe in his turn*) Where? I can't see it.
FIRST WOMAN: It's back in the front again.
CLEISTHENES: (*running round to the front*) No it isn't.
FIRST WOMAN: (*from behind*) No, here it is again.
CLEISTHENES: What is all this, a shuttle service across the Isthamus?
(p. 121)

The sight gag of the hide-and-seek phallus; the poet who dresses as a female in order to write about women; Euripides, the high tragedian, who trembles near the women of Athens – these are just some of the comic elements which make this play an exciting, brilliant parody of theatrical versions of women. Aristophanes' raucous, bawdy humour generates genuine laughter. On another level, however, the chameleon-like phallus is worshipped and celebrated within the festive response. For just as Mnesilochus conspires with his phallus to prevent the women from discovering his true identity, so do the Athenian (male) citizens of Aristophanes' audience conspire with themselves and the actors: what joy, what gaiety our phallus brings, how it binds us, male performers and male audience, in the gleeful power of possessing one.[2]

Here one must distinguish between the real penis and the dramatic phallus which is its costume-sign. Use of the phallus as a theatrical code encourages the audience to conflate the penis with the phallus: in Mnesilochus' case, the phallus acts both as an extension of himself and as an entity in its own right. The prop phallus promoting the *real* penis is a major source of Aristophanic comedy. There is no parallel joke for female characters. Unlike that of the phallus, the theatrical code for woman derives from her social clothing: costume apes costume, in this case, and not some real *part* of the woman. Such a coding assumes that an outer, separate and inanimate garment, one which physically contains women rather than extends them, somehow best expresses them as whole physical entities. While there is no end to the shape and escapades of the wily phallus, clothes are merely clothes and women are merely women, thus passively delineated and defined. Aristophanes' comedy tells us how easy it is to be a woman, a metonymic piece of skirt: Agathon, the poet, has merely to costume himself as a woman in order to write about women in his tragic poems; Euripides puts on the mask and dress of an old woman on stage and, *voilà!*, the manners make the woman! Mnesilochus' disguise as a woman is a more complicated dramatic re-invention – it takes up two pages of text and is full of comic twists. But Euripides' dressing of Mnesilochus is an ideal lesson in the male creation of 'woman'. For just as the tragic poet creates women in his successful plays, so he can now also create a flesh-and-blood woman before the audience's eyes. And what is this woman? She is a yellow gown, a wig, a head band, a girdle, with smooth, hairless skin, shoes, shawl – a list of items, of props. Later in the play when Mnesilochus enters the women's meeting, this 'invention-through-inventory' continues by listing the various ways that women fool and cuckold their husbands.

Thus the drama limits and reduces its imagined women to items of clothing and attributes of adultery. The clothes *are* the woman and the clothes that stand for them are instrumental to their well-practised deceit. Men, however, expand, develop, grow and celebrate through their costume-sign, the phallus.

Women as theatrical signs

The theatrical representation of women as symbols, signalled through their costume, can be usefully related to their representation in the purely visual arts. Marina Warner's book, *Monuments and Maidens* (1985) gives a historically comprehensive and often exhilarating account of this symbolic procession. Warner's argument centres on the visual arts and Western mythology. I would like to extend her thesis – that throughout Western history women ('woman' in fact) have carried male-imposed allegorical meaning and abstract ideas – to theatre.

In their role as symbols, signs representing things other than themselves, women did not have the capacity for originating speech and artifice. Women were, as Lévi-Strauss and others have demonstrated, not so much objects in their own right but the *medium* of exchange, tokens for maintaining (patriarchal) social and cultural meanings. The more symbolic and mediatory 'woman' becomes, the less she herself is and can be culturally creative. This is exemplified in the nature/culture split much discussed in feminist theory. Woman *is* nature, man *creates* culture. Therefore by 'being' nature, by representing nature, woman becomes a pure symbol. Whereas man is the subject, woman is the object, and objects can be transformed and used to carry symbolic meaning: thus man creates the Statue of Liberty as a woman; the classical muses, Truth, Knowledge and Nature itself, as women. Man's traditional icon of justice – a blindfolded woman holding a balance in her hand – is female. This purely symbolic, generic status assigned to 'woman' is stressed by the absence of any personal naming.

In 1602 a refined version of this classical symbolisation was systematised by Cesare Ripa, who demonstrated the ways in which the female body represented abstract ideas: Truth holds the sun in her hands, Charity feeds babies at her breast, and Liberty carries a *pilleus*, a felt hat worn by freed slaves of Rome. Ripa depicted a large number of his symbolic women as virginal: Faith, Hope, Prudence, Justice, Fortitude and Temperance. Ripa's *Iconologia*, which went through several reprintings, became a fundamental sourcebook for artists in the seventeenth and eighteenth centuries (Warner, 1985, p. 250).

This notion of women as symbolic objects, existing purely and passively as signs, in contrast to men who *use* signs, has a particularly striking relation to a theatre where for centuries only men took the stage. In this theatre, active, cultural man can and did assume many parts; passive, natural woman could not.

Indeed, the very act of men assuming the costume and mask of a woman reinforces the idea of woman as symbol, and so maintains male hegemony in the auditorium of cultural invention and ingenuity.

3

Historical precedents: women unmasked

The whole of her bodily beauty is nothing less than phlegm, blood, bile, rheum, and the fluid of digested food . . . If you consider what is stored up behind those lovely eyes, the angle of the nose, the mouth and cheeks you will agree that the well-proportioned body is merely a whitened sepulchre. (St. John Chrysostom, fifth Century)

There is yet another reason why the women did not wear masks – namely, that no mask could ever approach the enchanting effect of a lovely woman's face, whose beauty was obviously the chief requisite of her *role*. (Pierre Louis Duchartre, *The Italian Comedy*, 1929)

The actor's fall – the staging of Roman debauchery

The acting profession of the classical Greek period, linked as it was to religious festivals, was one of both privilege and good repute. Greek actors played an honoured role in the practice of the state religion, and as a result they often received special rewards for their performances.

When Roman culture gained ascendancy in the Mediterranean, the theatre's religious links disappeared, the importance and respectability of actors drastically diminished, and theatrical events often became little more than exercises in crowd manipulation. Indeed, the Romans built theatres all over their empire as part of their policy of keeping the crowd, the public, politically diverted and entertained. In the earliest period, however, the Romans looked to the Greeks as their theatrical masters, and many

31

productions simply rendered Greek scripts in Latin. The honour accorded to Greek actors, however, was not maintained, and during the Roman Republic the prejudice against actors multiplied: excluded from the rights of voting and holding public office, actors were forbidden to change their profession and their children were forced to follow in their footsteps. In effect, by the zenith of the Roman Empire, actors had virtually become social outcasts.

The variety of theatrical entertainments that existed in Roman days were seemingly endless – plays based on Greek models, rope-dancing, circus, pantomime, and farcical mimes. Additionally, the Romans gained historical renown for their staged military combats, the spectacles of the gladiators and other war-based sporting events. For the early Christian Church, all of these events were classified as 'theatre' simply because they took place in the same playing arenas as the more traditional drama. The Latin word *spectacula* was used by the Church fathers who condemned and denounced these 'spectacles' as the work of the devil. In order to receive baptism into the early Christian Church the initiative had specifically to renounce *spectacula* along with the devil and his other works.

Yet it is important to remember that the prejudice against the theatrical profession was well established before the attacks by the early Church fathers. Jonas Barish, in his book *The Anti-Theatrical Prejudice*, (1985, p. 42) identifies the source of such a bias as sexual. In accounts of theatrical activities during the Roman Empire there are numerous references to women performers, primarily as 'dancing girls' or mimes. It seems doubtful that women performed in scripted stage plays based on the Greek models involving the use of masks, but rather in the kind of theatrical entertainment which evolved from the street and the market-place: juggling, acrobatics, song, dance and mime, where both women and men took active part. The profession of prostitution was parallelled to that of the theatre, being viewed as a 'necessary evil' and linked by a sexual stigma:

> in the mimes and pantomimes women exhibited their bodies, castrated actors played feminine roles with much lascivious realism, and the dramatic fare ran heavily to bawdry and sexual excitation. Going to the shows must have seemed to many Romans like visiting the stews – equally urgent, equally provocative of guilt, and hence equally in need of being scourged by a savage backlash of official disapproval. (Barish, 1985, pp. 42–3)

The earliest historical references to mime, which is primarily a theatre of gesture and physical mimicry, depict it as coarse, lewd and indecent. One of the popular Roman festivals, the Floralia, by all accounts a riotous celebration, was also a favourite occasion for the performance of mimes. Founded two years after the introduction of Greek drama to the Roman stage, the Floralia sanctioned the appearance of nude mime-actresses. A common theme of these knock-about farces was conjugal infidelity, and a popular play which centred on this derived from Petronius's *Satyricon* in a story known as 'The Widow of Ephesus'. In this narrative, versions of which were used in a variety of theatrical productions, a virtuous widow resolves to starve herself to death while mourning her husband's death in his tomb, but a young soldier who is guarding corpses nearby sees the widow and tempts her with his food and drink and eventually leads her to love-making. Meanwhile one of the corpses the soldier has been guarding is stolen, and on discovering this the soldier anticipates death as his punishment for gross neglect of duty. The widow, however, prevents the soldier's execution by opening up her husband's coffin and replacing the missing corpse with his body (Ure, 1974, pp. 221–2).

The popularity of mime narratives such as 'The Widow of Ephesus' and the sanctioning of nude women performers conspire to promote a particular view of women as slaves to their unbridled sexuality. When Ovid, in the early days of the first century, crystallised the idea that women were not chaste until proven so, he was echoing a sentiment that had been played out by countless mime performances before him. A century later Juvenal, in his *Sixth Satire*, describes adultery – always assumed to be the woman's transgression – as the first crime of civilisation:

> To bounce your neighbour's bed, my friend, to outrage
> Matrimonial sanctity is now an ancient and long-
> Established tradition. All other crimes came later.
>
> (19–21)

Juvenal, like Aristophanes' comic character Mnesilochus, provides the reader with a detailed list of adulterous women as part of his *Sixth Satire* warning to men against matrimony: 'Marry a wife, and she'll make some flute-player/Or guitarist a father, not you' (76–7). Indeed, the original meaning of the word 'adultery' derives from the Latin for 'a wife's granting of marital advantages "to another (*ad ulterium*)" rather than to their owner, her husband' (Williman, 1986, p. 69).

Any credibility women as artists or creators achieved in theatrical performance became totally eradicated by plots which showed them merely transferring their adulterous tendencies from real life on to the stage: for example, in one historical account, the Roman Emperor Heliogabalus, at the beginning of the third century AD, ordered the realistic presentation of adultery on the stage as part of a mime performance. The Romans seem to have been obsessed by the combination of 'actual life' and 'spectacle', and with the blurring of any distinction between 'reality' and 'performance'. Another example of this obsession was their use of condemned criminals to appear on stage in literal 'murders' or 'crucifixions'. Such bloody displays, which at times undoubtedly combined copulation with murder, dramatically realised the early Christians' worst fears about the link between sex and death. It is hardly surprising, then, that the early Church included theatrical events in its attack on pagan ritual; and the fact that women themselves were performing the roles of female characters in mime performances strengthened the link between established social and cultural misogyny and prejudice against the theatre.

The Christian offensive: assaulting the imagination

The Christian barrage on theatre encompassed a wider front than paganism and its accompanying *spectacula*; it also led an attack on notions of artistic representation and, by inference, on the realm of imagination itself. In the impassioned condemnation of theatre entitled *De spectaculis*, Tertullian puts forward his own conspiracy theory: that behind Roman theatrical representation lurks the devil ready to ensnare innocent victims. For Tertullian, the very act of imagining is dangerous: 'The calling to mind of a criminal or a shameful thing is no better than the thing itself: what in act is rejected, is not in speech to be accepted' (quoted in Barish, 1985, p. 45) In other words, actors who play at being criminals are no better than actual criminals; likewise for the spectators who view such theatrical performance. The concept of mimesis, the art of representation through theatrical pretence, does not exist in Tertullian's view of play-acting, and he thus condones as well as condemns the

Roman reduction of theatrical performance to spectacle. Through its staging of actual murders and acts of adultery, or by presenting lion-torn humans as entertainment, Roman drama had eliminated the basic feature of Western theatre, mimesis. By also refusing to make distinction between real murder and play-acted murder (after which the 'victim' gets up and walks away), the Christian critic Tertullian reinforces the Roman cultural confusion between 'life' and 'art'.

Initially the critical onslaught by the Church had little effect: during the latter years of the Empire more than half of the calendar year was officially dedicated to various kinds of theatrical festival. Therefore Roman drama and its actors had plenty of opportunity to retaliate by ridiculing Christian ritual and symbols on the stage, much to the delight of its audience. Early Church hagiography contains several accounts of actors converting to Christianity both off and on the stage. St. Genesius, in the late third century, embraced Christianity while he was performing a mock baptism in a theatre performance in front of the Emperor Diocletian (Chambers, 1954, p. 10). This particular on-stage conversion is an example of the confusion between 'life' and 'art' working in the Christian's favour.

The medieval retrieval: theatre as Christian story-telling

Nevertheless the Church fathers did not relent, and their attacks proved ultimately effective. In the fifth century they succeeded in excommunicating all performers of mime; and as part of the conversion of Rome to Christianity, Justinian closed all the theatres in the sixth century. When theatre appears again as a major force on the Western cultural scene it is ironically the Church that promotes drama as a form of morality, mystery and miracle plays. This theatre, which parallels classical Greek tragedy and comedy in its relation to religious celebration, evolved inside the Church, being based on Catholic ritual and liturgy. When in the middle of the thirteenth century the productions became too large for the confining church walls, they moved outside into the surrounding streets or market square. As with the Greeks, productions cel-ebrated specific religious festivals, and the clergy used them as a way of disseminating religious stories, and visually spreading

Christian doctrine, codes and morals to a predominantly illiterate congregation. When the drama still took place within the small scope of the church, the priests themselves played most of the roles, but when the performances moved outside, actor-clerics increasingly shared roles with their secular audience. Although still controlled by the Church, productions now became community efforts, with local trade and crafts guilds sponsoring the productions at Christmas or Easter and taking great pride in constructing sets, special effects and, of course, costumes.

Despite the sense of community displayed in these productions, men took all the major roles. Modern historical analysis of this phenomenon of all-male casting finds it difficult to accept the Virgin Mary, for example, played by an adolescent boy or a mature male. (Recent historical research in this area has raised the suggestion that the onset of male puberty occurred later in medieval times, possibly as late as seventeen years, making young, unbearded men with high voices available for women's roles.)[1]

The main evidence for the male-only casting in England exists in the guild accounts of productions which list the name of the actor, his fee and his role. These remaining accounts are few, and from their meagre information we know that the roles of Mary, Anna and Eve were played by men. There is one documented exception to this in England, a stage direction in the play *Wisdom* which calls for six female dancers (Twycross, 1983, pp. 124–7).

Southern France and breaking the male theatrical monopoly

In France the cultural and social circumstance in relation to the position of women produced much more variety and geographical diversity. The surviving documents from two passion plays, the first at Mons in 1501 and the second at Valenciennes in 1547, list the performers and their delegated roles to reveal that men, boys and girls (*'jeunes filles'*) take part (Muir, 1985, p. 107). Male actors still take all the major roles, but it appears that in the Valenciennes performance both a young boy and a young girl are allotted the role of the Virgin Mary in her various scenes. So the contribution of young, pre-adolescent girls was permissible in northern France, but it seems that married women, whatever their age, did not act.[2]

More startling evidence from southern France records that in 1509 at Romans a production of the mystery play *Le Mystère des*

Trois Doms designated all but one of the female roles to women. These women performers all came from the local nobility and, with two exceptions, were married. Furthermore, it appears from the existing text, which includes the unusual feature of a prologue for four women, that the author had been encouraged to write as many roles for women as possible (Muir, p. 112).

How is it possible that acting practices in the south of France could differ so markedly from elsewhere in Europe? One answer might lie in the previous existence of female performers in that region, the women troubadours, who flourished there three centuries earlier. The poetry of more than twenty women troubadours has survived from the twelfth and early thirteenth centuries. It is thought that many more women than these extant poems indicate were actively involved in the court performance of poetry and music since Provençal, the language of southern France, includes a specific word for female troubadours, *trobaritz* (Neuls-Bates, 1982, p. 21). A recent study of this work, with translations of the women's poems, has revealed the special circumstances which, in spite of the Church's prevailing anti-women stance, made it possible for women to take an important role in one of the major secular literary movements in the West. These circumstances were primarily their noble birth, their control of feifdoms during their husbands' involvement in the crusades, and, perhaps most importantly, their ability to inherit land. At that time two laws governing inheritance in the Occitane south were inoperative in the north. The Code of Justinian (528–533) made it possible for a woman to retain her dowry; her husband could use it, but he did not own it. Thus if the death of a husband preceded that of his wife, her dowry would return to her, rather than pass on to his heirs. The Theodosian Code (394-395), effective in the south from the sixth century, gave sons and unmarried daughters equal shares in their deceased father's property.[3] In contrast, the Salic law which prevailed in northern France, England, Germany and Spain prevented daughters from inheriting from their father unless he had no sons; in addition, when a woman did marry, her dowry then became the absolute property of her husband (Bogin, 1976, pp. 8—36).

Religion is another aspect of Occitanian history relevant to the more mobile social position of women: the people of southern France were predominantly Cathars who believed in Christ without seeing the need for a wealthy, politically active Catholic Church. They believed to some degree in equality between men and women so that women could and did preach on equal footing with men. The Cathars presented an obvious doctrinal threat to the Catholic Church and became so numerous that in 1209 Pope Innocent III originated a new crusade – the Albigensian Crusade – which within fifty years of its institution virtually wiped out the 'heresy' and destroyed many of the major cities of the south.[4]

As a result of these crusades and their cultural annihilation of Occitania, the Catholic Church became rigidly entrenched in the south along with the Salic law. But the brief historical moment which preceded this, when women enjoyed a startling degree of political and artistic autonomy, gave rise to one of the great debates of the middle ages: the *querrelle des femmes*. Between 1275 and 1280 Jean de Meung completed the second half of *Roman de la Rose*. This long, acclaimed poem, the second half of which is an uncompromisingly vicious attack on women, exerted a powerful influence in both art and social life for the next two hundred years. Indeed, Marina Warner sees this debate and its surrounding controversy as having a historical and cultural impact equal to the publication of Darwin's *Origin of the Species* (Warner, 1983, p. 220). The three hundred copies of the manuscript which are still extant testify to its widespread popularity. The polemical controversy of the *querrelle des femmes* divided clergymen, royalty, and court officials between the Meung camp and that of Christine de Pisan, who in 1399 vigorously refuted the illogical, hate-filled *Roman de la Rose* with a clear-sighted and at times eloquent defence of women in her book *Le Dit de la Rose*.

What emerges is that the social and cultural atmosphere in France provided favourable enough conditions, or at least conditions that were not so rigidly hostile as in England or other parts of Europe, to permit its women to perform on its public stages. This 'permission' made it possible for the great playwrights of the seventeenth century – Corneille, Racine and Molière – to write all their plays in the knowledge that women could and would perform the roles written for them, a circumstance which, as we know, certainly did not exist on the English Renaissance stage.

Commedia families and the rise of the actress

There is another influence from within the theatre itself which exerted an important pressure on the social and cultural acceptance of actresses: the *commedia dell'arte*. The Italian comedy, improvised and nomadic, flourished from the mid-sixteenth century, entertaining most of continental Europe. Importantly, women were among the versatile performers of the *commedia* companies. Part of this can perhaps be explained by *commedia*'s possible but distant historic link with the Roman mimes. But more immediately relevant is the fact that many of the *commedia* companies were family-based structures where husband and wife teams often handed down their roles to sons or daughters. Evidence exists of such 'inheritances' lasting three or four generations. The family structure of the companies, linked with the precarious and unpredictable earnings of travelling players, made it economically necessary for the women to take part in both running the company and acting.

The playing of female roles by women in *commedia* companies happened gradually. Evidently the female servant roles were sometimes played by men, and even as late as the plays of Molière (which demonstrate an assimilation of certain aspects of *commedia* technique and style) certain male actors still specialised in the character parts of old women.

The *commedia* actresses often received high praise for their many talents – singing, dancing, playing guitar and bass-viol, and the writing of poetry. The co-operative, collective nature of these travelling companies was a vital element in their success, as this description by Niccolo Barbieri, a famous *commedia* actor from the early seventeenth century, indicates:

> The lovers and women study history, fables, rime, and prose, and the conceits of language. Those whose part it is to make folk laugh rack their brains to invent new farces, not from any wish to sin, nor to praise vice and folly in obscene words, but they strive to earn an honest living by arousing laughter with their covert quips and bizarre inventions. (Duchartre, 1966, p. 73).

The Catholic Church, however, maintained its centuries-old critical attack on the theatrical profession. Precisely at the point when the *commedia dell'arte* was most popular, the Church launched a new offensive against actresses through the issue from Pope Sextus V of a new edict in 1588 which banned the appearance of women on the stage (Duchartre, 1966, p. 262). In the wake of this ban the *Desiosi*, a *commedia* company managed by Diana Ponti, was prevented from performing until it substituted boys for its women performers (Gilder, 1960, p. 64). Enforced primarily in the papal states, this destructively influential prohibition lasted for nearly 200 years.[5] One of the few amusing effects of this edict occurs in *The Memoirs of Jacques Casanova*, where the author describes his attraction to a comely young actor named Bellino. Disturbed by the implicit homosexuality in his lustful feelings towards one of his own sex, Casanova with great relief discovers that Bellino's talent for acting goes beyond that of the stage: Bellino is a woman disguised as a man so that she can play female roles in the theatre (p. 70–2). In this instance social pressures and history provoke a cross-dressing scenario reminiscent of earlier Jacobean comedy.

The papal ban on women performers indicates a shift in the attitude of the Church to secular theatre: it moves from a condemnation of the whole profession to a much more specific and essentially misogynistic censorship of actresses. Such censorship not only prevents already-established actresses from performing, but those who do act (outside the papal states) are labelled morally suspect.

At the time when Italian actresses first appeared, their personal morality or their 'virtue' (for which read their supposed licentiousness) was constantly discussed and scrutinised. One of the most famous actresses of this period was Isabella Andreini (1562–1604), the leading woman of the renowned troupe, the *Gelosi*. She married the chief actor of the company, Francesco Andreini, and for twenty-five years they toured most of Europe. By all accounts Isabella was undoubtedly an excellent performer, but the quality which apparently sets her furthest apart from other women of her profession was her morality. Even Rosamund Gilder in her important reassessment of women in theatre, *Enter the Actress*, describes Isabella as

a pioneer actress and innovator in her profession . . . she took part in the creation of that world of pure theatre, that actor's world of movement and improvisation which had so great an influence on the European stage. Stately and beautiful, learned and virtuous, Isabella was at the same time a true child of the theatre. She could dance and sing, she could play hilarious comedy, and hold her own in the crudest farce. Her talents were multifarious, but unlike most of her contemporaries, *her virtue was above reproach.* (Gilder, 1960, p. 67, my italics)

In 1604, when Isabella died unexpectedly in Lyons, she received a magnificent funeral, and in denial of Christian custom and convention (which forbade the acting profession burial in consecrated ground) she was buried inside a church. A long Latin epitaph which recorded her many services to art also described her indomitable virtues.

Deciphering the unmasked female face

Thus, in the wake of *commedia dell'arte*, women had, against continued opposition, finally taken their place on the stage. What roles, then, did they play? Certainly not 'great' roles, as their parts of servants and young lovers testify. The four major masks of *commedia* are male: Harlequin, Pantalone, The Doctor, and Brighella, and all of its male characters exude invention and intrigue: Harlequin, of course, is one of the great clown lords of theatrical history. However, the female roles, which for the most part centre on love relationships, fall into two categories: the *inamorata*, a young female lover which Isabella Andreini made famous; and the female servant, sometimes called Columbina. The female servant proved a spirited comic match for her counterpart, Harlequin. Yet Columbina, and therefore the actress who played her with all the social and creative implications of this role, rarely initiated any major comic business. Instead she served as a foil, a side-kick, responding and reacting to the shenanigans of the male clown. Harlequin, in contrast, renowned for his disguises, chameleon-like changes, and his seemingly endless escapades, cleverly schemes, connives, and attempts to outsmart his master.

Duchartre, in his well-known study *The Italian Comedy*, explains the lack of interesting and challenging women's roles in this way:

> It was due to this absence of women from the stage for so long a time that the female *rôles* were not developed to any great extent in the *commedia dell'arte*, and hence never became as important characters as Pulcinella, Harlequin, and the others, who had a long tradition behind them. (Duchartre, 1966, pp. 263–4)

However, the absence of women on stage during the classical Greek period did not prevent the creation of important women's roles central to narratives such as *Lysistrata, Antigone* and *Electra*.

In his book, *The World of Harlequin*, Allardyce Nicoll discusses the role of the female servant (*servetta*) and depicts such characters as 'creatures' who inhabit a different comic world from that of the male servants:

> In the first place, only a few of their names became fully established: Franceschina was one of these during earlier years, Columbina and Smeraldina in later times became pervasive, and we can trace enduring traditions for Diamantina, Nespola and Ricciolina. Yet even these fail to reach *distinct individualisation*. (Nicoll, 1963, p. 95, my italics)

Nicoll's language here is unwittingly contradictory: far from lacking individuation, the female characters he cites are on the contrary individuals made fully particular by their singular names. Their individuality thus provides a contrast with their male counterparts, whose designated universal names – Harlequin, Pantalone, The Doctor – immediately reduce and delimit any sense of them as individuals. Nicoll continues his erroneous argument by aligning 'personality' with the male characters, while positing women's roles as less artistically creative, since, he asserts, these roles do not exist as characters 'in their own right':

> It is amply apparent that the names [of the female characters] themselves do not serve to designate personalities of the sort exemplified by Harlequin, Scapino, Brighella, Punch and Pierrot, *but are merely dependent on the choice of actresses interpreting the one single part*. No doubt one of these players performing, let us say, under the title of Rosetta produced an impression distinct from that of another actress who had selected the name of Suparella, but this does not mean that Rosetta was regarded by comedians or spectators as a *character which in its own right was to be presented differently from that of the other*. (Nicoll, 1963, p. 95, my italics)

The most telling differences in the women's roles, however, is purely visual: the absence of masks. Both Duchartre and Nicoll see this phenomenon of maskless women in a theatre of masks as an outward display of insufficient characterisation. Duchartre describes this absence as a lack of 'standardisation', a characteristic which for Duchartre implies individual status:

> Properly speaking, there were no masks for women in improvised comedy because the real mask was the standardisation of a character,

and no matter how frequently or how variously the Inamoratas, soubrettes, or matrons were introduced, these Flaminias, Sylvias, and Fiamettas changed in character and personality as often as different actresses were found to interpret them. (p. 266)

Undoubtedly the masks are a central ingredient – much celebrated and prestigious – of this improvised comedy. Jacques Copeau, the French director who revived *commedia* at the beginning of this century, reinforces this sense that masks had an almost mystical ability to generate a life and personality of their own:

> The actor who performs under a mask receives from this paper-mâché object the reality of his part. He is controlled by it and has to obey it unreservedly. Hardly has he put it on when he feels a new being flowing into himself, a being the existence of which he had before but never suspected. It is not only his face that has changed, it is all his personality, it is the very nature of his reactions, so that he experiences emotions he could have neither felt nor feigned without its aid. If he is a dancer, the whole style of his dance, if he is an actor, the very tones of his voice, will be dictated by this mask – the Latin 'persona' – a being, without life till he adopts it, which comes from without to seize upon him and proceeds to substitute itself for him. (Copeau, quoted in Nicoll, 1963, p. 41)

The tone of Copeau's panegyric upon the mask is reminiscent of the admiring regard for the phallus in the theatre of classical Greece. The phallus, linked as it was to celebrations of fertility and growth, provided an inspirational key to the comic (male) imagination. The wearing of the phallic apparatus, sanctioned by the religious festivals, obviously displayed the sign of male creativity. The power of the phallus, like the power of the mask, is histrionically prodigious. Copeau with his ·mask easily translates into Aristophanes with his phallus. The phallus, then like Copeau's mask, is a 'persona', 'a being without life till [the actor] adopts it'. Both phallus and mask are crucial tools to the patriarchal imagination, signs which transcend reality: 'religiously, philosophically and aesthetically the mask consecrates the effacement of immediate reality for the benefit of vaster reality' (Nicoll, p. 41).

So for Nicoll the absence of a mask for the female characters is as artistically bleak as the absence of a phallus. On the other hand, Duchartre, as we have seen from the introductory quote to this chapter, gives much more prosaic reasons why women do not wear masks: the chief prerequisite of an actress is her beauty, and wearing a mask would obscure this essential ingredient for an actress's success. Like Nicoll, he stresses this idea of actress-as-self but goes even further:

> The history of Isabelle, Francesquina, Flaminia, Columbina, or Zerbinette was rather that of the actress who played the *rôle* than that of the *rôle* itself. A *comédienne* was required to be pretty as well as charming. (Duchartre, 1966, p. 264)

We have seen in the previous chapter how the female costume acted as the theatrical sign for 'woman'. This sign does not disappear when women begin to perform their own roles. The costumes of the women were for the most part the personal clothing of the actress (a convention which carried on well into the nineteenth century) and so supported this enduring conflation of self and actress: the often magnificent dresses, especially for the leading actresses, could be worn in daily life for attendance at court as well as the stage: after all in both arenas the woman was simply her 'self'. Imagine, in contrast, Harlequin wearing his colourful, patchy, unreal costume anywhere other than the stage.

Of particular interest here is a subtext which says that women cannot in principle act a character, but can only perform aspects of themselves. This notion is corroborated by the absence of any mask standing for a female character, the lack of major female roles, no character name comparable to Harlequin, Scapino or Pantalone, no evidence of *lazzi* (comic business) for women, and by the blurred distinction between a woman's personal clothes and her costumes. If we look at the secondary material – the critical writing of Duchartre, Nicoll and Copeau – this constriction is upheld and advanced despite its evident contradictions. We have seen how both uchartre and Nicoll assert that the 'actress/character' lacks consistency. For Nicoll the part of a serving maid never developed a 'character in its own right', and for Duchartre there were so many actresses playing the various female roles that there was no possibility for 'standardisation' of character. Since I have demonstrated that the individual woman herself stood for the role, it follows that the possibility of creating a long-lasting 'character', one that transcends the mere 'self' of womankind, becomes impossible. In an effort to reinforce their idea of the undeveloped nature of female roles, Nicoll and Duchartre go out of their way to construct lists. Just as Aristophanes endlessly listed the characteristics of women, so Nicoll lists the numerous, and seemingly endless, names of women 'characters'. In particular, Nicoll spends some time discussing this as if the sheer wealth of female names from the archives of *commedia* performance justifies his theory of their relative unimportance. He has already acquainted us with Franceschina, Columbina, Smeraldina, Diamantina, Nespola, Ricciolina, Rosetta, and Suparella, and he continues his case by claiming that:

> Just at the first glance, these [names] may seem to be as diverse as their male companions, offering a rich array of individual names as variegated as those of the others. Armellinas, Corallinas, Olivettas and Spinettas flock in upon us, accompanied by numerous variants of similar kind, and we might well feel that these deserve separate attention. (p. 95)

But they don't. They are different from their male counterparts, the *zanni*; they live, as we have noted, in a different comic world, a world which defines them not by the attributes they possess, but by absences, deficits, lacks and shortcomings. Since women themselves have been relegated both in real life and in artistic representation to a position which reflects a historical view of them as deficient, as outside the realm of cultural creativity, it does not surprise us that their roles in performance, however individual, reflect this wider limitation.

Furthermore these women performers are characterised as fickle, mutable, lacking consistency. Again, this criticism is aimed solely at actresses but more comprehensively at women in general. 'Woman', the ideological concept, is, as we saw in Chapter 2, eternal and unchanging, but characteristic of her abstract consistency is her personal lack of it. She is, in other words, consistently inconsistent. It seems that actresses, by their very nature *as women*, can achieve no critical uniformity or steadfastness of character.

The male *zanni*, however, are constant and consistent; they have created 'real' characters, and the tangible evidence of these characters grins widely from their masks. The 'eternal' quality of these masks is clearly expressed in Copeau's description above. But while the mask is a 'being', existing in its own right, it is the male actor wearing it who brings it to life. When Harlequin performs before a large audience, the spectators witness a double act of creativity both from the actor who performs the role and from the creativity of the mask itself originated by some unknown Harlequin hundreds of years before. Isabella Andreini, the *innamorata*, enters the stage. She sings, plays the guitar, dances elegantly, and then bursts into a tirade against her faithless lover – an improvised speech in which she parodies both ideas of romantic love and turgid French tragedy. Her energetic, comic performance exudes style, wit, charisma. But she is maskless. She is merely playing herself.

4

Goethe, Goldoni and woman-hating

'It's not that I am jealous of her,' she exclaimed, with a quick proud look at me; 'not that I don't believe she's a great actress; but *I can't separate her acting from what she is herself.* It is women like that who bring discredit on the whole profession – it is women like that who make people think that no good woman can be an actress. I resent it, and I mean to take the other line. I want to prove, if I can, that a woman may be an actress and still be a lady, still be treated just as you treat the women you know and respect! I mean to prove that there need never be a word breathed against her, and that she is anybody's equal, and that her private life is her own, and not the public's!' (Mrs Humphrey Ward, *Mrs. Bretherton*, 1884, my italics)

It came over him suddenly that so far from there being any question of her having the histrionic nature, she simply had it in such perfection that she was always acting; that her existence was a series of parts assumed for the moment, each changed for the next, before the perpetual mirror of some curiosity or admiration or wonder – some spectatorship that she perceived or imagined in the people about her . . . It struck him abruptly that a woman whose only being was to 'make believe', to make believe that she had any and every being that you liked, that would serve a purpose, produce a certain effect, and whose identity resided in the continuity of her personations, so that she had no moral privacy, as he phrased it to himself, but lived in a high wind of exhibition, of figuration – *such a woman was a kind of monster*, in whom of necessity there would be nothing to like, because there would be nothing to take hold of. He felt for a moment that he had been very simple not before to have achieved that analysis of the actress. (Henry James, *The Tragic Muse*, 1890, my italics)

Against the background of *commedia*, where women were gaining access to the stage, it is useful to look briefly for contrast at three

47

influential theatrical arenas where the absence of women was staunchly maintained. The first two have links with educational establishments: the boys' companies in England, and the theatrical productions connected to the Jesuit schools and colleges on the continent. The third arena concerns the theatrical restrictions imposed by the Catholic Church in the papal states. This latter is examined through an eye-witness account: Goethe's essay of 1787 entitled 'Women's Parts Played by Men in the Roman Theatre'.

The boys' companies in England: Heywood's contest for liars

In the great wave of Renaissance humanism which swept England in the early sixteenth century, a strong programme of religiously inspired education for boys was instituted. One humanist ideal of learning was through playmaking, where religious doctrine and moral parables could be debated in public, creating a theatrical event which these educators believed spiritually edified both participant and spectator alike. Erasmus, for example, promoted the idea that study should 'hardly be distinguised from play' (Blewitt, 1986, p. 35). By the time of Queen Elizabeth the boys' companies attached to church-supported schools flourished in full artistic and monarchical favour. Indeed, the Children of St. Paul's were Elizabeth's favourite company, and she often invited them to play at court. In 1600 Richard Burbage turned the Blackfriars Theatre into a private stage which featured the Children of the Chapel Royal. These companies, with many of the leading play-wrights of the day in their service, for a short period of time outstripped the professional adult companies, and Shakespeare alludes to them in a well-known passage between Rosencrantz and Hamlet. Hamlet discovers from Rosencrantz that the famous company of tragedians from the city are touring the provinces, a sure sign of their falling upon hard times. They have been forced to tour because of a 'late innovation' – the sudden popularity of boys' companies. Rosencrantz describes the youthful players as:

> an aery of children, little eyases, that cry out on the top of question, and are most tyrannically clapped for't: these are now the fashion, and so berattle the common stages, – so they call them, – that many wearing rapiers are afraid of goose-quills, and dare scarce come thither. (II. ii. 362–8)

The importance of the boys' companies, historically either ignored as unimportant or simply overlooked, emerges in a recent study which states that

> the agents of drama in education, the boy actors, enjoyed an almost unrivalled success as entertainers . . . Not only did they popularize drama where it mattered most, that is, where evolution was possible, but they established its form, they alerted both playmakers and playwrights to the varieties of material that were susceptible to dramatic treatment, they demonstrated that plays could cross class barriers to engage the inheritants of both traditions [the classical revival and the popular drama], and they provided the model for an effective playing space. (Blewitt, 1986, p. 363)

The impact of the boys' companies on Elizabethan drama was by no means indirect; several of their 'graduates' – Kyd, Marlowe, Jonson and Middleton – went into the adult profession as playwrights. With this in mind, it is worth looking at two of the scripts written specifically for boy performances. The first, an early example, is an interlude written by John Heywood (c. 1497–1580), whose work with boys' companies is considered to mark the transition between medieval morality and mystery plays and the comedies of the Elizabethans. This most famous play of Heywood's, thought to have been performed by both professional actors and boys in 1520, is entitled *The Playe called the foure P.P.; a newe and a very mery interlude of a palmer, a pardoner, a potycary, a pedler.* The simple plot involves a group of four men, all lower class 'types', who meet on an open road and play a debating game over who can fabricate the biggest lie. Heywood's innovation was to take the traditional *disputatio* – an educational debate usually in Latin – and not only transform it into the vernacular by using native, Chaucerian characters, but also develop it into dramatic action. Theatre historians have stressed the innovative nature of Heywood's work; how, in educational terms, for example, it gave his young male performers the opportunity to improve their rhetoric. But another kind of 'teaching' informs Heywood's script, an instructive curriculum which academics have ignored: the script is a comic male discourse on the 'nature' of women.

The play's action originates from the Pedler's declaration: 'All things decayeth where there is no head' (p. 273). In order to establish a harmonious social hierarchy, the Pedler recommends that they have a tale-telling contest, with himself as the judge, where the man who tells the biggest lie will be the winner; the winner's reward will be the privilege of becoming the group's leader. The three men eagerly deliver their lies, all of which centre on anecdotal stories about women.

The first, by the Potycary (Apothecary), describes in flamboyant and scatological detail his medical treatment of a beautiful young woman with an anal blockage. The suppository he administered loosened her bowels so effectively that the force of the evacuation demolished a wall ten miles off! The second account, told by the Pardoner, involves another sick woman who died suddenly without the benefit of last rites. The Pardoner magnanimously decides ('for her soul health especially') to travel to purgatory to help her with his pardons (p. 284). Arriving to find she is not there, he realises she went directly to hell. Following her there he discovers, to his surprise, that Lucifer is quite happy to get rid of her:

> No devil in hell shall withold her!
> And if thou wouldst have twenty more,
> Were not for justice, they should go.
> For all we devils with this den
> Have more to do with two women
> Than with all the charge we have beside.
> Wherefore, if thou our friend will be tried,
> Apply thy pardons to women so
> That unto us there come no more.
> (p. 288)

Finding this woman more trouble than hell itself, Lucifer gladly expels her from his kingdom and requests the Pardoner to make more generous use of his pardons where women are concerned, since two women in hell cause more hardship that all its other inhabitants together.

The third story in this contest of lies comes from the Palmer. Unlike the descriptive, detailed and lengthy lies of the Pardoner and the Potycary, he adopts a straightforward, simple strategy. The Palmer's story is terse, crisp and to the point:

> Yet have I seen many a mile
> And many a woman in the while –
> Not one good city, town, nor borough
> In Christendom but I have been through –

And this I would ye understand:
I have seen women five hundred thousand
. . . [missing line] . . .
And often with them have long time tarried;
Yet in all places where I have been,
Of all the woman that I have seen,
I never saw, nor knew, in my conscience,
And one woman out of patience.

(p. 290)

The Palmer's tale of women's (im)patience elicits a vociferous reaction from all the men who recognise its superior quality: the Pedler, as competition judge, declares: 'know ye any [lie] so great?' (p. 290) and announces the Palmer the prize liar.

The ending of Heywood's interlude re-introduces and reiterates the theme of male co-operation and harmony which the Pedler advanced at the beginning. As the Palmer, declared winner of the lying competition and rightful leader of the group, abdicates his position, thus relieving the others of their subordinate role, the play ends in 'an exhortation to all to live righteously and with charity' (p. 68).

Heywood is not considered a major dramatist of the early English Renaissance, though modern re-evaluations of his work stress his importance as a transitional theatrical figure. These assessments emphasise the dramatic structure, the use of vernacular speech, the character types, as well as the *educational* value to the boy players (improving rhetoric, learning the value of social harmony) and audience. These all collude with Heywood's view that the subject of women initiates jokes and lies and, implicitly, praises the enactment of an interlude where women are the source of storytelling, voyeuristic fantasy, and deceit – the most blatant lie about women being to say something good about them.

The boys' companies in England: Jonson's search for a silent woman

The implication in Heywood's script that 'social harmony' relies on continual efforts to define, contain and restrict the female, exemplifies a tradition of anecdotal storytelling centred on the topic of 'woman' which appears with frequent regularity in the plays of this period. Another such classic is Ben Jonson's *Epicoene*, or *the Silent Woman*, which was first performed in 1609 or 1610 by the Children of her Majesty's Revels at Whitefriars. The script has an intriguing performance history: besides at least two additional performances at Court in 1635 or 1636, Dryden so celebrated the script in his *Essay of Dramatic Poesy* that it became the model for the new Restoration comedy. The first play recorded as publicly performed after the return of the exiled king, it received nearly one hundred performances between 1660 and 1752 (Jonson, ed. Partridge, p. 200). The plot has much more complexity than Heywood's and a much larger cast, with, significantly, five parts for women.

The main plot revolves around Morose, 'a gentleman that loves no noise', and his efforts to find a silent bride – primarily to prevent his nephew, Dauphine, whom he considers a wayward youth, from inheriting his fortune (Jonson, p. 27). Morose finds his ideal woman, Epicoene, 'who is exceedingly soft-spoken, thrifty of her speech, that spends but six words a day', and he plans to marry this personification of silence (p. 38). A loquacious friend of Dauphine, Truewit, tries to prevent the matrimonial match by visiting Morose with a tirade against both women and matrimony which he believes will banish thoughts of the altar. A sample of his 'true wit' advances a listing of alternative but apposite terrors associated with women:

> Marry, your friends do wonder, sir, the Thames being so near, wherein you may drown so handsomely; or London Bridge at a low fall, with a fine leap, to hurry you down stream; or such a delicate steeple i' the town as Bow, to vault from . . . (*He shows his halter*) or a beam in the said garret, with this halter, which they have sent, and desire that you would sooner commit your grave head to this knot than to the wedlock noose; or take a little sublimate [mercury sublimate, a violent poison] and go out of the world like a rat, or a fly, as one said, with a straw i' your arse: any way rather than to follow this goblin Matrimony. (Jonson, p. 50)

Truewit's tirade thunders on for another three pages, and shortly after he congratulates himself on its effectiveness: 'If ever Gorgon were seen in the shape of a woman, he hath seen her in my description. I have put him off that scent [marriage] for ever' (p. 61). But Truewit's censorious storytelling about the hazards of matrimony has exactly the opposite of its desired effect on Morose, who, thinking it is merely his nephew souring him by proxy on marriage, decides to marry Epicoene immediately.

But after the marriage Jonson transforms Epicoene from a silent, self-effacing girl into a talkative and dominant wife. (I explore the subtextual image of the speechless woman at work here more fully in Chapter 7.) Morose, exposed to endless female chatter, sets out in a panic to end the marriage as soon as possible. He turns to his wayward nephew Dauphine for assistance and, in a final desperate ploy to annul his matrimonial bonds, publically declaims his sexual impotence. Yet Jonson and his hero Dauphine reserve the ultimate comic twist for the ending: after persuading Morose to proclaim him as his deserved and sole heir, Dauphine disrobes Epicoene to reveal triumphantly that his uncle has married a boy costumed as a woman. Such sexual masquerading is similar to Aristophanes' play the *Thesmophoriazousae*, where the revelation of a man disguised as a woman plays a central part in both the plot structure and the comedy. There is another parallel, though: just as Aristophanes' character Euripides dresses his uncle as a woman, so Dauphine dresses Epicoene; and instructs him in creating the opposite stereotype of the silent woman – the domineering chatterbox. The message is clear for Jonson's boy players: learning female artifice is not only simple, but the defining of women through aesthetic (mis)representation is essential to comedy itself.

Jesuit spectacle and addressing the taboo of staging women

Such easy assumption of female dress both before and during the English Restoration was considered by the Jesuits too symbolically potent for their theatrical productions. Unlike the boys' companies in England where women, both as characters and subject matter, in-augurate dramatic action, Jesuit productions remained faithful to St Paul's injunction, 'Let women keep silent in church'; they banned not only women, but all female roles from their theatre. This ecclesiastical drama quickly became central to educational activity in Jesuit schools and colleges on the continent; the first record of a production is in 1551, only three years after the establishment of a college for day pupils in Messina. The productions subsequently developed from amateur, small-scale productions to large, 'professional' spectacles employing elaborate technical devices and magnificent costumes and sets. As with most contemporary school drama, their objectives focused on a didactic rendering of theological values designed to benefit both performer and spectator.

In reference to the position of women, the order set up precise regulations – *'nec persona ulla muliebris vel habitus introducatur'* – that no women characters or feminine dress should be used on the stage (Hartnoll, 1967, p. 598). In 1591 this early prohibition was revised: female roles could be used if they were limited to those absolutely necessary. Interestingly the Church fathers of this masculinised theatre found the prohibition both impracticable and virtually unworkable. Thus, for example, Jesuit priests in several provinces in Germany and Austria complained that finding material absolutely devoid of women for both religious *and* secular plays was extremely difficult. Nonetheless, the general prohibition remained in force until a dispensation in 1602 permitted female characters as long as they were modest, unassuming, and rarely used. Exceptions to this rule can be seen from the numerous productions around the story of Judith from the Old Testament, the popularity of plays about Esther, and the many productions on the lives of female martyrs.

Such productions were equally popular with local royalty and the general populace, sometimes being performed for the court and other times over several days in a festival atmosphere of the market-place. A celebrated aspect of Jesuit productions was their impressive visual stagings of religious scenes. In one account of a spectacular staging in Graz in 1640, dogs tore apart a life-like puppet figure of Jezebel, dressed in female magnificence (Hartnoll, 1967, p. 515). Here the emphasis on the dramatically visual clearly marries with the idea that the clothes stand for the woman. For Jezebel, as her story in the Old Testament makes clear, her dress, her clothing, her artifice are her whole nature and her crime: 'and she [Jezebel] painted her face, and tired her head, and looked out at a window' (2 Kings, 9: 30–31)

In spite of the suppression of the order in 1773, Jesuit drama had an undeniable effect (the full implications of which have not yet been fully investigated) on the historical development of secular, mainstream theatre. Like the boys' companies of England whose 'graduates' entered the professional theatre, many esteemed men of letters studied in Jesuit colleges. These include Corneille, Voltaire and Goldoni (whom we will consider in more detail in the next section) as well as less illustrious figures such as Dancourt (French dramatist and actor of the late seventeenth and early eighteenth centuries), Crebillon (1674–1762, popular playwright known as the French Aeschylus), and Le Sage (1668–1747, well-known novelist and playwright).

Goethe's view: men make better women

My final example of masculinised theatre brings together two theatrical practitioners, Goldoni and Goethe, with the Roman Catholic Church to reveal theatrical and social attitudes to women, actresses, female characters and cross-dressing. All three forces converge in Rome in 1787: Carlo Goldoni's play *La Locandiera* was produced there in that year; the papal laws banishing women from the stage were still in force; and Johann von Goethe, while on a visit to the city, witnessed the production and wrote about it in an essay entitled 'Women's Parts Played by Men in the Roman Theatre'.

Goldoni, as mentioned, studied with the Jesuits apparently as a result of his dramatic talent: at eleven Goldoni wrote a comedy which so astonished his father that he sent his boy to the Jesuits in Perugia. To theatre historians, Goldoni stands as the fundamental reformer of *commedia dell'arte*. Instead of allowing *commedia* actors to rely on their unwritten improvised comedy, which in some cases had degenerated into a series of obscene, rude gestures, Goldoni insisted that they learn his scripts. He also removed masks from the male *commedia* performer. Some contemporary critics evaluate him as 'the first naturalistic playwright in the history of drama' (Goldoni, ed. Davies, p. 9) – a somewhat large claim based on Goldoni's eventual shift from using stock *commedia* parts to more three-dimensional, recognisable, 'real' characters.

Considered best among his characters are the 'young women involved in the sex war'. One critic celebrates Goldoni's female creations with this assessment:

[A] selection of feminine traits, combined with a minutely careful observation of feminine talk, mannerisms and reactions, is revealed in his young women in search of husbands. They are playing a game according to rules nobody has taught them. *Theirs is the instinctive involvement in the battle for which nature has formed them.* (Davies, p. 17, my italics)

Already, before looking at Goldoni's script in any detail, we face a jaundiced secondary criticism of his work which pictures women as primarily instinctual and naturally formed to search for husbands. When one allies this view with the other critical claim that Goldoni's characters are 'real' – particularly the women – what emerges, both from Goldoni and from those critics who commend him, is the assumption that women are innately hunters of men and matrimony.

However, in his most popular and famous female portrayal, Mirandolina, Goldoni reverses his normal treatment of women and transforms his usual man-hunting female into its exact opposite: several men are desperate to marry the woman. Despite Mirandolina's departure from Goldoni's female stereotype, critics claim her as Goldoni's greatest portrait of female coquetry, a lively, forthright creature who runs an efficient, well-kept concern. Two of her guests at the inn, a wealthy count and an impoverished marquis, declare love for her and their readiness to marry her. Mirandolina is impressed neither by the money of the former nor by the title of the latter, and effectively and humorously keeps them at bay. A third character, the Baron, is a self-professed, vociferous woman-hater, who finds it utterly ludicrous that the count and the marquis should argue over a woman:

> Was there anything ever less worth arguing about! To argue over a woman! To upset yourselves over a woman! A woman? I can't believe it. Over a woman? Well, one thing's certain: that's something I'll never be in danger of arguing over. Women are by nature stupid, selfish, and dogmatic. The great tragedy of life is that they've made themselves indispensable. To put it plainly women bore me utterly, absolutely, and completely. (Goldoni, p. 196)

Although both the marquis and the count try to convince the Baron that their innkeeper truly differs from your normal kind of woman, the Baron remains implacable and resolute with his rebuffs: 'She's like any other woman'; and later, 'Women? They're all the same' (p. 197)

When the Baron uncompromisingly confronts her, Mirandolina decides to trick him into falling in love with her against his will: 'Yes, I'll use every art I have to conquer this enemy of women!' (p. 203). To ensnare the Baron she employs the effective ruse of appearing extremely truthful and honest; most importantly, she agrees ingenuously with him on his view of women:

Baron:	. . . I've no need of women.
Mirandolina:	Wonderful! Don't ever change! If you only knew, signore . . . but I shouldn't speak badly of my own sex.
Baron:	Do you know, you're the first woman I've ever heard talk like this?
Mirandolina:	I'll tell you a secret. When you're the mistress of an Inn like I am – well the things you hear! If men only knew they've every reason to be wary of my sex. They have my sympathy.
Baron:	*(aside)* What an unusual woman she is.

(p. 210)

Just as the Palmer's 'opposite lie' in Heywood's interlude wins the contest, so too does Mirandolina's 'opposite lie' win the Baron. Gradually, against his will, the Baron starts to warm to Mirandolina, and the aspect of her character which he appreciates most is her sincerity: '. . . she has a certain frankness about her, an openness. Quite uncommon' (p. 212). Later he comments: 'And one has to admit she's quite charming. Though what I like most is her frankness, her sincerity. Yes, that's just what most women lack. Sincerity in a woman is a fine thing' (p. 214).

By the end of the play the Baron has fallen madly in love with the innkeeper and rages so jealously that Mirandolina has to admit to herself that her scheming has ventured too far. In the presence of the Baron, the Marquis and the Count, three men of rank and money, she chooses her husband-to-be: the working-class servant in her employ. The Baron, outraged by Mirandolina's manoeuvre, leaves the inn cursing all womankind:

> You wretched woman, a dagger is what you deserve. And your heart cut out and shown as a warning to all women like you. Let me get out of your sight. I scorn and curse your female tricks, your tears, your lies. One thing you taught me, to my bitter cost. It's not enough to despise women. No! One should flee from the very sight of them. As I do now. From you!
> (p. 251)

The Count and the Marquis remain with Mirandolina, pledging their continued respect and admiration. She asks of them one last small favour: to find lodgings in another inn. Fabrizio, her husband-to-be, sees this expulsion of old would-be lovers as the necessary gesture that signifies the serious nature of Mirandolina's matrimonial intentions. Goldoni puts his final words in Mirandolina's mouth:

Your kind words, signori [*the Count and the Marquis*] will always mean very much to me – within certain limits. For in changing my state to that of a married woman, I shall learn to change my ways. [*She turns to face the audience.*] And you also may learn from what you have seen. Whenever you feel yourselves falling in love, and wonder whether you should yield or not, think of these *infinite tricks of women* – and remember Mirandolina! (p. 253, my italics)

La Locandiera was first produced in Venice in 1753, and later by Goethe in Weimar in 1777. In both these productions women actors played the leading role of Mirandolina. During his visit to Italy in 1787, Goethe, a theatre professional himself both as a playwright and a director, having only witnessed a woman in the role of Mirandolina, saw the all-male Roman performance. In his essay which details his reaction to the event, Goethe first recognises that this men-playing-women 'custom' has survived from the classical period, and that the production is therefore worth viewing as a museum piece. He presents the theatre of the 'ancients' as 'organised in such a way that either women could be more or less dispensed with, or else female roles were played by an actor who had prepared himself especially for them', and he observes that women were not allowed to perform during 'the best periods for art and morality' (Goethe, 1984, p. 98). But the main point of Goethe's essay is his belief in the superiority of male imitation (i.e. men playing women) over mere female being (women acting). He praises young male actors who have had to study women in order to portray them, and celebrates them as true 'artists'. But, more importantly, male imitation offers superior insights to the spectator: 'We come to know this nature [woman] even better because someone else has observed it, reflected on it, and presents us not with the thing itself but with the result of the thing' (p. 99).

For Goethe women do not take the stage to act; instead they serve as objects of admiration. Being unable to imitate, they are therefore unable to create, to make art. In the Roman production, with Mirandolina played by a man, Goethe enjoyed 'not the thing itself but its imitation'; he was entertained 'not through nature but through art'. When he compares this with an *actress* playing the final scene in which Mirandolina chooses her own marriage partner, Goethe cannot contain his agitation:

I am convinced and have myself been a witness to it, that a clever and understanding actress can earn much praise in this role; but the last scenes, if they are played by a woman, will always be offensive. The expression of that invincible coldness, of that sweet feeling of revenge, of malicious joy in the discomfiture of others, shock us in their unmitigated truthfulness. And when she finally gives her hand in marriage to her servant only so that she may have a manservant about the house, the trivial ending of the play hardly satisfies us. But on the Roman state we found no cold absence of love, no female wantonness – the performance merely reminded us of them. We were comforted by the fact that this time at least it was not true. We applauded the young man lightheartedly and were delighted that he was so well acquainted with the ensnaring wiles of the fair sex that *through his successful imitation of feminine behaviour he had avenged us for every offence women had made us suffer*. (p. 100, my italics)

Considering that Goethe produced the play himself, his 'directorial' interpretation is significant: he reads Mirandolina's decision to marry Fabrizio as exemplifying her scheming nature. Goethe cannot imagine her having genuine feelings of affection and love, and thus interprets her choice of husband merely 'so that she may have a manservant about the house'. In contrast to Goethe's construction, the script itself clearly signals the romantic interest that Mirandolina has for Fabrizio. Goethe merely discounts this and construes her declaration of love at the end of the play as inauthentic and deceitful.

Goldoni himself seems doubtful about Mirandolina's sincerity, as his authorial intentions bear an ambiguous relation to his creation: a strong, clever, witty woman whose sincerity, frankness and candour at times conflict with her coquetry and deceptive games. Goethe is not alive to any such ambiguity, since such would suggest that Mirandolina is a character of some internal complexity, that she does not merely exemplify consistent, acceptable, male-defined 'feminine traits'.

Goldoni characterises the Baron as self-important, pompous and ruthless, and part of our pleasure in the narrative derives from witnessing Mirandolina subvert him. At the height of her game-playing, however, Goldoni undermines Mirandolina's moral role by giving her the following lines: 'It may be a useful thing to be able to pretend and deceive. But the person who can deceive in one thing can deceive in another' (p. 223). Suddenly these lines, like some moral police force raiding the dramatic scene of a crime, question Mirandolina's actions: if she can so easily deceive the Baron, can't she just as easily deceive her future husband, Fabrizio? Are we really to believe her declarations of love to him at the end of the play? Mirandolina's final words to the audience appear to overturn her serious matrimonial declaration: 'Whenever you feel yourselves falling in love . . . think of the infinite tricks of women' (p. 253). Mirandolina's words return her to the female stereotype of the flirtatious coquette, fulfilling her 'natural role' in 'the battle of the sexes'.

Goethe's separation of 'art' and 'nature' ensures that he will be disturbed by Goldoni's ending. By aligning women with 'nature', Goethe could simultaneously deny them any role in creativity and assert that women performers are always assumed to 'be' themselves. It never occurs to Goethe that the actresses he saw in the role of Mirandolina were 'acting' in the sense of mimetic theatrical creation. So when Goethe watches an actress play Mirandolina, the end of this play is always 'offensive' because she presents herself in 'unmitigated truthfulness' when she expresses 'invincible coldness', 'sweet feeling(s) of revenge, of malicious joy in the discomfiture of others'. But when a man takes the role, Goethe and his audience can thoroughly enjoy the final scenes because they are not witnessing 'reality', only 'successful imitation', creativity, artistry; only a pleasurably distant reminder of 'female wantoness', and the 'ensnaring wiles of the fair sex', not a first-hand experience of this threat. Furthermore, such a successful man-as-woman imitation as Goethe experienced in Rome avenges 'us' (males) for every 'such offence women had made us suffer'. So where male actors play at being women, they aggressively and vengefully appropriate the female role out of self-righteous anger. Goethe's message is clear: women are created as artefacts, as images which stand for 'reality' or 'truth'; thus women as signs take artistic precedence over real women. Viewed at one remove they are, to Goethe, safer and less threatening because men have created them, and in creation lies control. Mirandolina played as a woman is 'offensive': she doesn't take marriage seriously, she uses men to her own end and she herself autonomously decides her partner. But Mirandolina played as a cross-dressed man is 'delightful': 'she' shows us the eternally manipulating, coquettish female and 'her' marriage to a male servant becomes a celebration of male-bonding in disguise.

The patriarchal checklist of femininity

A quality common to all the examples in this chapter – the boys'

companies, Jesuit drama, Goethe's essay – is the singular need of
male artists to *define* women. Such definition takes a variety of
forms, from actual imitation to textual description. Goethe, for
example, specifies the way young male actors learn to act women:

> They observe the facial expressions, the movements, the behaviour of
> women with the utmost care; they try to imitate them and to give their
> voices suppleness and sweetness . . . They are as keen about new
> fashions as women are. (p. 98)

Goethe's definition reveals a clear association between the female
body, physicality and external gesture. But Heywood, in *The Foure
P.P.*, shows an obsession with itemising female objects: the Pedler's
business is selling the paraphenalia of womanhood. In the first
encounter with the Potycary, Palmer and Pardoner, he attempts to
peddle his wares, describing himself as a specialist in women's
'triflings':

> Gloves, pins, combs, glasses unspotted,
> Pomanders, hooks, and laces knotted,
> Brooches, rings, and allmanner beads,
> Lace, round and flat, for women's heads,
> Needles, thread, thimbles, shears, and all such knacks.
>
> (p. 267)

The Pedler's self-pronounced expertise in the subject of women
stems from his direct involvement in selling women's objects. The
proof of his proficiency lies in his ability to itemise female 'needs':

> *Pardoner*:   (*to the Pedler*) Sir, ye seem well versed
> in women's causes.
> I pray you, tell me what causeth this,
> That women, after their arising,
> Be so long in their appareling?
>
> *Pedler*:   Forsooth, women have many problems,
> And they be masked in many nets,
> As frontlets, fillets, partlets, and bracelets;
> And then their bonnets and their poignets.
> By these lets and nets the let is such
> That speed is small when haste is much.
>
> (pp. 267–8)

Truewit in *Epicoene* similarly makes it his business throughout the play to present his endless erudition on the subject of women, listing, as we have seen, numerous reasons for avoiding matrimony. But his knowledge in this subject goes beyond the 'happy' realm of marriage into the wisdom of good grooming and beauty:

> O, a woman is then like a delicate garden, nor is there one kind of it: she may vary every hour, take often counsel of her glass and choose the best. If she have good ears, show 'em; good hair, lay it out; good legs, wear short clothes; a good hand, discover it often; practise any art to mend breath, cleanse teeth, repair eyebrows, paint, and profess it. (p. 33)

Later in the play Truewit resumes his cataloguing/defining of the female by describing ways for older women to survive male scrutiny:

> Women ought to repair the losses time and years have made i' their features, with dressings. And an intelligent woman, if she know by herself the least defect, will be most curious to hide it, and it becomes her. If she be short, let her sit much, lest when she stands she be thought to sit. If she have an ill foot, let her wear her gown the longer and her shoe the thinner. If a fat hand and scald [scabrous] nails, let her carve [gesture] the less, and act in gloves. If a sour breath, let her never discourse fasting, and always talk at her distance. If she have black rugged teeth, let her offer the less at laughter, especially if she laugh wide and open. (pp. 104–5)

Aristophanes is another playwright who relies on the notion of female definition for much of his comedy. We have seen how in the *Thesmophoriazousae* such an inventory becomes visual as well as textual when one male character dresses another in women's clothes in front of the audience. Aristophanes continues the inventory motif in *The Assemblywomen*, in which Praxagora, an articulate woman who has grown tired of the inefficiency of the governing men, tries to persuade her female friends to join her in taking over the running of Athens, because women make such 'efficient managers' at home:

> Women still sit down to do the roasting, as they've always done. They carry things on their heads, as they've always done. They hold the Thesmophoria Festival, as they've always done. They bake cakes, as they've always done. They infuriate their husbands, as they've always done. (The other women begin to join in, with increasing gusto, when

this phrase recurs.) They buy themselves little extras on the side, as they've always done. They drink their wine neat, as they've always done. They enjoy a bit of sex, as they've always done. (pp. 29–30)

In this particular speech the women characters themselves perform the list, turning it into their own ritualised group chant. The rhythmic repetition of 'as they've always done' percussively drums in the notion of woman eternally the same. Significantly, they refer to themselves in the third person, not the first person. This was Aristophanes' nod and wink to the audience, since, of course, male actors were performing the roles.

The idea of inventories, catalogues or lists is of special interest in the world of the theatre, where words and text can be reinforced by visual imagery. Michel Foucault, in his book *The Order of Things*, quotes:

A certain Chinese encyclopedia [invented by Borges] in which it is written 'that animals are divided into: (a) belonging to the Emperor, (b) embalmed, (c) tame, (d) sucking pigs, (e) sirens, (f) fabulous, (g) stray dogs, (h) included in the present classification, (i) frenzied, (j) innumerable, (k) drawn with a very fine camel hair brush, (l) et cetera, (m) having just broken the water pitcher, (n) that from a long way off look like flies.' In the wonderment of this taxonomy, the thing we apprehend in one great leap, the thing that, by means of the fable, is demonstrated as the exotic charm of another system of thought, is the limitation of our own, the stark impossibility of thinking *that*. (p.xv)

The list, Foucault tells us, generates an immediate awareness of personal limitations. For him, this Borgesian inventory tied maniacally together by alphabetical categorisation and by the co-presence of the items on the printed page, makes one sensitive to the inability of thinking 'that'. But this interpretation, this 'wonderment of taxonomy' which offers Foucault an insight into his own imaginative restrictions, does not work in an 'order of things' where men are the sole arbiters of artistic creation and what is being listed is 'women'. Far from making man aware of *his* limitations, this dramatic dictionary of the female, this endless enumeration and itemisation of women, has just the opposite effect: it gives him power by classifying *her* limitations. When related to women in drama, Foucault's notion of 'the impossibility of thinking *that*', becomes emphatically reversed. For these male playwrights find it all too possible to think *that* about women. Driven to create a patriarchal checklist of the feminine, they revel in the lists of apparel, physical gesture, habits, tricks, occupational functions.

In Chapter 3 such listing concerned itself with women's names, the actresses of *commedia*. Here it concerns their traits and the (im)possibilities of their creativity. When 'women' are so external and assumable as to be listed and acted into existence, the construction of their gender encounters little resistance. Within a patriarchal order which gives men Pygmalion-like powers of creativity, shouldn't they *be* considered the experts in how women act? Agathon, the proficient poet in women's dress, is not the comic exception but the more common and obvious rule. So 'woman' becomes a disposable sign worn and discarded like a costume, a dress, make-up, a gesture. It is thus in the cultural artefact of theatre, where acting is considered literally and metaphorically as the wearing of a mask, that the sign called 'woman' finds its boldest and most forceful statement in the convention of men playing their roles.

5

Masques and masking

MRS SQUEAMISH: And that demureness, coyness, and modesty
that you see in our faces in the boxes at plays, is
as much a *sign* of a kind of woman as a vizard-
mask in the pit.
MRS DAINTY FIDGET: For, I assure you, women are least masked when
they have the velvet vizard on.
(William Wycherly, *The Country Wife*, Act V, scene iv, 1674–75,
my italics)

. . . she might do what she liked with her face. It was an elastic substance,
an element of gutta-percha, like the flexibility of the gymnast, the lady who,
at music hall, is shot from the mouth of a cannon. He coloured a little at this
quickened view of the actress; he had always looked more poetically,
somehow, at that priestess of art. But what was she, the priestess, when one
came to think about it, but a female gymnast, a mountebank at higher
wages? She didn't literally hang by her heels from a trapeze, holding a fat
man in her teeth, but she made the same use of her tongue, of her eyes, of
the imitative trick, that her muscular sister made of her leg and jaw. (Henry
James, *The Tragic Muse*, 1890)

Varieties of royal performance: continental queens acting

In 1632 William Prynne published his infamous *Histriomastrix – the
Player's Scourge, or, Actors Tragedie*, an hysterical and vicious
attack on the theatre in general and vilification of women on the
stage in particular: 'And dare then any Christian woman be so more
then whorishly impudent, as to act, to speak publicly on a Stage
(perchance in man's apparel, and cut hair, here proved sinful and
abominable) in the presence of sundry men and women?' (Cotton,

1980, p. 39). The severity of Prynne's punishment for this publication – he had his ears cut off – matches the contemporary extremity of his crime: his attack seemed to aim directly at the Queen herself.

The Queen was Henrietta Maria, wife of Charles I and sister to Louis XIII, who began performing on the English stage well before the Restoration. In 1626, the newly arrived sixteen-year-old Maria acted at court in a masque which she both wrote and directed. Unfortunately the script has not survived, but several witnesses from the English nobility recorded the event: 'I have knowne the time when this wold have seemed a straunge sight, to see a Quene act in a play but *tempora mutantor et nos*' (times change and so do we). The ambassadors from the continent were much more open-minded, however, as such court performances were common in Italy and France and they praised the Queen highly (Cotton, 1980, p. 38).

The court masque was a major source of entertainment for nobility and royalty both in England and on the continent, a licensed indulgence for elaborate, usually ostentatious display. In its inception, masque was not considered 'theatre', as the rudimentary script often consisted of no more than a series of poetic speeches to flatter the reigning monarch or celebrate a royal event such as a marriage or ambassador's visit. Ben Jonson was commissioned by Queen Anne in 1605 to write a masque, and the resulting work, *The Masque of Blackness*, was the first of its kind to have a serious and poetical text. When Queen Anne and her ladies 'performed' in Jonson's first masque they were there to play a symbolic version of their royal selves, since a major requirement of the masque was the creation of valid theatrical symbols which the royalty could enact without relinquishing their royal status. Queen Anne's 'performance' consisted primarily of her presence in the masque itself, where she and her ladies, magnificently costumed, simply appeared and danced. All the speaking parts in masques went to professional male actors.

Twenty years later, with Charles I on the throne, his wife Queen Henrietta Maria decided not merely to appear in a court masque, but to speak as well. The reaction of the audience, although diplomatically selected for the occasion, was surprise and censure. Despite Queen Henrietta Maria's introduction of a practice commonplace in France, the monarch speaking and singing the text, the masque still maintained its symbolic nature with no question of her or her ladies playing an immodest or common 'character'. As late as 1639 the King and Queen presented a masque entitled *Salmacida Spolia* by William Davenant, whose text begins its list of *dramatis personae* with the names of the reigning monarchy, a reference which underscores the monarchy's *real*, not representational, role:

The King's Majesty (under the name of Philogenes) and his Lords

The Queen's Majesty and her Ladies. (Davenant, p. 346)

In *Salmacida Spolia* the Queen descended on to the stage from 'a huge cloud of various colours' wearing a magnificent costume of an Amazon: 'Amazonian habits of carnation, embroidered with silver, with plumed helms, baldrics with antique swords hanging by their sides – all as rich as might be' (p. 358). Despite the frequency of such productions (more than one hundred during the reigns of James I and Charles I), no expense was spared.

While outside the majestic confines of Whitehall debate raged not only over the nature of kingship, but also over the nature of women, inside we see the final gorgeous (pre-Restoration) image of woman-as-symbol. *Salmacida Spolia* was the last court masque produced before the King was arrested and all theatres closed; it was an exorbitant final theatrical display of defiance of the revolutionary reality enveloping the court, a visual and textual exorcism of a discordant spirit identified in Davenant's masque as a 'Fury'. This malicious creature wages chaos and disorder over the world but is thwarted by none other than King Charles I, 'Philogenes', or the 'Lover of his People'. The masque rewards the King for such prudence with a heavenly vision of his Queen and her many female attendants in celestial descent fully costumed as Amazons.

As a political allegory the masque transparently constructs a symbolic healing of contemporary social division. Over and above such symbolism, there is an ironic premonition in this final performance by the Queen: when the theatre returns in 1660, ordinary women will perform on the public stage for the first time as a function of masculine drama not far removed from the Queen's final 'mask'. For while the Queen overtly played a symbol, actresses of the Restoration will do so unintentionally.

When a queen plays both herself and the symbolic role of the monarch, we witness a merging of female self with symbol, a fusion which we have already seen in the *commedia dell' arte*, where Italian actresses performed without masks the role of stereotyped (young lover, maidservant) 'self'. The Queen's performances in the masques of the English court manifestly celebrated such a merging in an elaborate, conspicuous spectacle – a conflation we shall see again in Restoration drama, where women actors in their less high-flown dramatic paradigm fulfil such a dramatic doubling of self and symbol.

The revolutionary potential of women acting

How could such a fusion of self and symbol have been possible in the English Restoration, which boasted women playwrights as well as actresses? In the acting profession, as we have seen, the notion of women performers remained unthinkable, beyond discussion, for centuries. How better, one might ask, to denote the purely symbolic role of women than to have young apprentice boys play their parts? Since men were the creative source of symbols rather than instances of them, their active role in cultural creation allowed, indeed their versatility demanded, that they assume women's roles. Actual women could not take part in their own aesthetic representation: a symbol could not generate another symbol. The very nature of female 'otherness' required a kind of vacuum necessarily filled with male-originated meaning, much as in medieval France an un-married woman was categorised as a *femme vacante*, her emptiness filled only through a marriage contract (Duby, 1985, p. 67).

Thus in this situation the creation of stage women was easily accomplished: as creators of women men were perhaps best suited to act out their inventions on stage. Just as unmarried women seemed to them empty of meaning until married, women them-selves were meaningless signs – vessels waiting to be filled with male values and constructions. It is this notion of woman as an empty sign that played upon both the public and the court stages where boys fulfilled the role of woman and symbolism fulfilled the role of Queen.

Why was rupturing this sign seen as such a threat? Even women with symbolic auras such as the Queen did not win unanimous acceptance in a performance role. In 1626, when Queen Henrietta

Maria spoke lines in a court masque, this 'did not give complete satisfaction, because the English objected to the first part being declaimed by the queen' (Cotton, 1980, p. 38). Three years later when a professional French company gave a public performance in London, the women actors were viciously pelted offstage:

> Furthermore you should know, that the last daye certaine vagrant French players, who had beene expelled from their owne contry, *and those women*, did attempt, thereby giving just offence to all vertuous and well-disposed persons in this town, to act a certain lacivious and unchaste comedye, in the French tonge at the Blackfryers. Glad I am to saye they were hissed, hooted, and pippin-pelted from the stage, so as I do not thinke they will soone be ready to trie the same againe. (Thomas Brande, 1629, in Bentley, 1956, vol. 1, p. 25)

Of course, a woman who spoke in public broke the age-old Pauline code about the necessity of women's silence. Yet breaking silence is only one aspect of the potential revolutionary power of the woman who takes the stage. Not only do actresses speak in a public space, but they show activity, versatility, a potential for social mobility. They contravene the dictum of the stable, stationary, and permanent symbol. It is through this speech and this mobility that an audience would witness female creativity in conception, in action. Allowing women to act, to make characters publicly on the stage, would permit them to be manifestly creative. To men, to society, after centuries of denying this possibility, of promulgating 'woman as nature' and promoting an idealised woman as an eternal symbol, the presence of a woman creating a role on a stage is a revelation. The safeguarded territories of women in the home, men in the world, no longer apply. All the world is indeed a stage, and the stage is a world: for through their presence on the pretend world of the stage, women enter the real world.

By entering the world in this way, women also take part in the most collaborative of all art forms. The stage has the potential to show women and men – performers all – sharing in a creative effort. Men and women tread the boards equally, they must learn to share the stage space in order to work together towards a public production. Unlike other more solitary art forms such as writing or painting, theatre exists in living moments of collaboration and compromise; and the art form itself, as any theatre practitioner knows, is written on the wind. It is just that quality of 'life', the using of real time and real people to create a theatre production, that has revolutionary potential.

But it was not to be. There was no revolution. When Charles II returned to England in 1660 he did more than restore the monarchy; he restored 'woman' as a sign to the stage. On 21 August 1660 a royal warrant decreed that women must perform on the stage so that the plays would be 'useful and instructive representations of human life' (Fraser, 1984, p. 419). Here other motives less rationally enlightened were no doubt in operation: Charles II felt that an all-male theatre promoted homosexuality. He wanted to avoid the criticism levelled at the homosexual court of his grand-father, James I, and to this end Charles II wanted to appear to favour women. And 'favour' women he did. His famous affair with the actress Nell Gwynne archetypally represents the rags to riches scenario where a young, lower-class woman vaults into fame and fortune as a result of her selection by a man of rank and power. As reigning monarch, Charles II set the tone of the age known for its casting-couch auditions. It was the expected custom for the men of the court to keep a pretty actress – just one of their many expenses in an age of public display. Any potential power a woman might have had on stage became diffuse and deflated by the way the Restoration drama objectified her. Her stage mobility gave her potential for social mobility, but her status as a commodity on public display neutralised this possibility. What better place for an aristocrat to exhibit his most recent acquisition than in a public theatre, framed excellently by the proscenium, with the dressing room procuring their privacy? (Indeed, Queen Anne, who reigned from 1702 to 1714, passed a law which banned members of the public from going backstage *during* the performance.) So far from revolutionising women's place in the social world by their presence on the stage, they became objects of exchange both as actresses *and* as the characters they played in the popular Restoration comedies, the plots of which often offered little more than an opportunity for men to bargain over women's dowries.

The feminisation of theatre

Alice Clark's conclusion in *Working Life of Women in the Seventeenth Century* (1919) contrasts the growing demand for actresses with the decline in other professions, where women became progressively excluded from other areas of professional work, even in previously deemed 'female' occupations such as midwifery, weaving and corset-making. Theatre became a well publicised profession available to women; and with this, theatre itself became identified as a feminine domain. This 'feminisation' of theatre, together with all that it implies – the social and cultural marking of professional actresses as scarcely more than prostitutes and the ensuing ostracisation – has not disappeared even today. As Molly Haskell points out in her analysis of film images of woman, *From Reverence to Rape,*

> The idea that acting is quintessentially 'feminine' carries with it a barely perceptible sneer, a suggestion that it is not the noblest or most dignified of professions. Acting is role-playing, role-playing is lying, and lying is a woman's game. (Haskell, 1973, p. 123)

This deceptive role-playing aligns itself to theatre itself – a profession which traditionally relies on an inequality between the audience and the performer – by the potential domination of the silent spectator. Thus actors find themselves in the 'feminine position' in relation to power. When women begin to act for the first time, they highlight this 'feminine position': both women and performers find it necessary to their survival to sell something to someone who is in a dominant position (Phelan, 1988, p. 124)

Another Restoration development which aligns itself to this notion of a theatrical feminisation was the creation of the 'breeches parts', where women cross-dress as men. 'Breeches parts' are a natural response to Charles II's warrant requiring women actors to play women's roles. As we have seen, numerous plays from pre-revolutionary England used cross-dressing: women characters, such as Viola in *Twelfth Night*, Moll Cutpurse in *The Roaring Girl*, Rosalind in *As You Like It*, and Portia in *The Merchant of Venice*, dress as men or boys in these plays. The change is dramatic: where previously boys played womens' roles dressed as men, now actresses play women who dress as men. Accounts estimate that between 1660 and 1700 nearly one-third of all new plays written contained 'breeches' parts. Actresses who disguised themselves as boys or men not only displayed their legs publicly but provided the means for new sexual innuendoes: one actress so disguised in *The*

Plain Dealer, for example, had her breasts felt by one of the actors on stage (Fraser, 1984, p. 423). The sight of women dressing as men, considered a threat to society twenty years earlier, had now become a sexualised theatrical commodity. Thus the subversive quality of woman-as-man became merely a popular effect in Restoration comedy.

As we saw earlier, women could not take part in their own aesthetic representation; a symbol could not generate another symbol. And yet, with the Restoration, they apparently did. How are we to explain this?

The plays of this period – a period which produced the celebrated comedy of manners – have been described as presenting 'a world of inverted moral values', where 'cuckolding has become almost the serious business of life', and the familiar 'battle of the sexes' which ridicules marriage and celebrates clandestine affairs and intrigues. And roles for women? The scripts present 'assured young women who are going to reappear with little variation or distinction of personality in the comedies for the next forty years' (Hartnoll, 1967, p. 283).

With such a bleakly unanimous view of female characters, how was it possible that actresses achieved such popularity? As Katherine Eisaman Maus has pointed out, the pre-civil war spectators appeared relatively uninterested in the offstage lives of the male actors. But in the more intimate, court-aligned Restoration theatre, with its smaller, more select audience, the personalities of both the men and women performers became central to notions of theatre itself. As Maus (1978, p. 598) says, 'Actresses as well as actors were praised not for their ability to depict any character with equal skill but for their ability to inform their dramatic portrayals with the force of their personal talent and idiosyncratic vision'. Furthermore, 'Restoration theatre did not really challenge the actor to submit himself to the demands of a fictional role; rather it provided, at least for the leading players, manifold opportunities for self-expression' (p. 599). This aspect of Restoration theatre had serious implications for the newly arrived actress: first, its cult of personality reaffirmed the established view that women are not cultural creators, but merely their natural selves; secondly, since society viewed theatre as a profession of role-players, a long-held prejudice – that women are continual and constant role-players by 'nature' – is reasserted and reconfirmed when they join ranks with professional actors.

The impact of the English queens performing in court masques before the civil war cannot be underestimated. Just as a pre-Restoration Queen of England could and did act the role of the Queen of the Amazons, so a shameless, assured young woman could act the role of a shameless, assured young woman. An example of this actress/role confusion can be found as early as 1661, when Hester Davenport became widely known as her character name 'Roxalana' after appearing successfully in that role in *The Siege of Rhodes* (Fraser, 1984, p. 425). Hester, like the *commedia* actresses and those pre-revolutionary Queens of England, cannot 'act', she can only 'be'. In fact, the Restoration theatre provided a dramatic double-bind in which the actress/role confusion thrived: by disguising themselves on stage, women demonstrated their 'natural' proclivity for deceit and falsehood. The double vision behind this is clear: to work in theatre, they must be experts in disguise, but because they are women, disguise is not seen as artistic creation, but rather as a natural part of that sign called 'woman'.

This actress/role confusion has another dimension which requires a further reconsideration of the beginnings of Western theatre. The mask and exaggerated costume of the Greek theatre provided an automatic distancing device between the role and the male actor-self. This sense of distance informs our cultural notions of artistic creativity. *Webster's Dictionary* defines the verb 'to create' as 'to originate; to bring into being from nothing; to cause to exist'. Works of art exist in their own right; the male actor, then, creates a role that is separate from himself, and his mask and costume provide him with the means for this separation. In other words, male actors have created a space between themselves and the roles they have played. Despite the fact that men eventually performed without masks, they have maintained this sense of space in relation to their roles. But for women, as we have seen, there was no mask or exaggerated costume; thus, the space for artistic illusion located between the role and the self was absent. With no distancing device between role and self, the male-controlled female role takes dominance over the more tenuous, uncharted notions of female self. In a sense, the self is absent, and this *femme vacante* becomes integral to the representation of women in patriarchy, where women are rendered invisible within the dominant narratives of history. Just as women were physically absent from their initial aesthetic representation on the Greek stage, so too they are 'absent' from their roles on the Restoration stage. Hester Davenport disappears in favour of 'Roxalana'. The male-generated 'Roxalana' takes precedence over Hester; male control of female image-making still reigns supreme.

The relationship of women to disguise (which will be more fully developed in Chapter 10) is particularly redolent with meaning during the Restoration. Not only did actresses disguise themselves for their roles, but female spectators – of which there were two categories, those in the boxes (aristocratic) and those in the pit (prostitutes) – began wearing masks or 'vizards' to the theatre. This 'fad' for wearing masks went beyond theatre attendances, and some women began wearing them on other social occasions. Allardyce Nicoll, in his historical overview of the Restoration, cannot understand the attraction such masks had for women: 'Ladies of quality seem not to have minded being taken by their friends for *femmes d'amour*' (Nicoll, 1928, p. 14). But one can easily imagine that it must have been tremendously liberating to walk the streets of London with one's identity momentarily voided by the simple black mask. It is also tempting to imagine such disguise as a subversive act: if women are deemed to be natural disguisers, then wearing an anonymous black mask flouts such a definition openly by calling attention to the means of disguise: the mask. Since the physicality of a woman's face – her beauty or lack of it – so centrally influenced her success in life, then eradicating and neutralising this face was equally anarchistic.

The potency of theatrical manpower

A feminist analysis of an Indian classical dance performance known as 'gotipua' explores this notion of female absence. The custom of 'gotipua' – young boys performing dressed as girls – has existed since the fifteenth century. At a recent performance of this dance, an eleven-year-old boy named Gautam, dressed in a vivid pink costume with stylised female make-up, smiled seductively at his audience. Peggy Phelan articulates the impact of this boy/woman:

> No one forgets that the dancer is male; the invocation of the nonmale is controlled by the security of the performer's male body. As a substitu-tion for the female in the sphere of visual desire, Gautam's dance questions the function of erotic substitutions – what Freud called fetishes

– in the incitement of desire which all performance exploits. The fetishized 'female' image so perfectly encoded in Gautam's costume, make-up, and movement works not to bring the female into the spectacle of exchange between spectator and performer but to leave her emphatically outside. In place of the female, a fetishized image is displayed which substitutes for her and makes her actual presence unnecessary. (Phelan, 1988, pp. 110–11)

Phelan's analysis of this non-Western dance tradition can, as we have seen, equally apply to the Western theatrical convention of men playing women's roles. Freud assigns additional attributes to fetishes: for him they function as a phallic substitute. So men-as-women performances generate a significant homoerotic desire; Gautam, the 'gotipua' dancer with his choreographed tableaux of seductive femininity, is a reassuring projection of the fantasy of male narcissism. The absent female is not only filled with male-generated meaning, but also male-generated desire.

Such male-generated narcissistic desire informs several of Shakespeare's plays in which the repercussions of adultery are central. As Shirley Nelson Garner points out in her essay 'Male Bonding and the Myth of Women's Deception in Shakespeare's Plays', Shakespeare seems to suggest a male *need* for adultery from which the potency of male relations can be confirmed and endorsed. As Garner states when discussing *Much Ado About Nothing*, *Othello*, *Cymbeline* and *Winter's Tale*, the four plays central to her argument:

[that] Shakespeare wanted to depict his male characters as needing to be betrayed is further affirmed by their determination to believe that they are betrayed. When a moment comes that the contrary might be true, that the women they suspect might be faithful, they insist on their falseness . . . The male characters' certainty of betrayal allows them to unleash their pent-up misogyny and fear of women as they plot vengeance, revile their beloveds and women in general, and persecute and even murder or attempt to murder the innocent women who love them. Their distrust also allows them to break their bonds with those women and return either imaginatively or actually to an exclusive male community. (Garner, 1983, pp. 4–5)

Restoring the theatrical sign 'woman' in 1660 effectively rehabilitated this notion of an 'exclusive male community' through the popular masculine pastime of cuckolding. Eve Kosofsky Sedgwick, in her book *Between Men: English Literature and Male Homosocial Desire*, says: ' "To cuckold" is by definition a sexual act, performed on a man, by another man' (p. 49). Cuckolding is something one man does to another, a reaffirmation of their male (not necessarily sexualised) desire for one another, where men simply traffic through women to achieve their real goal: ratification of their masculinity. While a woman's presence is essential to this confirmation, to her it confirms only her 'otherness'. In a detailed discussion of *The Country Wife*, Sedgwick views cuckoldry as one way in which men 'attempt to arrive at satisfying relationships with other men'. Furthermore, 'men's heterosexual relationships in the play have as their *raison d'être* an ultimate bonding between men; and that this bonding, if successfully achieved, is not detrimental to "masculinity" but definitive of it' (p. 50).

Much as Gautam's homoerotic performance as a woman is 'the fantasy of exchange *between* men *about* women' (Phelan, 1988, p. 111), so too the cuckolding narratives of the Restoration stage (where men simply use women to reaffirm their male desire for one another) invest men with a centrality that validates their position as the essential cultural creators and relegates women to the position of signs which men *make*. Thus theatre becomes a medium which both allows men to admire and revere their own artefacts and at the same time perpetuates their illusion of having created woman. It is these illusory signs of women, these imaginary females, that the rest of this book explores.

Part II

Archetypal Images of Women in Theatre

6

The penitent whore

Oh woman, woman, woman, woman, woman,
The cause of future and Originall sinne,
How happy [had you not] should we haue beene.
(Nathan Field, *The Woman is a Weathercock*, III, i. 193–5, 1609–10)

Hugo wrote *Marion Delorme*, Musset wrote *Bernerette*, Alexandre Dumas wrote *Fernande*. Thinkers and poets throughout the ages have offered the courtesan the oblation of their mercy and, on occasion, some great man has brought them back to the fold through the gift of his love and even his name. (Alexandre Dumas fils, *Là Dame aux Camélias*, 1848)

So she followd love for love's sake only, now and then, as she would have followed art if she had been a man – capriciously, desultorily, more in frolicsome spirit of *camaraderie* than anything else. Like an amateur, in short – a distinguished amateur who is too proud to sell his pictures, but willingly gives one away now and then to some highly-valued and much admiring friend. (George du Maurier, *Trilby*, 1895)

The newest member of the world's oldest profession: Marguerite Gautier

Hrotsvit's tenth-century play *Paphnutius* proposes possibly the earliest theatrical representation of the penitent whore with the role of the popular and wealthy prostitute Thais. The monk Paphnutius approaches her to repent and give up her evil life. Overcome by the monk's fervent aura of sanctity and righteousness, Thais publicly burns all the objects of her profession – jewellery, clothing, gold – in full view of her many lovers as her first step towards Christian transformation. She then isolates herself in a convent for three years, after which her soul leaves her body and soars heavenward to join Christ, her 'heavenly husband', in paradise. Several elements of this story recur in most, if not all, of the harlot/saint narratives. The first is that the woman is both beautiful and evil and her transgressions are entirely sexual – she sells her body to men. Secondly, once she repents and asks forgiveness, she willingly accepts, indeed embraces, physical suffering and deprivation. In the case of Thais, she exists in solitary confinement in a filthy cell, lives on bread and water, and speaks to no one for three years. The third recurrent narrative feature requires that the woman must die, and that her death be viewed as a release from physical torment and pain, a mortal resolution to a life of decadence and decay.

The popular myths of the harlot/saint developed a wide following, not least because their stories proved that no one, however steeped in sin, stood beyond the reach of grace. Unlike the Virgin Mary, who over time became more and more remote as an idol due to the Church's insistence on her total purity, harlots/saints were commonplace and accessible. Furthermore, they sinned in a way which society expected of them and so fulfilled Ovid's mysogynistic premise that all women are whores until proven otherwise. The Virgin Mary's death receives no mention in the New Testament, but the deaths of harlots/saints formed a central part of their story, with a variety of their morbid relics available for worship and sale (Warner, 1978, pp. 228–9).

A variety of harlots/saints exist in Christian hagiography; one in particular combines acting with prostitution: the popular Pelagia, an actress from eighth-century Antioch, who like Thais was both wealthy and beautiful – so beautiful in fact that the bishop was terrified to meet her for fear that even a fleeting glimpse of her would tempt him to sin. Pelagia, in a *volte-face* manoeuvre characteristic of the harlot/saint narratives, longed to meet the bishop to beg him to baptise her, gave away all her wealth to the poor, disguised herself as a man, and became a hermit in the desert where she fasted in isolation.

The leader of these holy women, of course, is Mary Magdalene, who throughout the history of the Catholic Church has often eclipsed the Virgin Mary in popularity. Unlike the mother of Christ, Mary Magdalene had a privileged and intimate friendship with Jesus during his ministry and was a central witness at his resurrection.[1] Theatrically, Mary Magdalene figured often in medieval mystery plays, where the resurrection was occasionally presented from her unique viewpoint. Yet it was not until half a millenium later, when theatre had long removed itself from its religious context, that a new version of this popular eternal prototype emerged: Marguerite Gautier, La Dame aux Camélias. In a preface to one of the many English translations of the playscript the translator states: 'Marguerite Gautier is today theatre's most famous Magdalen, and Dumas's play has outlived its century to become a classic of its kind' (Dumas, ed. Smith, p. 178).

Alexandre Dumas fils wrote *La Dame aux Camélias* as a novel in 1847 and then adapted it for the stage in 1852. The phenomenal popularity of the book and the play relieved Dumas of huge debts accumulated in his hitherto erratic and unsuccessful writing career and was instrumental in his election to the Academie Française in 1874.

But the popularity of *La Dame aux Camélias* did not simply reflect a short-lived interest in the Parisian *demi-monde*, or a middle-class flirtation with a romanticised bohemia. The original actress for the role of Marguerite Gautier, Eugénie Doche, played the role over six hundred times; and numerous continental actresses, including Eleanor Duse and Sarah Bernhardt, who aspired to careers as tragic actresses, saw this highly coveted role as an enhancement to an already established reputation. This century in New York alone there have been over forty productions of the play, with actresses including Ethel Barrymore, Eva Le Gallienne, Tallulah Bankhead, and Colleen Dewhurst.[2] Marguerite Gautier, therefore, 'the theatre's most famous Magdalen', has had over a century's worth of seemingly endless replication. At the time of writing, a new English translation of the novel has just been published with a detailed introduction. The back cover describes the story as 'irresistible': Marguerite Gautier 'has long since attained the status of myth. Dumas's subtle and moving portrait of a woman in love is a timeless antidote to the cynicism of every age' (Coward; see Dumas, 1986). Why is this so? (Perhaps more interesting, why have the publishers decided to publish a new translation now – a translation which continues past centuries' mythmaking and never once in its lengthy introduction mentions feminism or why this text might interest women?) How has Marguerite Gautier achieved such status when her predecessors are aligned specifically with religious martyrdom, and she herself comes from an entirely secular age? To understand the creation of her myth we must examine the historical and cultural background which preceded her story.

'A little world of sentiment made for women to move in': the rise of sensibility and the emotional terrain of women

An important cultural phenomenon to study first is the ideological change that occurred in the theatre itself between the Restoration and the eighteenth century. By the end of the seventeenth century the characteristic combination of wit, satire and comedy which reflected the tastes of the predominantly male and aristocratic audience of Charles II, as well as the structuring Restoration themes of sex and money, had grown stale. The audience had changed; it was becoming more middle class and more varied – more women attended performances. In 1698 Jeremy Collier published his pamphlet *A Short View of the Immorality, and Profaneness of the English Stage*, which attacked the Restoration theatre and gave a clarion call for a theatre of virtue and morality. Collier's pamphlet initially elicited an enthusiastic debate on the nature of dramatic art itself, but its long-term legacy was the creation of a sentimental drama which began to develop in the late seventeenth century and became the popular theatrical mode of the eighteenth.

Janet Todd (1986, p. 2), in her book *Sensibility*, describes sentimental literature as arousing 'pathos through conventional situations, stock familial characters and rhetorical devices . . . such literature buttonholes the reader and demands an emotional, even physical response'. Sensibility itself, defined by the *Oxford English Dictionary*, is the 'capacity for refined emotions, a readiness to feel compassion for suffering and to be moved by the pathetic in literature or art'. The sentimental impulse is not new; it has recurred repeatedly in literature, but the innovative element in the eighteenth-century context is the significant positioning of such an emotional consciousness at the centre of the stage.

Sentimentalism infiltrated all literary genres, but the 'cult of sensibility' primarily thrived in fiction between 1740 and 1780. As Todd explains,

> This fiction initially showed people how to behave, how to express themselves in friendship and how to respond decently to life's experiences. Later, it prided itself more on making its readers weep. In addition, it delivered the great archetypal victims: the chaste suffering woman, happily rewarded in marriage or elevated into redemptive death, and the sensitive, benevolent man whose feelings are too exquisite for the acquisitiveness, vulgarity and selfishness of his world. (Todd, 1986, p. 4)

So sensibility, that state of sentimental communion with the self, set the fashion in mid-eighteenth-century England. Women's economic worth had declined since millinery, dressmaking and midwifery became male-dominated professions, and accordingly her value, constructed in terms of 'sensibility', increased. Promoting the belief that women were essentially emotional creatures prone to tears, passion and hysteria became the central motif of the popular novel. For a brief period emotionalism became a positive attribute of 'men of feeling', though the satirists Pope and Swift deplored such sentiment, viewing it as a damaging 'feminisation of culture' (Todd, p. 43).

Significant in this context is the large number of women novelists who worked in the eighteenth century, creating a split between the classical university-educated 'male' literature and the sentimental literature available to the growing lower middle class through the newly created circulating libraries and cheap, mass publishing. In the world of the sentimental novel, sensibility was available to all, not merely the upper classes or aristocracy, and it was therefore valued above wealth and titles. The intrinsic subject matter of sentimental literature, focusing as it did on emotional consiousness, became the self.

Since the cult of sensibility offered a way of acting in the world and a response to the events of life, the major source of narrative for women writers was autobiography. Women novelists' use of the self as primary subject matter won initial applause for its spontaneity, its artlessness, its intuition – all desirable attributes of sensibility. It was often the case that even when writers wrote purely fictional novels they presented the work either through the seemingly autobiographical device of a diary or letters. And conversely: in the 1796 novel, *Memoirs of Emma Courtney*, the author Mary Hays used her own personal love letters as the letters of her fictional heroine.

Much of this fascination with women's sensibility was both echoed and reinforced by the ideas of Rousseau, who dominated late eighteenth-century English literary-philosophical thought. He stressed the concept that woman was aligned to nature and, like his contemporary Diderot, emphasised the need to train and prepare girls for a life in the home as wife and mother. Diderot thought that women, with their violent emotions and uncontrollable passions, needed to be understood so that men could control and direct such natural qualities. Both these men contributed to the growing debate about women which flourished in the early days of the French Revolution – a debate which opened up the questions of women's education, ownership of property, full citizenship, holding office, and divorce. As Jane Rendall points out,

> In the history of feminism, the 1790s is often seen as a critical decade . . . [for] . . . it was only in the context of a world in which revolutions in America and France opened up the possibilities of reshaping the social as well as the political order that radical changes in the relationship between the sexes began to seem feasible. (Rendall, 1985, p. 33)

This was a short-lived but energetically charged period which in many ways paralleled the fervour over social and political change prior to the civil war in England.

But organised women's groups in Paris received a defeat in 1793 when the government outlawed all women's clubs and disdainfully reminded women, with Rousseauean confidence, that their place was in the home. The only victory for these politically active women seems a minor one considering the issues at stake: in 1792 legislation was passed granting divorce on grounds of mutual consent for the first time in France (Rendall, 1985, p. 53).

Archetypal homilies and the assuaging of fear through melodrama

In the Revolution's cultural arena the new theatrical genre of melodrama emerged. In the academic study of theatre, melodrama has been primarily isolated and marginalised for one significant reason: its status as a 'popular' theatrical form, enjoyable and enormously accessible, deemed it less worthy of serious critical attention, and the playwrights themselves provoked academic and artistic suspicion both for their success and prolific output. However, a recent study by Peter Brooks entitled *The Melodramatic Imagination* depicts melodrama as a theatrical genre not only obviously worthy of study but essential to comprehending nineteenth-century theatre in its social and historical context. As Brooks puts it,

> The origins of melodrama can be accurately located within the context of the French Revolution and its aftermath. This is the epistemological moment which it illustrates and to which it contributes: the moment that symbolically, and really, marks the final liquidation of the traditional Sacred and its representative institutions (Church and Monarch), the shattering of the myth of Christendom, the dissolution of an organic and hierarchically cohesive society, and the invalidation of the literary forms – tragedy, comedy of manners – that depended on such a society. Melodrama does not simply represent a 'fall' from tragedy, but a response to the loss of the tragic vision. It comes into being in a world where the traditional imperatives of truth and ethics have been violently thrown into question, yet where the promulgation of truth and ethics, their instauration as a way of life, is of immediate, daily, political concern. (Brooks, 1985, pp. 14–15)

So in a world where the ancient, engrained and codified framework of God and Monarch is destroyed, some solace lies in watching the battles of Good and Evil, of victims and villains, in a theatre where the ultimate climax imposes a moral vision; a claim that, against all the odds, simple yet fundamental goodness always wins. This battle plays again and again in the theatres of Paris for a middle-class audience hungry for the affirmation supplied by the melodramatic narratives which endlessly replicate the bourgeois moral universe.

Diderot made a conscious effort to establish a new genre of theatre that would fall between comedy and tragedy, and wrote numerous plays where he attempted to make such a novelty appealing to the bourgeoisie. Far from the naturalism of a century later, Diderot wanted to 'exploit the dramatics and excitement discoverable within the real, to heighten in dramatic gesture the moral crises and peripeties of life'. Such theatre would emphatically spell out for the middle-class comfort of its spectators the simplicity of familial truths and the moral message of the universe (Brooks, 1985, p. 13)

Rousseau, it appears, coined the word melodrama in 1770 when he attempted to create a new emotional theatrical expressivity which fused spoken soliloquy, pantomimic gesture, and orchestral accompaniment. But it remained to the playwrights a generation later – Pixerécourt, Caigniez, Ducange, Cuvelier – to push the melodrama to the centre of Parisian theatrical life. Pixerécourt alone wrote over one hundred and twenty plays, and between 1800 and 1803; reigned as the 'Corneille of the Boulevards' (Brooks, p. 24).

Brooks's view of melodrama offers a theatre of overt signs which straightforwardly declare their archetypal symbolic meaning. Pixerécourt's play of 1819 entitled *La Fille de l'Exilé* demonstrates such symbolism in its narrative, which describes

> the perilous journey of Elizabeth, a sixteen-year-old daughter of the exiled Stanislas Potoski, from Siberia to Moscow to seek the czar's pardon for her unjustly persecuted father. Along the way . . . she seeks shelter with a humble boatman who turns out to be none other than Ivan, the author of her family's disgrace, formerly a rich Boyard, now himself ruined, repentant, and punished by the death of his own daughter . . . A Tartar attack ensues, and Ivan's life is threatened. Elizabeth rushes forth from the cabin, takes the cross from her neck . . . suspends it above Ivan's head, saying, 'Wretches! bow down before this revered sign, and do not forget that in this vast Empire any being placed under its protection is inviolable.' . . . The Tartars are taken aback and let fall their arms. Ivan, who understands the deeper heroism of the gesture, turns to Elizabeth: 'Angel from heaven! It is you, my victim, who protects my life!' (Brooks, 1985, p. 24)

The sign Pixerécourt uses here is the cross; at other times in the story he employs a gravestone, a lightning bolt and a flood. But it is Brooks's major contention that the central sign in this play, indeed in the genre of melodrama itself, is *virtue*. And who carries the sign of virtue? A woman. When the Tartars lay down their weapons at Elizabeth's heroic stance, Ivan explains to them the implications of her gesture in the full-blown, grandiose phraseology of melodrama. The Tartars murmur admiration for such strength and fortitude in a woman; and when Ivan continues his panegyric to explain that Elizabeth, his victim, saved the life of her persecutor, the once war-like Tartars fall spontaneously on their knees in a spectacular display of humility and homage to her virtue.

When at long last Elizabeth arrives in Moscow to win her exiled father's pardon and the restoration of his title and lands, the czar says of her: 'Placed above her sex by her sublime actions, she has become at once its glory and its model' (Brooks, p. 27). This statement greatly resembles Sedulius's well-known description of the Virgin Mary:

> She . . . had no peer
> Either in our first mother or in all women
> Who were to come. But alone of ąll her sex
> She pleased the Lord.
>   (in Warner, 1978, p. 365, n.1)

Indeed, this theatrical genre elevates its women to the position of eternal goodness; the young heroine almost always embodies virtue, a righteousness, integrity and moral purity that must struggle throughout the narrative against the oppressive and powerful efforts of the villain. Melodrama, then, is a theatricalised battle of good and evil, virtue and villainy, female and male, which ends in the public recognition and celebration of virtue and the eradication of iniquity, corruption and wrong-doing.

The major source for melodrama (although it freely pillaged a variety of narrative forms) was the nascent novel itself, in particular the English sentimental novel and the Gothic novels of Ann Radcliffe. If, as Brooks says, the novel was 'the first medium to realize the importance of persecuted women, struggling to preserve and impose the moral vision' (p. 87), then it is no less true that melodrama, with its insistence on clear, obvious, unambiguous symbols, centres the innocent, virtuous, saint-like woman as its major theatrical sign.

Harlot/saint and virtuous woman

It is my contention in this chapter that in the middle of the nineteenth century a collision occurred between two female images: the harlot/saint of Catholic hagiography and melodrama's virtuous woman. This collision created a new theatrical character – Marguerite Gautier – a role duplicated and repeated continuously on the stage since its first appearance in 1852; a figure who combines a mixture of age-old views and prejudices with a more modern, secular vision of the purity and goodness that restore moral order.

The story of *La Dame aux Camélias* is straightforward:

Marguerite is a young, beautiful courtesan in Paris kept by a variety of wealthy, aristocratic men. Inadvertently she falls for the bourgeois yet gallant Armand Duval, a man who cannot keep her in her accustomed style. Duval passionately returns Marguerite's love, so much so that he is willing to tarnish his family name and spend his future inheritance on her. Marguerite, experiencing love for the first time, wants to keep separate her relationship with Duval from her business as a prostitute: she refuses all his offers of money, and together they retreat to the country where they share a temporary but idyllic existence. Set against this dual existence of a thriving, healthy passion and the commercialised exploitation of prostitution is Marguerite's tenuous health: she is consumptive. In the fresh air of the country, away from the rigours of her Parisian life, she prospers. But the happiness of both Armand and Marguerite is interrupted by a visit from Armand's father, who has tried every available means to prevent his son from continuing the liaison. M. Duval approaches Marguerite without his son's knowledge and convinces her that the relationship must end. 'If you really love Armand, you would give him up' is the father's trump card. She reluctantly agrees to abandon Armand for her former life, a decision she well knows to be suicidal. In order to carry out M. Duval's wishes, she must convince Armand that she no longer loves him. Though thunderstruck by this revelation, Armand accepts it and turns cruelly against her. Once Marguerite returns to Paris and the luxurious decadence of her previous existence her health declines rapidly. Armand visits her on her deathbed, declaring his love for her, and Marguerite dies blissfully in his arms.

How is it, when chastity conventionally symbolises woman's essential goodness, that a prostitute has vaulted into a position of prominence and usurped the centremost theatrical role of the sign of virtue?

During the period when Dumas fils wrote this work the materialistic bourgeois family had firmly entrenched itself in a position of social power; increasing industrialisation was adding to its wealth; and divorce laws no longer threatened it, since the victorious legislation hard won during the French Revolution was abolished in 1826 and was not restored for nearly sixty years. Paris witnessed a steadily growing, if barely surviving, presence of working-class women on minimal wages. That these women had to turn to prostitution to support their families was commonplace, but they were joined there by a new class of women, coined *demi-mondaines* by Dumas fils, who were cultivated by aristocratic backgrounds and education but impoverished by the loss of their fathers and acceptable suitors in the many wars of the Empire. Such women became prostituted into being the kept women of wealthy married men, offering intellectual and cultural amusements beyond the expected sexual liaison.

The mixture of high life and prostitution contrasted mordantly with the staid, materialistic existence of the bourgeoisie; and in 1845–48 Henri Murger wrote a series of short stories, *La Vie de Bohéme*, which celebrated this variance, wherein the sons of industrial magnates rebelled by leaving the family home to live a carefree irresponsible, impoverished life of both artistic and sexual freedom. Pivotal to this Bohemian ideal of free living was the notion of woman as muse, as inspiration for male creativity. For male painters in the mid-nineteenth century this notion assumed a justificatory importance, for it protected their work with female models from hints of artistic licentiousness. The Bohemian mythology enveloping these women was that they piously scorned conventional morality; their beauty inspired the artist and was indeed essential to his creativity; they were sexually generous, and were almost certainly the artist's current sexual 'oeuvre'.

At this time the classic myth of Pygmalion, first recorded by Ovid in his *Metamorphosis*, enjoyed a revival as it joined the painter's canon of oil subjects throughout Europe. The restored popularity of this myth clearly relates to the Bohemian vision of the artist and his model: the sculptor Pygmalion, disenchanted with the de-graded, depraved women which populate the world, decides to sculpt his own vision of feminine perfection. His stone creation of femininity, as symbolically fixed as the male-created muses of Ripa's classifying dictionary, radiates beauty, gentleness and obeisance. The goddess Aphrodite sees Pygmalion pining for his stone woman, pities him and brings the statue to life. Thus Pygmalion gains possession of female perfection, the ideal erotic object shaped to the pattern of his own desires and wishes. The Pygmalion story completes the Bohemian myth of male creativity: the male artist moves from being inspired by his female model to the ultimate act of creating her.

Versions of these two self-regarding myths – the myth of Pygmalion and the myth of Bohemia – proliferate in the middle to late nineteenth century. Puccini adapted Murger's story into his famous opera *La Bohéme*, in which the working-class seamstress Mimi provides an inspiration to the artist Rodolpho. Indeed, it is Mimi's death near the end of the story which inspires Rodolpho/ Puccini to sing what is often considered one of his greatest tragic arias.[3]

Another enormously popular example was George du Maurier's *Trilby*, which was written in 1894 and staged in London a year later.[4] In du Maurier's novel, which he based on his own Bohemian lifestyle in Paris twenty years earlier, Trilby is a naive, unassuming and stunningly beautiful artist's model. All the artists in the small English colony in Paris are impressed by her and the most sensitive, Little Billee, falls passionately but voyeuristically in love with her. But Trilby's socially unacceptable life as a model clashes with Little Billee's bourgeois family background, cordoning off any serious thoughts about marriage. Instead the muscian Svengali, a clear parallel to Pygmalion, hypnotises her; although she is off-key and tone deaf by nature, whenever she is under his creative spell she transforms into a talented, charismatic singer. Tours of the major concert halls of Europe ensue with great personal acclaim.

A distinguising feature of many of these narratives is their autobiographical source. Henri Murger wrote *Scènes de la vie de Bohème* from his own Bohemian experiences, as did du Maurier in *Trilby*. Although Puccini for the most part used Murger's narrative, he based the character of Mimi in his opera on his own maid with whom he had an affair. Certainly one aspect which helped to sensationalise Dumas fils's novel and play was its proximity to real events in the author's life: he gave his initials to his leading male character, Armand Duval, and a well-known libertine of the time came to the theatre every night to admire his portrait as one of Marguerite's lovers (Dumas, ed. Smith, p. 177). Marguerite herself was based on a famous Parisian courtesan with whom Dumas had had an eleven-month affair, Marie Duplessis. Her death in 1847, at the age of 23, was widely reported; her beauty was described as 'miraculous' and 'exquisite', and she was said to have had a 'natural elegance and distinction'. The praise for this once impoverished, illiterate peasant girl was lavish: 'She is, first of all, the best dressed woman in Paris; second, she neither flaunts nor hides her vices; thirdly, she is not always talking or hinting about money; in short, she is a wonderful courtesan.' Franz Liszt, after an affair with her late in 1845, wrote: 'She was the most absolute incarnation of Woman who has ever existed', and her obituary described her 'indefinable but genuine air of chastity' (Coward, in Dumas, pp. x–xi).

In short, one would almost imagine that the many journalists, writers and artists who wrote about Marie Duplessis, both before and after her death, were writing about the Virgin Mary and not about a celebrated, infamous courtesan. In fact, during the same period there was also a great deal of talk about the nature of Christ's mother. While Marie Duplessis held forth at the height of her power and notoriety in Paris, the centuries-old debate about the birth of Christ's mother was drawing to a slow, laborious, yet spectacular close. In 1854, two years after the play based on Marie Duplessis's love affair with Dumas opened to great acclaim in Paris, Pope Pius IX proclaimed

> The Virgin Mary the Immaculate Conception, the only human creature ever to have been preserved from all taint of original sin. Pius' Bull, *Ineffabilis Deus*, now declared this be to dogma, a mandatory belief for all those who acknowledge the spiritual authority of Rome. Pius also thereby made impossible any interpretation of Christ's incarnation as the full embrace of the ordinary condition of man. Not only he, Christ, was exceptional; so was his mother, his only human parent. (Warner, 1978, p. 236)

Four years later the Pope's dogma seemed to be divinely ratified when a fourteen-year-old girl in Lourdes saw a vision of a beautiful girlish figure dressed in azure with the sun radiating from her feet. Bernadette Soubirous began to draw large crowds of spectators when she went into a trance in front of the grotto where her vision appeared. When the girl, at the request of her local church, asked her vision who she was, the figure replied, 'I am the Immaculate Conception' (Warner, 1978, p. 250). After submitting the girl to rigorous questioning, the Catholic Church ended by supporting her claims and declared Lourdes a place of pilgrimage.

As Church dogma catapults the Virgin Mary into greater prominence (another example of male-created female perfection – Mary is declared immaculately free from original sin) the devotion to Mary Magdalene, a much more 'human' saint, increases. This dynamic tension between perfect and human female figures may explain why *La Dame aux Camélias*, with its central character of a courtesan redeemed by love, became extremely popular despite its initial ban by the censor. Original in its combination of melodrama and the well-made play, Dumas's work had as a result a nascent psychological realism. As one critic states, 'What [Dumas] did was to bring the theatre into more direct touch with life and human problems than it had aspired to since before the Romantic movement' (Kaplan, 1983, p. 37).

However, if Dumas made innovative advances towards a closer awareness of human problems in his script, the ultimate pronouncement in the play is still the age-old message of Mary Magdalene: a woman 'sins' sexually, a male intervenes in her sinfulness, she repents, she suffers, she dies, she is forgiven. With Mary Magdalene the male intervention was Jesus, with Thais it was Paphnutius, with Pelagia it was a bishop. Such male intercession, in these cases, derives from God, from divinity, from the Roman Catholic Church. In post-revolutionary France, however, the divine male presence has lost its validity and is replaced by the bourgeois father, the new law of the patriarchy. Marguerite Gautier, a business-minded courtesan, poses no threat to the patriarchal order until she falls in love, recognises her own desire, and breaks open the continuum of power in the hands of bourgeois men. This fissure, forced open by her love for Duval, a love which will remove him from the male line of inheritance and power, must be closed at once. When Duval's father confronts Marguerite they reach a brief but exhilarating stalemate. She claims her right to her own life, her right to autonomy, her right to love and be loved. The deadlock is resolved only by Marguerite's capitulation – a denial of her own desire that will, as she knows, lead ultimately to the entire eradication of her self.

The patriarchal world rewards and celebrates such self-sacrifice: in language couched in religious epithets Armand's father asks Marguerite to 'prove to me you truly love my son' by giving him up. After Marguerite agrees to end her relationship with Armand, his father is 'overcome despite himself' and calls her a 'noble girl'. Marguerite says to herself:

> Thus, no matter what she does, a fallen woman may never rise again. God, perhaps, will pardon her, but the world remains inflexible! What man could wish to call her 'wife', what child would wish to call her 'mother'? (*To Duval*) You are right, sir. Everything you tell me I have told myself a thousand times. I must obey . . . I shall die of this, sir, and perhaps then God will forgive me! (Dumas, p. 196)

Rewards of patriarchal icon-making: decaying bodies and profit-making relics

As with the long, drawn-out martyrdoms of the penitent whores before her, Marguerite must suffer physically before she dies. She is consumptive, pale, weak; she spits blood, she finds it difficult to breathe. It is essential to this quasi-religious narrative that her beauty deteriorates and decays. Mary Magdalene supposedly 'expiated her wicked life in conditions of grim austerity' (Warner, 1978, p. 229). In the famous statue *La Maddalena* by Donatello, the male sculptor creates an old, thin, ugly, repellant, hag-like creature smothered in long strands of hair.

Not only does the penitent whore endure physical pain and torment in life, but after death her body remains a source of fascination. The cult of Mary Magdalene thrived in southern France with its myth that she and two other Marys from the Gospels were washed ashore after fleeing persecution in the holy land. Her body was supposedly discovered in the crypt of St. Maximin's church in Aix-en-Provence in 1279, where consequently her relics have been worshipped ever since (Warner, 1978, p. 228).

Equally there was a particularly fantastical obsession with Marguerite's decomposing body. In the novel, Dumas's patriarchal checklist of female body parts provides a detailed, morbid description of Marguerite's exhumation:

> The dampness of the earth had rusted the screws, and it was not without considerable effort that the coffin was opened. A foul odour emerged, despite the aromatic herbs with which it had been strewn. 'Dear God! Dear God!', Armand murmered, and he grew paler than ever. A large white winding sheet . . . had been completely eaten away at one end, and allowed one of the dead woman's feet to protrude . . . [A grave-digger] suddenly uncovered Marguerite's face. It was terrible to behold and it is horrible to relate. The eyes were simply two holes, the lips had gone, and the white teeth clenched. The long, dry, black hair was stuck over the temples and partly veiled the green hollows of the cheeks, and yet in this face I recognized the pink and white, vivacious face which I had seen so often. (Dumas, p. 38)

An important element in the worship of saints is the presence of the body; the remains must remain. When the penitent whore becomes canonised, her decaying body proves her humanity and provides a powerful emphasis on her ultimate earthly punishment rather than her heavenly glorification – as if it is particularly gratifying that female beauty, first deemed so central to a woman's life, can then prove to be so fickle, so ephemeral, just a mere façade of blood and bones. Marguerite Gautier's decomposed body is not only the artist's ultimate *memento mori*; it is his supreme revenge on a woman whom he encouraged to use her beauty for wealth and notoriety.

The opening chapters of Dumas's novel depicts Armand Duval as a man possessed by a driving obsession to see Marguerite's dead body. Viewing the decomposed corpse overwhelms Duval with mental and physical anguish: 'he no longer seemed capable of walking without staggering; his teeth chattered, his hands were cold, violent, nervous convulsions took possession of his entire body' (p. 39). Once recovered from what the doctor calls a 'brain fever', the healthy Armand is impelled to tell his martyr's miraculous story: 'But I must tell you the story; you shall turn it into a book which no one will believe' (p. 41).

Dumas's book was written quickly in June of 1847; Marie Duplessis had died in February of that year and was buried in a temporary grave. When her body was moved a few weeks later there is a strong likelihood that Dumas attended the exhumation. He certainly did witness the auction or prior viewing of Marie's possessions described in the opening pages of his novel. For not only relics of the body are essential to this myth of secular canonisation; like Thais and Pelagia before her, Marguerite Gautier is defined by her possessions, expensive jewellery, clothing, gold, by the signs of her successful business transactions. Thais burned all her riches, Pelagia gave hers to the poor, but Marguerite's wealth, in the style of a materialistic bourgeois age, is auctioned off after her death to pay her earthly debts, recalling Heywood's misogynistic Pardoner who sold saint's relics to aid his customers' salvation. Marguerite's auction not only emphasises the modern importance of buying, selling, ownership and property that quantified her sexual status, but simultaneously offers a calculated tabulation, an itemised inventory enumerating her capitalistic worth.

The initial appeal of the book, therefore, came from a public fascination with the dissolving line between myth and reality, a great voyeuristic interest in a woman whose real relics the artist Dumas had miraculously made fictional. After the play based on her life opened in Paris, Marie's grave was nightly strewn with flowers, bouquets of fresh camellias. At a revival of the play in 1859, Clémence Prat, Marie's neighbour and go-between in arranging her sexual liaisons, actually played the role of Prudence which Dumas had based on her. After seeing Sarah Bernhardt's magnificent portrayal of Marguerite, Dumas was so impressed that he sent her a copy of his novel with his original last letter to Marie inside the cover. The artistic use of the self initiated by the sentimental novelists of the previous century finds an echo in Dumas's use of this letter in the text of his novel.

Finally, we must return to the connection between the role of prostitute and actress (one that we have examined in earlier chapters). This prejudicial link encourages fantastical speculation from Baudelaire in 1863:

> What can be said of the courtesan can also be said, with reservations, of the actress: for the latter, too, is a manufactured confection and a thing of public pleasure. But where the actress is concerned, the conquest and the booty are more noble, more spiritual. Her business is to win general favour not only by her physical beauty, but also by the talents of the rarest order. If on one side the actress is akin to the courtesan, on the other side she is akin to the poet. (Baudelaire, 1986, p. 67)

Behind the fictional Marguerite Gautier stands the real Marie Duplessis – a doubling of myth and reality which brought Dumas's novel its immense popularity. When this narrative moves into the theatre, such a doubling resonates: the actress, that 'manufactured confection', who plays the role of Marguerite brings with her the age-old theatrical prejudice so aptly put by William Prynne: 'Women-Actors, notorious whores' (Cotton, 1980, p. 39). So behind the dramatic actress stands an imagined prostitute, and unlike other archetypal theatrical roles for women, the penitent whore fulfils the patriarchally created belief that acting women are merely being themselves.

7

The speechless heroine

Why should women only above all other creatures
that were created for the benefit of man, have
the use of speech?
    (Francis Beaumont, *The Woman-Hater*, 1606)

The wives tongue towards her husband must bee neither keene, nor
loose, nor countenance neither swelling nor deriding: her behaviour not
flinging, not puffing, not discontented; but savouring of all lowlinesse
and quietnesse of affection. Looke what kinde of words or behaviour
thou wouldst dislike from thy servant or childe, those must thou not give
to thine husband: for thou art equally commanded to be subject.
(William Whately, *A Bride-Bush: or a direction for married persons*,
1619)

An impossible nirvana: Jonson's quest for a silent woman

In 1606 an edition of Libanius' *Sixth Declamation* was published in
Paris with Latin and Greek translations in parallel columns of text.
Libanius was a fourth-century Greek scholar who conducted a
school of rhetoric in Constantinople, and his work declaims the
downfall of a man fooled into believing his bride to be soft-spoken
and self-effacing. After the wedding, his illusion of a gentle
feminine silence is shattered; not only is his new wife loud but
insatiably talkative, and he pleads desperately for legal permission
to commit suicide.

    Three years after the publication of Libanius' text Ben Jonson
wrote *Epicoene, The Silent Woman* (considered his most popular
comedy in his lifetime) in which he uses Libanius' story as the
central plot. It was commonplace among writers of the era to draw

upon classical work for a variety of uses: dramatic frameworks, plots and philosophical discourse. Besides Libanius' story, Jonson used Ovid's *Ars amatoria (The Art of Love)* and Juvenal's Sixth Satire Against Women. From these classical writers, Jonson elicits and combines two opposing views of the relation of artifice to women: Ovid's proposal that nature is improved by art, hence encouraging the use of cosmetics by women as admirable; and Juvenal's view that such artifice negates nature and gives further proof of the falseness of womankind (Barish, 1956, p. 214). Also common among his fellow playwrights was Jonson's interest in the stereotypical attribute of female talkativeness, as Linda Woodbridge documents in detail:

> According to literary pronouncements, female speech is less rational than male speech in general; authors' diction often characterizes female speech as meaningless sound, babbling, prating, chattering: 'a prating wrangling toung,/A womans ceaselesse and incessant babling' (Haughton's *English-men for My Money; or, A Pleasant Comedy Called A Woman Will Have Her Will*, Sig. Cv); 'women will be prating' (*Arden of Feversham*, xiv, 201); 'a long-tongued babbling gossip' (*Titus Andronicus*, IV. ii. 150); 'tame a shrew and charm her chattering tongue' (*Taming of the Shrew*, IV, ii. 58). (Woodbridge, 1984, p. 210)

Thus since female speech is irrational, endless and incessant, these writers either neutralise any attempt at speech by their woman characters, or make it the butt of jokes. (An example in Jonson's play, *Epicoene*, is when Morose declares 'a woman's chiefest pleasure' to be that of 'taking pleasure in [her] tongue' (p. 68).)

We have already looked in Chapter 4 at Truewit's talent for verbosity and assurance when it comes to discussing and defining women. Equally articulated in this script by Jonson is the search for the 'silent woman' and the relationship of 'speech' itself to the indiscriminately talkative characters of the play. One critic states that 'Speech is central to this play about society because to Jonson it is central to human life itself' (Jonson, ed. Partridge, p. 12). Furthermore, since 'language most reveals a man, Jonson uses it as a principal mode of social and moral discriminations' (pp. 13–14). Clearly language is both a theme and a technique to Jonson, who uses his characters' relationship to the 'word' to humorous and satirical effect. Thus Morose, who seeks a 'silent wife' and loves listening to his own egomaniacal discourse, expects the rest of society to be quiet. But despite the eloquent range of male characters in the play Jonson presents us with only deviant women who lip-serve the age-old stereotype of talkative female: Madam Haughty, Madam Centaure and Mrs Mavis are designated by Jonson as 'Ladies Collegiates' (insatiable talkers, dominant women who have formed a salon with pretensions to cultural knowledge and court gossip); while Mrs Trusty and Mrs Otter are labelled as 'Pretenders', those lesser 'privileged women' who hope to gain entry into the ladies 'college'.

Supporting this non-silent stereotype of femininity is Jonson's eponymous 'silent woman', a desirable but unobtainable goal. Indeed, one of the male characters has spent months looking for one! When finally Morose meets Epicoene he registers both surprise and delight at her self-effacing aura of silence and immediately puts her to the test with a barrage of questions: Can she answer him by 'silent gestures' (II. 5. 37)? In the society of the court where women are expected stylishly to display verbal wit and amorous discourse, can she 'bury in [her]self with silence' (II. v. 50)? Morose's final cross-examination, 'the utmost touch and test of [her] sex' (58–9), converges on fashion:

> I do also love to see her whom I shall choose for my heifer to be the first and principal in all fashions, precede all the dames at court by a fortnight, have her council of tailors, lineners, lace-women, embroiderers, intelligences [fashion news from France], and then come forth varied like Nature, or oftener than she, and better by the help of Art, her emulous servant. This I do affect. And how will you be able, lady, with this frugality of speech, to give the manifold – but necessary – instructions for that bodice, these sleeves, those skirts, this cut, that stitch, this embroidery, that lace, this wire, those knots, that ruff, those roses, this girdle, that fan, the t'other scarf, these gloves? Ha? What say you, lady? (59–70)

The fascination of this speech lies in its close proximity to a speech delivered earlier by Truewit to Morose in Act II, scene 2. Here, as we saw in Chapter 4, in order to discourage Morose from the notion of marriage, Truewit verbally assaults him with a detailed accounting of the many faults of women. Truewit's harangue is an endless display of his supposed knowledge of the character, desires and frailties of women, involving a woman's relation to her clothing and appearance. Truewit tirades against fashion:

Then, if you love your wife, or rather dote on her, sir, O, how she'll torture you and take pleasure i' your torments! . . . she will not hurt her beauty, her complexion; or it must be for that jewel or that pearl when she does; every half hour's pleasure must be bought anew . . . she must have that rich gown for such a great day, a new one for the next, a richer for the third; be served in silver; have the chamber filled with a succession of grooms, footmen, ushers, and other messengers, besides em-broiderers, jewellers, tire-women, sempsters, feathermen, perfumers . . . (II. 2. 76–97)

Truewit's inventory of femininity mirrors Morose's later speech on the same theme: he inverts Truewit's Juvenalian vices into ideal requirements, an Ovidian eulogy to the exemplary artifice of wives by appropriating Truewit's image of a fashion-crazed wife in a manner which serves to give him sanity and power. When Morose asks Epicoene how, 'with this frugality of speech', she will be able to give numerous instructions for creating her wardrobe, she replies softly, 'I'll leave it to you, sir' (II. 5. 71). 'Admirable creature!', replies Morose, '. . . she has brought a wealthy dowry in her silence' (79–80). Thus not only does silent Epicoene propose to hold her tongue in daily domestic existence with Morose, but she will abdicate her role in the creation of her social self. Morose's Pygmalion-like fantasies of dominance and creative control over his wife and her social costume quickly disintegrate. Once married, Epiocoene sheds her silence to reveal the 'real' woman transformed into an outspoken, demanding, relentlessly verbose female.

The stereotype of female talkativeness – and by implication the impossibility of being quiet – is the central conceit which Jonson conspicuously fails to question in *The Silent Woman*. Although Jonson punishes Morose for his self-centred, uncompromising nature, this punishment reinforces the stereotype: marriage to a woman who is, like all women, insatiably garrulous. When the end of the play reveals Epiocoene to be a young boy in disguise planted by Morose's wayward nephew, Jonson has played a marvellously witty, visual double-cross on us all. This humorous cross-dressing, however, is double-edged: even women who *pretend* silence are impossible to find, therefore one needs young boys to impersonate them.

Before the revelation of Epicoene's deception, Morose's only escape from marriage, short of suicide, is publicly to proclaim his impotence and ask for an annulment. As Partridge, Jonson's editor states: 'Speech seems to be associated with healthy and normal social activity – except by the egotistic Morose' (Jonson, ed. Partridge, p. 13). Analysing Jonson's treatment of speech as healthy and socially normal creates a gender-blind assertion which relates only to the male characters. The play's talkative women, The Collegiates, are shown as deviants from Jonson's ideal of soothing, silent, self-effacing 'woman', and their abundant speech is used comically to categorise a group of lower-middle-class women with aggressive pretensions to a cultural and social milieu to which they have no right. The speech Jonson assigns to these women expresses no natural self, but a self that is built out of overheard courtly argot and classical smatterings.

Truewit introduces us to these women when he describes them to Morose's nephew, Dauphine, at the beginning of the play:

> Why, is it not arrived there yet, the news? A new foundation, sir, here i' the town, of ladies that call themselves the Collegiates, an order between courtiers and country-madams, that live from their husbands and give entertainment to all the Wits and Braveries o' the time, as they call 'em, cry down or up what they like or dislike in a brain or a fashion with most masculine or rather *hermaphroditical* authority, and every day gain to their college some new probationer. (I. 1. 67–74, my italics)

Later when the ladies meet Dauphine and enthusiastically begin to shower unwanted attention on him, Truewit continues his analysis:

> Did I not tell thee, Dauphine? Why, all their actions are governed by crude opinion, without reason or cause; they know not why they do anything; but as they are informed, believe, judge, praise, condemn, love, hate, and in emulation one of another, do all these things alike. Only, they have a natural inclination sways 'em generally to the worst, when they are left to themselves. (IV. 6. 57–63)

For Jonson his 'Female Collegiates' are hermaphrodite harpies who would invade the masculine domain of knowledge and spoken discourse. Their inadequacy in this campaign provides a great source of the play's comedy; and their sexual ambiguity, informed by their misappropriated male speech, is anything but socially normal.

We have already noted in Chapter 1 the obsessive Renaissance preoccupation with women who dress as men, a preoccupation which could be said to have culminated in 1620 with the publication of two pamphlets, *Hic Mulier* and *Haec-Vir*. The former subjects women who dress in male clothing to a full frontal attack; the latter counters with the defence that women have been forced into such drastic dressing by the current trend in male effeminacy. An earlier disparagement of women who trespass sexual boundaries by cross-dressing is Phillip Stubbes's *Anatomy of Abuses*, published in 1583. Stubbes sees these male-attired women as literally and physically evolving into actual men:

> The Women . . . haue dublets & Jerkins as men haue . . ., & though this be a kinde of attire appropriate onely to man, yet they blush not to wear it, and if they could wel chaunge their sex, & put on the kinde of man, as they can weare apparel assigned onely to man, I think they would as verely become men indeed as now they degenerate from godly sober women, in wearing this wanton lewd kinde of attire. (Woodbridge, 1984, p. 139)

Stubbes continues his chastisement: 'Wherefore these Women may not improperly be called *Hermaphrodita*, that is, Monsters of both kindes, half women, half men' (Woodbridge, p. 140). Jonson's textual references to the cross-dressing controversy suggest a familiarity with Stubbes's work: besides the analoguous use of 'hermaphrodite', Jonson also refers to the issue of women wearing the doublet (i.e. men's clothing), when Mrs Otter recounts her dream of appearing in a 'crimson satin doublet' (III. 2. 64). The naming of the Collegiates also reflects contemporary confusion over the man-woman. As Edward Partridge says,

> Both 'Centaure' and 'Otter' suggest the sexual ambiguity of women. The Renaissance had inherited the centaur, a half-horse, half-man, from the Greeks. The Elizabethans were so uncertain about the otter that they could not decide whether it was flesh or fish, and even thought that both sexes of the Ichneumon (a mongoose which they considered a kind of otter) bore young, 'having seed in themselves, whereby they conceive'. (p. 174)

Furthermore, the Greek word 'Epicoene' itself means a person with characteristics of both sexes.

The difference between these two Renaissance perceptions of woman-as-men is that Stubbes finds the powerful source of transformation in women's dress, while Jonson identifies it in women's attempted appropriation of male speech. But for both men such behaviour is a monstrous aberration.

A great deal of Jonson's comedy relies on the talkative female stereotype, and his suggestion that the 'silent' woman does not exist must be seen in relation to the prevalence of this notional figure. The traditional Christian dichotomy of womankind – virgin and whore – had been secularised by Chaucer. As Linda Woodbridge argues, 'after the confrontation between Patient Griselda and the Wife of Bath in *The Canterbury Tales*, the central confrontation between opposing female character types in literature was that between the Patient Grissill figure and the aggressive liberty-minded woman, either a shrew or a whore' (Woodbridge, 1984, p. 211). Although the self-effacing, silent Patient Griselda does not exist in Jonson's play, she was a popular female type used often by his contemporaries in the early seventeenth century so that, as Woodbridge points out:

> *Patient Grissil*, acted ca. 1600, *How a Man May Choose*, acted ca. 1602, *All's Well that Ends Well*, acted ca. 1602, *The London Prodigal*, acted ca. 1604, *The Fair Maid of Bristow*, acted ca. 1604, *Othello*, acted ca. 1606, all have heroines who remain patient and submissive through scenes of gruesome abuse by their husbands. (Woodbridge, 1984, p. 211)

The Patient Griselda figure presents a two-fold difficulty: she appears to condone such abuse through her silence, *and* there is the uncomfortable suggestion that she is lucky, in the first place, to have been selected for marriage by her husband. When any verbal protest from the woman invokes the instant accusation of 'shrew' or 'whore', her silence within these patriarchal narratives is assured.

King Lear and the goodness of a speechless daughter

The idea of the speechless woman takes on a new dimension when male writers elevate her to a 'heroine'. In the original story by Chaucer, Patient Griselda is a character who courts martyrdom, not heroism; her exaggerated and overblown 'patience' and obedience were contrasted with the outspoken, dominant Wife of Bath. Similarly, the female characters in Woodbridge's list above represent not so much heroism as martyrdom to their silent, self-effacing personalities. But what happens to the conventional silent stereotype when speechlessness finds a new link with strength and assertiveness? The greatest example of this occurs in Shakespeare's

King Lear, when Lear asks his daughters, 'which of you shall we say doth love us most/that we our largest bounty may extend' (I. i. 52). Although her older sisters Goneril and Regan can easily articulate the facile, false love which gains them a share in their father's kingdom, Cordelia finds any such answer – treating love as a commodity, as something to be bought and sold with the currency of a suitably ritualised response – an impossibility.

LEAR:	. . . what can you say to draw/a third more opulent than your sisters? Speak.
CORDELIA:	Nothing my lord.
LEAR:	Nothing?
CORDELIA:	Nothing.
LEAR:	Nothing will come of nothing. Speak again.
	(I. i. 90)

As Brian Rotman observes in his book, *Signifying Nothing*:

> In forcing Cordelia to outbid her sisters, Lear coerces her into the world of exchangeable commodities where, before the play has started, he has trapped himself. Cordelia's attempt at silence comes from the intuition that any answer to Lear's question would make sense only in a world where love, as she has to understand it, is absent. (Rotman, 1987, p. 80)

Of course, it is Cordelia's silent horror at her father's fixation on transactions which require, for him, the buying and selling of natural love, which provokes and initiates the action of the play.

> For Cordelia, confronted with Lear's question about love – 'how much' – the only response, the only one possible in her moral universe, is silence. Her 'nothing', her failed attempt to remain silent, to stay outside the language of commodities set up by Lear, becomes for him an answer . . . to his question: obsessed by the need to close his deal Lear converts her unarticulated refusal to enter the deal and make a bid . . . into a bid. (Rotman, 1987, p. 81)

Cordelia's refusal to enter into Lear's love market, although undoubtedly an heroic action, is intrinsically linked to her femaleness. Can we imagine a son acting in the same way? Even Lear's long-standing friend and confidant, Kent, attempts to reason with the king verbally. Though Kent is commanded by Lear to stop speaking and is eventually banished from the kingdom, this fails to prevent him from using speech, logic and reason.

This idea of the silent woman as heroine, as a model offered and advocated for womankind, incorporates the notion that nobility at its most articulate suffers in silence. Thus Cordelia must suffer in dramatic silence, banished both from the kingdom and literally from the play until the last act, when her return to the narrative only initiates the ultimate silence of her death. Both male 'creators', father and playwright, define her by her silences, her softness, her quietness. As her father says of her, 'Her voice was ever soft,/ Gentle and low, an excellent thing in woman' (V. iii. 274–5). Yet her father gives her an ultimatum – an injunction to speak – which contradicts this parental restraint on her language.

Eighteenth-century versions of silence: Cibber's Lady Easy

The figure of a speechless heroine appears and then absents herself from drama in a multitude of ways. In *A Winter's Tale*, for example, the strong, articulate women, Hermione and Paulina, are removed from the plot in Act III, scene 2. Hermione's 'silence' is contrived by a dramatic 'death' that lasts sixteen years; Paulina helps to hide her during that time, and not until the end of the play do both women return to the dialogue. Some eighteenth-century versions of the play removed the Hermione/Paulina characters entirely, leaving a truncated version in which Perdita, Hermione's sixteen-year-old daughter, became the central female voice: a new voice that is young, compliant and unthreatening.

Theatrical artisans of the century enjoyed replicating the naive and innocent Perdita. What began as MacNamara Morgan's musical afterpiece at Covent Garden in 1754, David Garrick developed as the main performance piece at Drury Lane. Despite Garrick's failed attempts to revive the full-length *Winter's Tale*, his abbreviated musical version, *Florizel and Perdita*, remained popular until the end of the century (Dash, 1980, pp. 271–2). Dash, describing Garrick's adaptation, opines:

> by removing the first half of the play, they cut out Leontes' passion-wracked passages, his intense spurts of jealousy, and his arrogance. Since characters in drama are defined by their interactions with other

characters, the omission of the early scenes affected not only the portrait of Leontes but also those of Hermione and Paulina. Contrast, action, and reaction all help to project an image. Hermione's strength becomes unnecessary if there is no challenge, no contest, for her to face. And Paulina's role as the voice of conscience also loses its meaning. By revising, excising, and emending, both Morgan and Garrick, substituted weak women for strong, and strong men for weak. (Dash, 1980, p. 274)

The permutations of female speechlessness find another dimension for women who lived in the eighteenth century in Colley Cibber's *The Careless Husband* (1704). Here Lady Easy is plagued by her husband's open, thoughtless adultery. Although she opens the play with a monologue in which she despairs over her husband's licentiousness (having just discovered his latest female conquest to be her own maid), she ends her speech by figuratively biting her tongue: 'My eyes and tongue shall yet be blind and silent to my wrongs' (I. i. 11–12). The play itself is usually viewed critically as a dramatic bridge between standard Restoration drama and the new eighteenth-century sentimental drama. As Appleton, editor, critic, of Cibber's plays, puts it, 'Wearied of the pre-marital love-chase, dramatists turned instead to the post-marital quarrel, and their plays are dominated by a succession of provoked, jealous, and suspicious husbands, and wives' (Cibber, 1966, p. xiv).

Cibber's play deviates from this conventional pattern in that the 'post-marital quarrel' never occurs because of Lady Easy's refusal to engage in an argument. As Chaudhuri (1983, p. 7) pointedly observes, 'Throughout this action, Lady Easy moves silently about, seeing all and saying nothing. On the few occasions when she does speak, her characteristic forms of utterance are the aside and the question, both designed to insinuate her presence without asserting her position'. How, then, does Cibber dramatically resolve the requisite quarrel when one of his spouses is so self-effacing and passive as to avoid the possibility of any cathartic outburst which could lead to a resolution? At the end of the play Lady Easy discovers her husband, 'without his periwig', and her maid side by side, sleeping in two easy chairs. Confronted with this concrete evidence of infidelity, Lady Easy 'starts and trembles some time, unable to speak' (V. v.) She then launches into a monologue in which she fantasises confronting him through the use of language:

I'll throw this vizor of my patience off,

Now wake him in his guilt,
And barefaced front him with my wrongs.
I'll talk to him till he blushes, nay till he
Frowns on me, perhaps – and then
I'm lost again.

(V. v. 7–12)

But the fantasy of articulation is short-lived in the face of the frown
it conjures. A few lines later she reminds herself:

I have vowed obedience. Perhaps
The fault's in me, and nature has not formed
Me with the thousand little requisites
That warm the heart to love.

(V. v. 15–17)

This monologue denies the wife's right to discourse by blaming her
lack of physical, non-verbal allure for her husband's indiscretions.
But she does communicate her presence to her husband through a
sign: she drapes her scarf over his bare head. This gesture is 'the sign
of her knowledge, and of her impotence. It is this dramatically
signified absence that finally provides Sir Charles with the space for
his transformation. By repressing herself, Lady Easy has given her
husband the chance to *become* the good man he inherently *is*'
(Chaudhuri, 1983, p. 8). His transformation is cataclysmic: on
discovering the scarf he realises his wife has witnessed his adulterous liaison, is overcome with his transgressions, and immediately
decides to repent his many sins.

In the following scene Sir Charles approaches his wife to ask
forgiveness. The adjectives he uses to describe her are 'soft',
'generously tender', 'virtuous'. He carefully and gently asks her to
tell him why she left the scarf: 'Be easy in the truth and tell me'. But
even here Lady Easy shirks the opportunity: 'I cannot speak – and I
could wish you'd not oblige me to it. 'Tis the only thing I ever yet
refused you, and though I want a reason for my will, let me not
answer you' (V. vi. 96–9). Lady Easy's rewards for never answering
back are significant: her husband proclaims his 'new-born love' for
her and asks her to 'take what yet no woman ever truly had, my
conquered heart' (V. vi. 115–20). Indeed, the scene of their
reconciliation is an extended tribute (dramatic form merging with
dramatic repression) to Lady Easy's speechlessness in the face of

her husband's transgressions. Her husband says, 'Virtues, like benefits, are double when concealed' (V. vi. 87); thus playwright Colley Cibber concludes, celebrating the speechless heroine as the ideal woman rewarded for her exemplary, 'womanly' behaviour: suffering in silence.

This 'ideal' woman, with her indistinguishable characteristics of silence and virtue, appears again as the central female figure in early nineteenth-century melodrama. As seen earlier in relation to the dramatic narratives of the penitent whore, melodrama is a theatre of signs – both pictorial and metaphorical – where conflict occurs when the sign of virtue (usually a woman) falls in the face of evil. As Peter Brooks says,

> Virtue, expulsed, eclipsed, apparently fallen, cannot effectively articulate the cause of the right. Its tongue is in fact often tied by the structure of familial relationships: virtue cannot call into question the judgements and the actions of a father or an uncle or a guardian, for to do so would be to violate its nature as innocence. (Brooks, 1985, p.31)

But there is an important criterion here which Brooks overlooks: 'virtue as innocence' comprises woman; her speechlessness in the face of wrongdoing, of evil, occurs because she cannot 'call into question the judgements and actions of a father'. In sum, the woman cannot transgress the laws of the patriarchy, and as Brooks says, 'This imposed silence and passivity may be represented by a vow, usually in the name of the father, which cannot be violated' (p. 31). Furthermore, it is the heroine's silence, her passivity, her total submission to the laws of the father which engineer the melodramatic plot.

This patriarchal law of silence operates in Hubert's play *Clara, ou le malheur et la conscience*, in which the heroine must change her name and run away destitute as a fugitive for three months because she has been wrongly charged with infanticide. She has pledged silence to the real criminal, the man she believes to be her father. Like Lady Easy, another woman abdicates her voice to play out the consequences of a narrative which her silence, paradoxically, has engendered. Thus the function of the woman's speechlessness is two-fold: it creates an image of the ideal woman, mobile, gestural, but silent, on the stage *and* at the same time allows the sadistic pleasure of the narrative itself – the witnessing of innocent virtue in battle with evil – to emerge from the woman's self-imposed silence. But there is an explicit difference between Cibber's neophyte sentimental comedy and later French melodrama: Lady Easy's silence arises implicitly as the mark of a woman's goodness, her virtue, whereas the melodramatic heroine overtly pledges her silence to her father. So the dominant theatrical mode of the nineteenth century creates a narrative context in which virtuous women support and uphold the laws of the father. The theatrical image of a virtuous woman in early nineteenth-century France is overblown, excessive, and as grotesquely alive as Marguerite Gautier is dead; after all, Dumas fils forced her, like Hermione, to leave the 'narrative' of life. In the aftermath of the French Revolution (a moment in history when women were asserting their political voice but were abruptly forced to leave *that* narrative), the virtuous, silent heroine lives in the splendour of theatrical artifice embraced and popularised by the patriarchy.

Silence personified: the classical ballerina

While the melodramatic heroine played out the importance and necessity of female silence, her counterpart in dance gained cultural ascendancy. In 1820, usually considered the year of the birth of classical ballet, Carlo Blasis published his book *Treatise on the Dance*, which became the dancer's manual for many technical rules, including the importance and value of the ninety-degree turn-out of the feet. Although this codification of dance technique was important, the debut of Marie Taglioni two years later marks the beginning of the great Romantic movement in ballet. Her greatest success was *La Sylphide* in 1832. Choreographed by her father and designed by the French painter, Eugène Lamy, Taglioni, in her white tulle skirt, made the perfect artist's model for male-inspired notions of femininity, female dress, and movement.

The art form of ballet clearly differs from theatre, but their boundaries often overlap and collide, and this period witnessed the simultaneous emergence of the melodramatic heroine and the Romantic ballerina. Dance, by its very nature, obviously creates a non-verbal theatrical performance. Significantly the elevation of the female dancer to an icon, placed high on a pedestal of 'feminine' perfection, both parallels and transcends the creation of the

melodramatic heroine. This icon is a divine creation in the eyes of
one nineteenth-century dance critic seeing Taglioni dance in *La
Sylphide*:

> There is a sequence of furtive, aerial steps, something ravishing beyond
> description . . . The irresolute flight of a butterfly, those round tufts
> which the mild wind of April plucks like down from the cups on flowers
> and balances in the air . . . Really Taglioni is no mortal. God could not
> have imagined the cherubim better. (quoted in Guest, 1966, p. 115)

Taglioni received critical credit for revolutionising ballet by rescuing it from the staid classical style which, as Ivor Guest points out,
'expressed itself in the *danse noble*, with its mannered poses, its
stiffness, its stereotyped smiles, and above all its applause-catching
tricks' (p. 115). But however revolutionary in its outward form, the
essential impulse in Taglioni's dance remained stiffly stereotyped in
its representation of women, as another contemporary description
shows:

> Imagine our joy one evening when, unsuspecting and by pure chance,
> like finding a pearl by the roadside, we were presented not with the *danse
> noble*, but with a simple, easy, naturally graceful Taglioni, with a figure
> of unheard-of elegance, arms of serpentine suppleness and legs to match,
> and feet like those of an ordinary woman, even though she be a dancer!
> When we first saw her so much at ease and dancing so happily – she
> danced like a bird singing . . . Taglioni continues her triumphs, every day
> *learning to become more of a woman* and less of a dancer than ever.
> (quoted in Guest, 1966, p. 115–16, my italics)

In ridding herself of the artificial tricks of neoclassicism and
engaging with what seemed a 'natural' style (although to us
Romantic ballet looks anything but natural) Taglioni 'learned to
become more of a woman'. And what is this Romantic image of
'woman'? She is 'graceful', 'elegant', 'light', 'furtive', she transforms into a bird singing, a butterfly in flight, a tuft of a flower cup in
the April wind. Of course, the Romantic choreographers imbedded
in their narratives the attributes of the ballerina which developed
this idea of woman as ideal object, the floating, perfect, doll-like
icon of femininity.

The Romantic ballerina became such a popular image that the
notion of ballet became aligned to notions of femininity, so much so
that by the 1840s a strong prejudice had grown against male

dancers. Men were excluded from the *corps de ballet* whenever possible: the new ballet scenarios cut the number of male charac- ters, or allowed males to act but not dance, or, if they *must* dance, allowed them only for the sturdy elevation of the ballerina. The prejudice against men was well documented, as the ballet critic Jules Janin demonstrates in a passage from 1840:

> Speak to us of a pretty girl dancing who displays the grace of her features and the elegance of her figure, who reveals so fleetingly all the treasures of her beauty. Thank God, I understand that perfectly, I know what this lovely creature wishes us, and I would willingly follow her wherever she wishes in the sweet land of love. But a man, a frightful man, as ugly as you and I, a wretched fellow who leaps about without knowing why, a creature specially made to carry a musket and a sword and to wear a uniform. That this fellow should dance as a woman does – impossible! That this bewhiskered individual who is a pillar of the community . . . a man whose business it is to make and above all unmake laws, should come before us in a tunic of sky-blue satin . . . a frightful *danseuse* of the male sex . . . Today, thanks to this revolution which we have effected, woman is the queen of ballet. (quoted in Guest, 1966, p. 21)

Janin's nature/culture dichotomy views women as the 'natural' dancers and tells men to remain who they are: the sturdy elevators of the military machine and choreographers of our culture. The focusing of attention on women in the Romantic ballet reinforces the notion that woman creates only physically, with her body, a body linked to nature and therefore 'natural', whereas it is male choreographers and scenario writers who generate and control the 'creativity' of dance. There is a laboured irony behind this idealised and romanticised ballerina: in order to achieve her 'natural' state of perfection she has to spend years in training, she has to develop a powerful, physical presence which involves the distortion of her legs and feet, to endure great hardship and deprivation – all to learn a technique which paradoxically makes invisible the real woman, and creates instead an ethereal, dream-like, passive image floating across the stage. It is not coincidental that dance, specifically the Romantic ballet, a voiceless and speechless performing art, focuses almost relentlessly on the female performer and elevates her to a position of mute feminine perfection.

8

The wilful woman

Wife beating . . . was a recognised right of man, and was practised
without shame by high as well as low . . . Similarly . . . the daughter who
refused to marry the gentleman of her parents' choice was liable to be
locked up, beaten and flung about the room, without any shock being
inflicted on public opinion. Marriage was not an affair of personal
affection, but of family avarice, particularly in the 'chivalrous' upper
classes. (Trevelyan's *History of England*, quoted by Virginia Woolf in *A
Room of One's Own*)

Would that we were not daily forced to hear that one man has murdered
his wife because he suspected her of infidelity; that another has killed his
daughter on account of a secret marriage; that a third has caused his sister
to be murdered because she would not marry as he wished! It is great
cruelty that we claim the right to do whatever we list and will not suffer
women to do the same. If they do anything which does not please us there
we are at once with cords and daggers and poison. (Matteo Bandello,
Renaissance writer, who first wrote down the tale of the Duchess of
Malfi)

Autocratic and immature, the term 'wilful' has a certain double
edge: applied perjoratively to a child, it conveys headstrong,
obstinate, self-willed. But used in a wider context it also implies
strength, autonomy, decisive action. A person who performs
'wilful' actions intends them deliberately, not accidentally. In this
chapter I argue that the 'wilful woman' is a central female image in
our theatrical canon; an image riven by its own double edged
meaning of adult strength and childish obstinacy; a source of
anarchy, an attack on the status quo, and therefore traditionally
presented as an 'evil woman'. Additionally, there is a subtext to the
term 'wilful' in the world of the theatrical patriarchy which views

111

women simply *as* children, at times uncontrollable and destructive, incapable of maturity and adultness.

If we look at four major female characters in classical theatrical tragedy who are often described as 'wilful' – Clytaemnestra, the Duchess of Malfi, Miss Julie and Medea – their transgressions are primarily sexual: they have 'wilfully' chosen their own sexual partners. As we can see from the quotations which open this chapter, such independence of mind and power have attracted the cords, daggers and poison of the patriarchal scenario. Such women must be punished: therefore, Orestes kills his mother Clytaemnestra; the Duchess of Malfi is brutally murdered by her brothers; and Strindberg takes Miss Julie's life. Only Medea survives, even though her own wilful vengeance has included murdering her children. As a result, or perhaps to the purpose, Euripides elevates her in her heavenly chariot to mythical status as 'female monster'; she survives, but as the evil woman of all time.

The hideous blast of contrary winds: treacherous Clytaemnestra

The story of Clytaemnestra is told in Aeschylus' trilogy *The Oresteia*, which chronicles the aftermath of the Trojan War. Her husband, Agammemnon, returns home after a ten-year absence – triumphant, proud, displaying his war prize Cassandra, a Trojan princess taken as his concubine. During Agammemnon's absence, Clytaemnestra, ruling in her husband's place, has defiantly taken her own lover, Aegisthus. Clytaemnestra ceremoniously fetes her husband on his return, feigns affection and concern, lowers him into his bath, and stabs him. Prior to Agammemnon's departure to Troy, he had sacrificed their daughter, Iphigenia, to the gods to win favourable winds in his sails, and Clytaemnestra justifies her murder of Agmmemnon by his murder of her daughter. Orestes, the son of Clytaemnestra and Agammemnon, kills his mother to avenge his father's death. Orestes' matricide provokes his mother's Furies to action and they pursue him in retribution. In the final play. Orestes stands trial, with Athena as judge and Apollo as his defence against Clytaemnestra's Furies. In this scene Apollo's main defense rests on the power of the male parent over that of the female:

  APOLLO: . . . mark the truth of what I say.

The mother is not the true parent of the child
Which is called hers. She is a nurse who tends the growth
Of young seed planted by its true parent, the male . . .
. . . And of this truth,
That father without mother may beget, we have
Present, as proof, the daughter of Olympian Zeus:
One never nursed in the dark cradle of the womb
(656–65)

Here Apollo cleverly focuses the judicial proceedings on the judge
herself: the 'proof' that mothers are not the 'true parents' is shown
by Athena herself, who was born fully developed from her father's
head. However, Apollo's defence does not convince all the jurors,
and the twelve votes are divided equally until Athena casts her
deciding vote in Orestes' favour.

   Such misogynistic myth-making never questions the authority of
Athena's decisive ballot, as Froma Zeitlin points out in her seminal
essay on the *Oresteia*:

   Clytaemnestra, the female principal, in the first play is a shrewd,
   intelligent rebel against the masculine regime, but by the last play,
   through her representatives, the Furies, female is now allied with the
   archaic, primitive, and regressive, while male in the person of the young
   god, Apollo, champions conjugality, society, and progress, and his
   interests are ratified by the androgynous goddess, Athena, who sides
   with the male and confirms his primacy. Through gradual and subtle
   transformations, social evolution is posed as a movement from female
   dominance to male dominance, or, as it is often figuratively phrased,
   from 'matriarchy' to 'patriarchy'. (Zeitlin, 1978, p. 151)

'Archaic', 'primitive', 'regressive' – Zeitlin's words suggest that
Clymaemnestra comes to represent some archetypal quality –
wilful, unruly, monstrous – of womankind which is embodied on the
stage by the presence of her writhing Furies. Clytaemnestra, like
Eve in another founding myth of the patriarchy, loses any sense of
individuality and signifies the transgressions of *all* women. As
Homer describes her in *The Odyssey*, 'By her utter wickedness of
will she has poured dishonour both on herself and every woman that
lives hereafter, even on one whose deeds are virtuous' (XI, 433–5).
We see here a pattern in these two literary myths of female
punishment, where one female act of hubris brings a curse on the
entire House of Women: all women must suffer because of Eve,

just as all women must accept male dominance because of Clytaemnestra. The character of Clytaemnestra stands for all women who through their strength and search for autonomy undermine and pervert the 'normality' of male power.

Such perversion by strong women threatens the entire race in Aeschylus' play *The Suppliants* (the first play of a trilogy, and, the only extant portion) where the Daniads, fifty daughters of Daneus, rebel against proposed marriages to their male cousins. These militant virgins are forced to undergo the marriage ceremony but on their wedding night they murder their numerous bridegrooms. Here Aeschylus multiplies Clytaemnestra's single husband-murder into a massacre threatening the extinction of the entire human race. Another mass marital murder takes place in a lost play by Sophocles, in which Aphrodite cursed the Lemnian women by giving them an evil odour that turned their husbands against them; the women responded by killing all the men in their community and establishing a manless society. Zeitlin views these male-visions of masculine slaughter as an 'Amazon' complex

> which envisions that woman's refusal of her required subordinate role must, by an inevitable sequence, lead to its opposite: total domination, gynecocracy, whose extreme form projects the enslavement or murder of men. That same polarizing imagination can only conceive of two hierarchic alternatives: Rule by Men and Rule by Women. (Zeitlin, 1978, p. 153)

The ultimate message here is that the male notion of democracy really presents a polar *impasse*: female self-assertion results in annihilation of the male.

Such a diametrical opposition of men and women informs Euripides' play of the Clytaemnestra story, *Orestes*. Similar to Aeschylus' trilogy, the dichotomy produces a condemnation of *all* women: here the Messenger reports Orestres' trial speech which views the eponymous hero's matricide not only as being in his 'father's cause', but also in defence of *all* men:

> In your defence, no less than in my father's cause,
> I killed my mother. For if wives may kill husbands
> And not be guilty, you had best lose no time,
> But die today, before your wives make slaves of you.
> To vindicate her would be a preposterous act.

As things stand now, the traitness to my father's bed
Has paid for it with her life; but if you now kill me
The law is void; the sooner a man dies the better,
Since wives lack but encouragement, not enterprise.
(935–43)

Here Orestes affirms Zeitlin's contention that classical male playwrights view the nature of hierarchical power as one of oppositions: men against women. Sophocles distributes outraged male vanity among the other male characters in his play as they continue their descriptive disputation of Clytaemnestra's evil:

Orestes, son of Agammemnon should be
Honoured with crowns for daring to avenge his father
By taking a depraved and godless woman's life –
One who corrupted custom; since no man would leave
His home and arm himself, and march to war, if wives
Left there in trust could be seduced by stay-at-homes,
And brave men cukcolded.
(924–30)

Vase paintings often portray the godless Clytaemnestra with an axe in her hand running towards an open door – a reinforcement of this Aeschylean view of her as the evil, anarchic, unruly female (Keuls, 1985, p. 338). But Clytaemnestra's personification of corrupted, depraved femininity, her Furies, go through a startling metamorphosis after the trial which vindicates Orestes, when Athena transforms them into the Eumenides – gentle, pacified priestesses, who will 'agree to accept marriage sacrifices and to use their powers of fertility for the state' (Foley, 1981, p. 152). The destructive creature who 'corrupts custom' is dramatically transfigured into a life-giving female who promotes marriage and female devotion to the male.

In all these stories of the male-genocidal females, one female character refuses the anarchic actions of her sisters, choosing instead a submissive loyality to the male line. Just as the Eumenides reincarnate Clytaemnestra as a 'good' woman, in the Lemnian massacre a good daughter spares her father out of filial piety. In the myth of the Danaids, a single woman refrains from murdering her new husband. And in the Homeric episode of the Amazons, one of the leaders, Antiope, is captured by Theseus and alters her warrior-like persona to become a faithful wife and mother.

The legendary Amazons were extremely popular – particularly so to the Athenians as a fable for rebellious, unconventional, disorderly women. Eva Keuls provides evidence of their appeal:

> From Classical antiquity in its entirety, over eight hundred portrayals of Amazons have survived. Nowhere else are they more numerous as in Athens; representations of Greek heroes stabbing and clubbing Amazons to death could be seen everywhere in painting, sculpture and in pottery decoration. (Keuls, 1985, p. 4)

The Amazons, of course, had no husbands to murder as they chose to live in a community without men. It is precisely this autonomous choice to live outside the patriarchy, paralleled in Clytaemnestra's decision to choose her own sexual partner, that is aesthetically punished and condemned from the epic amphitheatre to the household vase. The Amazons are shown to be not *real* women, but aberrant, deformed 'monsters' who prefer self-mutilation to a submissive life with men. Just as the Amazons are denied their status as 'women', so too Clytaemnestra is denied her status as 'mother'. In both these denials, the mythical conclusion is a kind of counter-genocide, a destruction of reputation and an ultimate subjugation.

Precious whores and irregular crabs: Webster's *Duchess of Malfi*

What we witness in the story of Clytaemnestra is a double murder: the literal murder of the matriarch, and the murder of her status as a women and a mother. Such doubling of death, of a reality and the language which conveys it is also a central element in Webster's *Duchess of Malfi*. The widowed Duchess wilfully contravenes an injunction by her brothers, the Cardinal and Ferdinand, against a second marriage by secretly marrying Antonio, a steward in the Duchess's household. When the brothers discover this, they plot to kill her along with her husband and children. Before this literal murder takes place, the brothers attempt on numerous occasions to control and implicitly destroy their sister through language:

FERDINAND: You are a widow:
  You know already what man is; and therefore
  Let not youth, high promotion, eloquence –

<blockquote>
                                                    No,
CARDINAL: Nor anything without addition, honour,
  Sway your high blood.
FERDINAND: Marry! They are most luxurious
  Will wed twice.
CARDINAL: Oh, fie!
FERDINAND: Their livers are more spotted
  Than Laban's sheep.
DUCHESS: Diamonds are of most value
  They say, that have passed through most jewellers' hands.
FERDINAND: Whores by that rule are precious.
</blockquote>

(I.ii.4–10)

Through such murderous figures of speech the Cardinal and Ferdinand insist that the Duchess keep wearing her widow's weeds, occupying a safe, inert, social position. And they polarise the Duchess's desire for personal action and mobility as whorish:

<blockquote>
CARDINAL: You may flatter yourself,
  And take your own choice; privately be married
  Under the eaves of night –
FERDINAND: Think'st the best voyage
  That e'er you made; like the irregular crab,
  Which, though't goes backward, thinks it goes right
  Because is goes its own way; but observe,
  Such weddings may more properly be said
  To be executed than celebrated.
</blockquote>

(I.ii.25–32)

Through such metaphorical slanders the Duchess's mobility is viewed as an aberration: the journey of an 'irregular crab'. Autonomous women go through life 'backward', courting condemnation and death: the ultimate position of stasis.

When later in the play Ferdinand discovers that the Duchess has secretly remarried, she is instantly 'a sister damned: she's/loose i' th'hilts;/ Grown a notorious strumpet' (II.v.3–4), a 'Cursed creature!' (31), and later an 'Excellent hyena!' (39). In Act III, scene ii, Ferdinand confronts the Duchess directly with a knife, calling her a 'screech-owl' (86) and a 'vile woman' (97); in the following scene, he describes her to his brother as 'damned'. 'Methinks her fault and beauty,/Blended together, show like leprosy,/The whiter, the fouler' (III. iii. 64–6).

In seeking the death of the Duchess, Ferdinand continuously kills her through language, where in order to effect this second murder she must become no longer a Duchess, or a sister, but a whore, an animal, a leper. In fact, her attempts at movement within the patriarchal scaffolding of her society are deadly simple and straight-forward: she chooses to move from static, childless widow to active, creative wife. In retaliation for the Duchess's mobility, Ferdinand used language both to sanction her real murder and justify his metaphorical action.

The Duchess fights this downwardly spiralling redefinition of herself in direct and forceful speech. At the end of the scene in which Ferdinand rushes at his sister with a drawn dagger, she seeks to convince him of her status as a happily married woman:

> DUCHESS: You are in this
> Too strict, and were you not my princely brother,
> I would say, too wilful. My reputation
> Is safe.
> FERDINAND: Dost thou know what reputation is?
> I'll tell thee, to small purpose, since the instruction
> Comes now too late.
> Upon a time Reputation, Love and Death,
> Would travel o'er the world; and it was concluded
> That they should part, and take three several ways.
> Death told them, they should find him in great battles,
> Or cities plagued with plagues. Love gives them counsel
> To inquire for him 'mongst unambitious shepherds,
> Where dowries were not talked of, and sometimes
> 'Mongst quiet kindred that had nothing left
> By their dead parents. 'Stay', quoth Reputation,
> 'Do not forsake men; for it is my nature,
> If I once part from any man I meet,
> I am never found again.' And so for you:
> You have shook hands with Reputation,
> And made him invisible. So, fare you well.
> I will never see you more.
>   (III. ii. 114–34)

In his speech Ferdinand makes clear the power of male language over the female. His tale, which ranks 'Reputation' on a level with 'Love' and 'Death', demonstrates the masculine power of words to determine the course of her existence. Thus, since 'Reputation' is 'what is geneally said or believed about a person', clearly one's reputation relies on the voices or beliefs of others.[1] It matters not to Ferdinand that the Duchess herself believes in or asserts the safety of her reputation; the very fact of his utterance invalidates any claim she has to it. Since this is built on words alone and not on deeds performed in a real world, he can destroy her name with his words. In the semantic world of Webster's play, women have no say in their definition.

The embattled Duchess appears to accept verbal annihilation; in response to Ferdinand she ignores his allegory on 'Reputation' and shifts her tactics with another argument:

> DUCHESS: Why should only I,
>   Of all the other princes of the world,
>   Be cased up, like a holy relic? I have youth
>   And a little beauty.
> FERDINAND: So have some virgins
>   That are witches. I will never see thee more.
>   (III. ii. 135–9)

But on the battleground of male and female language, the Duchess' strategy is a mere skirmish compared to the abruptness and brutality of Ferdinand's outright attack. His language transforms her once and for all from the archetypally 'good' woman to the archetypally evil: from virgin to witch.

The scene just prior to Ferdinand's discovery of his sister's marriage shows his brother, the Cardinal, with his mistress, Julia. Webster no doubt intended to expose the Cardinal as lecherous and lascivious, like his brother, and to emphasise the amorous double standard that exists in the world of the play, for when Julia tells how she deceived her husband to keep their rendezvous, the Cardinal calls her 'a witty false one' (II.iv.5). Countering this casually attributed falseness, she points out that the Cardinal had approached her and initiated their liaison: 'You have prevailed with me/Beyond my strongest thoughts: I would not now/Find you inconstant' (6–8). But inconstancy is a characteristic assigned only to women:

> CARDINAL: We had need go borrow that fantastic glass
>   Invented by Galileo the Florentine
>   To view another spacious world i' th'moon,
>   And look to find a constant woman there.
>   (15–19)

The cosmos of Webster's play exposes a distinct relativity in its rules for men and women. It is a world where finding a constant woman is as impossible as finding a patient one in Heywood's or a silent one in Jonson's; where Cardinals may have mistresses but widows who marry are murdered; a world dominated by 'Reputation' and the power of the male word.

The articulation of male dominance continues in the Duchess's final scene, when she confronts Bosola, her executioner, with the words 'Who am I?' Bosola, continuing the obsessive redefinition initiated by Ferdinand, engulfs her in a final onslaught of language:

> Thou art a box of worm-seed, at best but a slavatory of green mummy. What's this flesh? A little crudded milk, fantastical puff-paste. Our bodies are weaker than those paper-prisons boys used to keep flies in, more contemptible, since ours is to preserve earth worms. (IV.ii.123–9)

The Duchess, however, resists. Bosola's barrage of language will not transform her, will not prevent her from preserving an ultimate self-identity to the end: 'I am Duchess of Malfi still' (IV.ii.143).

The story of the Duchess of Malfi was first told by the Italian Renaissance writer Matteo Bandello, who based its narrative on real events, some of which he possibly witnessed. An extremely popular story during the Renaissance, writers throughout Europe replicated it in a variety of versions; after Webster, Lope de Vega dramatised it for the Spanish stage. It appears that the majority of the tellers of this tale retain Bandello's original condemnation of the Duchess's actions: that she *did*, after all, marry beneath her station. Webster innovatively calls such moralising into question when he points out the double standard and hypocrisy of the brothers, their utter corruption and lack of compassion; importantly, he creates a strong, autonomous Duchess. Yet despite Webster's challenging, non-conventional approach, numerous critics have continued to interpret the Duchess's actions as mendacious and deceitful – one, for example, describing Webster as the 'stern justicer of human error – of the folly of Antonio and the Duchess' (Hunter, 1969, p. 302). Another critic, in discussing an audience's response to the play, says: 'we are unsure of whether the Duchess is guilty or innocent' (Moore, 1966, p. 126).

However, such moralising justifications have been called into question by recent feminist critics,[2] as a blinkered misreading of Webster:

to assert that Webster's Duchess deserved torture and death because she chose to marry the man she loved and to bear his children is, in effect, to join forces with her tyrannical brothers, and so to confuse the operations of some poetic justice, of which we should approve, with precisely those examples of social injustice which Webster does everything in his power to make us condemn. (Hawkins, 1975, p. 341)

Miss Julie's loss of self: half man and half woman

Just such a confusion between poetic justice and social injustice operates centuries later in a radically different period of drama: Strindberg's Miss Julie again contains a wilful woman who like the Duchess of Malfi breaks the female taboo by choosing her sexual partner outside her class. Miss Julie's wild, disorderly behaviour precipitates the breaking off of her recent engagement to which Jean, the footman of Julie's father, the Count, gives witness:

They [Miss Julie and her fiancé] were down in the stable-yard, and she was 'training' him – as she called it. And what do you think she was doing? She was making him jump over her riding whip – just like teaching a dog tricks. He jumped it twice, and each time she caught him a stinger with the whip. And then the third time, he wrenched it out of her hand, broke it in pieces, and then cleared out. (p. 79)

This initial description clearly prepares us for the entrance of Miss Julie, who is not the refined lady she should be: unconcerned about her dress, she dances with servants, loves to ride horses, prefers common beer to refined wine.

By contrast, the other female character of the play, Kristin, the cook, clearly knows her place as a woman and a member of the lower class – waiting on Jean, the footman, and enjoying this subservient position. The play becomes a scene of intimate conversation between Miss Julie and Jean, who prompt one another with reprimands and reminders of their rightful station. This scene culminates offstage in Jean's room and (although they respond spontaneously when a group of singing peasants approach) it is clear that Miss Julie chooses to have this sexual encounter. On their return to the kitchen they discuss eloping, running away from their life under the Count, but slowly their previous intimacy dissolves and ends in hatred and accusations. For as the scene finally makes clear, Miss Julie, true to her changed identity, cannot return again to the life she lived before, although Jean shows the facile flexibility to do so.

Near the end of the play the transformed Miss Julie approaches desperation:

> MISS JULIE: What would you do in my place?
> JEAN: In your place? Let me think . . . A woman of your class, who's gone wrong . . . I don't know. Yes, I do though.
> MISS JULIE: (*she picks up the razor, and makes a significant gesture*) Like this?
> JEAN: Yes. But *I* wouldn't do it, mind you – that's the difference between us.
> MISS JULIE: Because you're a man and I'm a woman? What difference does that make?
> JEAN: Just the difference there *is* between man and woman.
>
> (Strindberg, pp. 116–17)

Strindberg, famous for his obssession with the pugnacious relations between men and women, clearly wants to set up inviolable divisions between the sexes. It is just this sense of division, this sense of sexual warfare, that will destroy Miss Julie, for as she says shortly after:

> You see he [her father] taught me to despise my own sex – to be half woman and half man. Who's to blame for all this – my father, or my mother, or myself? Myself? I haven't a thought that I don't get from my father, nor an emotion that I don't get from my mother. Even this last idea that all human beings are equal – that came from my fiancé – and then I call him a beast for his pains . . . But who's to blame? Still, what does that matter? I'm the one who has to bear the blame and take the consequences. (p. 117)

It has been the patriarchal absence of Julie's father from the play and the action which has allowed the evening's drama to develop; now at its end, when the sound of the Count's bell signals that he has returned home and expects to be served, Jean actively resumes his subservient demeanour while Miss Julie becomes paralysed at the thought of her father's renewed presence in the house:

> Oh, I'm so tired; I can't do anything: I can't repent, I can't run away, I can't stay; I can't live, I can't die. Help me now! Order me, and I'll obey you like a dog. (p. 118)

Jean cannot help Julie, however, for the sign of the patriarch is too potent: 'I can't order you now – not since the Count spoke to me – I can't explain it, it must be this livery I've put on my back' (p. 118).

But Miss Julie persists, begging Jean for some kind of action, some kind of decision: ' . . . pretend you're the Count and I'm you . . . Oh, haven't you ever seen a hypnotist on the stage?' (p. 118). Jean slowly gives the razor to Miss Julie, but in the end neither of them has the will to further action. It is the father who provides the final impetus, who makes the decision, a dramatic moment whose authority stems from the implication that after all Julie's 'crime' is a crime against the patriarchy, which now will punish her. The final stage directions read:

> Two sharp rings from the [Count's] bell. Jean shrinks for a moment, and then staightens himself. He says: 'It's horrible – but there's no other way out. Go . . .' With a firm step, Miss Julie goes through the door. (p. 119)

This finality of 'no other way out', no possible alternative, no choice, gives Miss Julie her firmness of step, a gesture characteristically implying strength, reserve, decisiveness. But, of course, Miss Julie makes no decision here, except the joint decision with Jean that they have 'no choice'. Yet earlier before the Count's return, Jean, Miss Julie and even Kristin discussed at length a variety of wistful possibilities:

> MISS JULIE: . . . When we get to Hamburg, we'll go to the zoo . . . and . . . to the theatres and the Opera. And when we get to Munich, there'll be the museums . . . And it's not far from there to Switzerland – and the Alps – think of the Alps, with snow on them in mid-summer; and oranges grow there, and laurels that are green all the year round. (p. 114)

Of course, such talk is idyllic and overblown, but there are moments, such as Jean's suggestion of running a hotel, of working for himself, that are realistic. Such pragmatic flashes give a specific focus to Strindberg's ultimate message: there *is* no option, no choice in this world where the hierarchy of gender and class reigns supreme.

We must remember Strindberg's specification that Miss Julie is a naturalistic product of her genetic past; her dead mother's disorderliness and unconventionality have wilfully warped her genes. She says:

My mother wasn't a noblewoman – her people were quite ordinary. She was brought up according to all the theories of her time about the equality and freedom of women and all that. She could never bear the thought of marriage; when my father proposed she swore that she would never be his wife, but she married him in the end. As far as I can make out, I was born against her wishes. (p. 102)

There is a clear implication here by both Strindberg and the 'noble half' of Julie that nobility cannot concern itself with concepts like the 'freedom of women'. Once Miss Julie's mother gained exposure to such ideas, she began to hate the idea of marriage and of bearing children, but nevertheless, the potential new woman succumbed to patriarchal pressure and married to produce Julie:

I was to learn everything a boy does – just to prove that a woman's as good as a man. I had to wear boy's clothes . . . I had to groom the horses, and harness them, and hunt; I even had to learn farm work. On our estate, the men were given women's work and the women men's – till everything went to pieces, and we were the laughing-stock of the whole neighbourhood. At last my father seemed to have woken up from his trance; he asserted himself at last, and things were run his way. (p. 102)

Miss Julie's mother is pictured as a perverse woman who replaces 'Rule by Men' with 'Rule by Women'. For her, women's equality and freedom simply equals performing traditionally male-oriented work. This 'world turned upside down', this rule by a disorderly woman, caused havoc, confusion, and eventual destruction of the matriarchal house. The reason why such madness was permitted in the first place is explained by this wife's witchlike spell over her Count: when the spell is broken, when the bell rings, he wakes from his trance to restore the old fatherly order.

Despite her mother's attack on the patriarchy and her attempts to impel Julie after her – 'She taught me to mistrust and hate men . . . she hated the whole sex – and I swore to her that I'd never be a slave to any man' (p. 103) – Miss Julie exists not as a free woman but as a torn and riven individual, 'half woman and half man'. For Julie, such a division gives her no wilful access to an autonomous self: 'I haven't a self.' She accepts her androgynous state as a biological aftermath of the sex war between her parents. And she subdivides her own attributes in terms of a traditional, stereotypical sexual agenda: intellect or 'thoughts' from her father, 'emotions' from her mother.

Unlike the Duchess of Malfi, Miss Julie recognises no sense of self, no independent will. Her unruliness and disorderliness derive not from inner strength and personal power, but from the opposite, from the anarchic absence of 'self'. Miss Julie is Strindberg's 'battle of the sexes' personified; her selfhood, whose existence she denies, manifests itself in a psychotic struggle between her male and female halves. Like the Duchess, however, whose self was murdered by language prior to her actual death, Miss Julie fulfils the textually articulated notion of no-self when, razor in hand, she listens to prompting from the father-in-her-head, exits the stage and, literally, kills herself.

There is a large narrative leap from the woman killed by evil, villainous men to the woman who affirms her position of no-self by committing suicide. In both dramas, however, women transgress the patriarchal laws and are punished accordingly. (The fact that Strindberg chooses to place the patriarchy in the mind of Miss Julie deserves a study of its own.) So Clytaemnestra is killed by her son, the Duchess of Malfi by her brothers, and Miss Julie, in effect, is killed by the laws of her father. It is important, however, to look at another classical female theatrical character with mythical impact who wilfully chooses her own husband but, instead of dying for this, takes action and murders others: Medea.

Strains of ancient music: plucking the strings of moderation in Medea

Medea's crime is the ultimate female transgression: she is a mother who kills her own children. But unlike other mythical exemplars of infanticide – such as Oedipus' father who abandons his son on a mountain, or Agammemnon when he sacrifices his daughter, Iphigenia – Medea has become the mythical pariah of womankind. As the psychologist Phyllis Chesler says in her book *Mothers on Trial*:

> Any woman capable of breaking male law – sexually, reproductively, theologically, or economically – may also be *capable* of infanticide. Her *capacity* is unforgiveable. The fear of the disobedient woman is the fear of the unwed mother; is the fear of the spurned wife turned rebel; is the fear of the witch; is the fear of Medea. (Chesler, 1986, p. 44)

The story of Medea, a priestess, granddaughter to the sun-god endowed with magical powers, is part of one of the earliest known Greek myths: Jason and his quest for the golden fleece. Medea meets Jason as he attempts to steal the golden fleece in order to regain the Greek throne of Iolcus which has been usurped by his uncle Pelias. On the island of Colchis, Medea's father, Aeetes, agrees to surrender the fleece if Jason can conquer the magical, powerful forces that protect it. Falling in love with Jason, Medea chooses to marry him, against the wishes of her father, and as a result betrays her father and brother when she helps Jason to escape the island of Colchis with the fleece. However, when Jason and Medea arrive with the golden fleece in Iolcus, Pelias refuses to surrender the throne as promised, so again through sorcery Medea charms Pelias' daughters into murdering their father. This still does not gain Jason the throne, however, and the pair flee Corinth. Here Jason abandons Medea to marry Creusa, the daughter of the Corinthian king. As a result of this brutal betrayal, grief-riven Medea kills Creusa, her father, Creon, and murders her sons by Jason. At the end of the drama, Medea survives.

Medea's story can be seen as one of betrayal, poisoned passion, and enchanted violence – a mythical rendering of the ultimate evil woman whose vengeance knows no imaginative bounds. As Eva Keuls (1985, p. 335) says, 'In her tragic persona, [Medea] became the perpetrator of the ultimate act of impotent rage against male supremacy – the murder of her own masculine offspring.' In some sense the fascination in this story and its sheer repetition over the centuries is a cautionary warning: *this* is the ultimate outrage. Phyllis Chesler states:

> The crime of maternal infanticide has long been associated with Medea in the patriarchal imagination. Medea's crime is one of essential being. Medea is a proud and powerful woman. Her sacred power has been forbidden, debased, condemned --and eroticized, as a sexual crime. The *idea* of Medea threaten's men's trust in their wives. The *idea* of Medea therefore threatens all women's highly circumscribed access to a (man's) child. (Chesler, 1986, p. 48)

The plight of wayward Medea, then, parallels the plight of self-willed Clytaemnestra: both are denied the natural rights of motherhood by patriarchal justice. Clytaemnestra's denial occurs in a civilised, apparently democratic, trial. Medea, through her own violent actions, destroys her right, and eternally remains to prove the patriarchy right.

Euripides' play *Medea* had its first production in Athens in 431 BC and served as the source for a variety of stagings: Seneca used Euripides' play as his main source for his Roman version; Ovid recounts the tale with great detail in his *Metamorphoses* and also wrote a tragedy based on the story, which, highly praised in antiquity, did not survive; Corneille created his version in seventeenth-century France, drawing on both his Greek and Roman inspirational models to perpetuate this myth of the matriarchal monster.

For our purposes here we will consider Euripides' play, which has often been interpreted as a promotion of the Greek ideal of moderation. The female chorus, in fact, puts forward the play-wright's ideal of moderate perfection:

> Love may go too far and involve men in dishonour and disgrace. But if the goddess comes in just measure, there is none so rich in blessing. May you never launch at me, O lady of Cyprus, your golden bow's passion-poisoned arrows, which no man can avoid.
> *May Moderation content me, the fairest gift of Heaven.* Never may the Cyprian pierce my heart with longing for another's love and bring me angry quarrelings and never ending recriminations. May she have respect for harmonious unions and with discernment assort the matings of women.
> (Euripides, *Medea*, 630–42, my italics)

Throughout the play the sustaining, benign Chorus supports Medea (taking absolute exception to the infanticide) and expresses compassionate sympathy for her plight as the abandoned woman. But as one critic says of the chorus,

> their speeches generalize Medea's experience into the female condition of slavery, oppression, and pain. But the Corinthian women of the Chorus in fact covertly support female subservience. (Durham, 1984, p. 56)

In fact, such support of female subjugation is found in the play's emphasis on moderation. The Nurse, at the beginning of the play on the day following Jason's marriage to Creusa, warns Medea's children to avoid her:

> Beware of her fierce manner, her implacable temper. Hers is a selfwilled nature . . . Soon, it is clear, her sorrow like a gathering cloud will burst in

a tempest of fury. What deed will she do then, that impetuous, indomitable heart, poisoned by injustice? (100-10)

And immediately after hearing Medea's raging voice from within, the Nurse reaffirms her earlier comment:

> Moderation! Firstly, the very name of it is excellent; to practise it is easily the best thing for mortals. Excess avails to no good purpose for men, and if the gods are provoked, brings greater ruin on a house. (122–6)

Behind such admonishments of measure, however, Durham (1984, p. 56) locates a firm rule: 'The play's plea for moderation . . . discloses its real message: be moderate, be human, be normal; that is, be female – according to the rules laid down by men.' But Medea does not behave according to men's rules: for Creon she is a 'wizard possessed of evil knowledge' (238). Later he fears her because she is 'cunning and silent' (321). And at the end of the play Jason angrily asserts that she is 'not a woman at all, but a tigress, with a disposition more savage than Tuscan Scylla' (1345–6). Earlier Jason has already displayed his feeling about the unfortunate but necessary female function: 'There ought to have been some other way for men to beget their children, dispensing with the assistance of women. Then there would be no trouble in the world' (572–4).

Thus the 'reproduction debate' used by Aeschylus in his arguments against Clytaemnestra's maternal rights resurfaces in the Euripidean Medea narrative, which, according to Eva Cantarella,

> divided Greek thinkers from the very beginning. Is the child, they asked, born solely from the father or from the mother too? The very terms of the question bespeak a singular attitude. The incontrovertible biological fact that the child is born from the mother . . . was cancelled at the outset, sometimes radically. (Cantarella, 1987, p. 52)

Already in the *Oresteia* we have witnessed how Aeschylus used theatre and a theatrical trial to celebrate and legitimise the father-right, to enact the denial and eradication of the mother. But the theatrical event did not merely assert the ritualised claims of the father; it recorded the legal reality of Athenian citizens' rights. These 'rights' were quite specific on the issue of children: the father *owned* his children and had the legal right to practise infanticide, as Cantarella explains in her discussion of the classical periods:

'Exposure (*ektesis*) of newborns was a practice allowed by law and accepted without difficulty by the social conscience' (p. 43). Centuries later the Romans were to elevate this life-giving/life-taking father-right into an important social ritual:

> At birth, in a highly symbolic rite, newborns – male and female – were deposited at the feet of the father. He – without explanation or justification – either recognized the child as his by picking it up . . . or withheld his recognition by leaving it where it was. The recognized child became a member of the *familia*; the unrecognized child was abandoned to the river or left to die by starvation. Exposed children were more likely to be girls than boys. (Cantarella, 1987, p. 115)

In addition to this 'ownership' of Medea's children by the father, her rights as an Athenian were further circumscribed. Helen Foley points out that 'the Athenian citizen woman's status was derived entirely from kinship with males, and her primary function was to produce a male heir for the *oikos* (household) of her husband' (Foley, 1981, p. 130).

With these Athenian 'democratic practices' in mind, let us review Medea's crime. First, her children are not legally hers. They belong to Jason who, as we have seen, controls their life and their death. While Jason is married to Medea, their sons are his legal heirs, but when Jason rejects Medea and marries Creusa, not only does he rob Medea of all wifely status, effectively relegating her to the level of prostitute, but he grievously damages their sons' legitimacy and right to inheritance. Although as illegitimate sons they still have some claim to their father's estate, society now places them in a lower social position than legitimate sons. Such isolation is increased by the fact of their mother's exile from her homeland and the absence of any protection from her family. In this illumined context, Medea's murder of her children shows its proper significance: she prevents them from becoming second-class citizens in their own father's household and moreover prevents the traitor Jason from having the all-important male line continue and maintain his *oikos*.

Medea realises she will suffer all her life for her actions; her own immediate death would be too easy and would end her sorrows too conveniently. In her final speech before she exits to kill the children, she says:

I can delay no longer, or my children will fall into the murderous hands of those that love them less than I do. In any case they must die. And if they must, I shall slay them, who gave them birth. Now, my heart, steel yourself. Why do we still hold back? . . . Before you is a course of misery, life-long misery; on now to the starting post. No flinching now, no thinking of the children, the darling children, that call you mother. This day, this one short day, forget your children. You have all the future to mourn for them. Aye, to mourn. Though you mean to kill them, at least you loved them. Oh! I am a most unhappy woman. (1234–47)

Despite her resolve to do the horrendous deed, Medea must continually goad herself to perform the crime in full awareness of its horror. But placed in the cultural society context of classical Greek life, Medea's infanticide becomes the disturbing appropriation of a traditional male role as the ultimate arbiter of family life.

'Evil' women like Medea, Clytaemnestra, Miss Julie and the Duchess of Malfi necessarily question the rights of a male-dominated society. At the same time they serve as examples of strong, wilful women who are punished for daring to question, to seek autonomy, to make their own choices. Indeed, the whole notion of female choice is brought into question by these archetypal figures. Does woman have free choice? Is she an existential character who can choose? Does she have the freedom to create herself through the power of choice? Or does this classical image of the 'wilful' woman teach us a male lesson: that female autonomy will always be punished? Certainly these women have been doubly penalised: by the narratives which emprison them and by criticism, both contemporary and historical, which by finding them 'guilty' affirms their punishment as just.

We have already considered how, according to some critics, the Duchess of Malfi 'warranted' her fate; a brief look at a recent introduction by Moses Hadas to the *Medea* text also exposes an implicitly prejudiced view. First, Hadas states that 'Medea's conduct is by no means justified'. Hadas describes her first speech as undoubtedly 'a fine feminist harangue but not appropriate to her own situation'. Consequently Jason's actions become 'justified brutality', and Jason's situation stirs a universal sympathy: 'Moderns can understand that a young noble abroad on a dangerous mission might have become involved with a passionate barbarian who saves his life and honor, and in later years, returned to conventional society, having grown weary of her erotic intensity'

(Euripides, *Orestes*, ed. Hadas, p. 31) This introduction entirely ignores the play's significant historical context, where both women and children were legally owned by males. It also ignores the clues that Euripides has left us in this text that suggest a more positive ambivalence towards powerful women, an ambivalence which, for example, finds voice in a beautiful choral ode where the women of the chorus, as they question the prejudiced morality of men, begin to imagine a utopian world while at the same time wearily affirming women's undermined status in the real world:

> Back to their sources flow the sacred rivers. The world and morality are turned upside-down. The hearts of *men* are treacherous; the sanctions of Heaven are undermined. The voice of time will change, and *our* glory will ring down the ages. Womankind will be honoured. No longer will ill-sounding report attach to our sex.
>
> The strains of ancient minstrelsy will cease, that hymned our faithlessness. Would that Phoebus, Lord of Song, had put into woman's heart the inspired song of the lyre. Then I would have sung a song in answer to the tribe of males. *History has much to tell of the relations of men with women.*
>
> (409–31, my italics)

The world they imagine, however, is one that is oddly 'turned upside-down'. For only in such an inversion of Athenian democracy, of Strindberg's nineteenth-century Naturalism, of Webster's world of Jacobean revenge, can men be viewed as 'treacherous' and the 'wilful' woman 'honoured' for her rightful strength.

Ironically, Euripides' women of the chorus give voice to their lack of cultural voice: if only women had access to song, to poetry, to art, then they could tell *their* story; however, Euripides' play, to the contrary, tells of 'the relations of men with women' and not of that other truly democratic possibility: 'the relations of men *and* women'.

9

The golden girl

I'm quick with the trigger
With targets not much bigger
Than a pinpoint on number one,
But the score with a feller
Is lower than a cellar,
Oh you can't get a man with a gun.

When I'm with a pistol
I sparkle like a crystal,
Yes, I shine like the morning sun.
But I lose all my lustre
When with a bronco buster,
You can't get a man with a gun!

(sung by Annie Oakley in *Annie Get Your Gun*
music by Irving Berlin, lyrics by Herbert and
Dorothy Fields, 1946)

Real pioneer women and mythical melodramatic heroines

The American West has been mythologised as a particularly male domain – a filmic horizon of flat plains, rugged hills, treacherous mountain ridges and commanding precipices in which cowboys, ranchers, gamblers, bandits and sheriffs create a human existence that parallels the variety and rawness of the landscape. Within this world the men are actively mobile, whether on horseback, stagecoach, wagon or train. Indeed, mobility and movement are often definitive of the 'lone western hero'. The women, if they exist, are peripheral figures, for the most part stationary and static: in a home as a 'good' woman, or in a saloon as a 'bad' woman. If they move at all – such as in a stagecoach or in a wagon train – they are shown to be fragile and in need of male protection, always potentially 'at risk'.

The real female pioneers of the American West differed radically from their romanticised filmic stereotype. The pioneer woman took an active and often hazardous role in settling the West; she fought adversity, physical hardship and extreme deprivation in a hostile, unknown terrain. The historical and social reality of the pioneer woman was formed at the same time as the bourgeois Victorian lady developed into a dependent, ornamental and inactive female. In Europe this notion of a decorative, leisured wife gained ascendancy in the eighteenth century and stood in opposition to the 'common' woman who worked to help support her family; by the next century this ideal had firmly established itself in the Victorian middle class, as Sheila Rowbotham describes in her book *Hidden from History*:

> Leisure for women became an indication of status just when the bourgeois man elevated the dignity of labour against the indolence of the aristocracy and of the poor. The beginnings of capitalism required singleness of purpose and ceaseless uninterrupted endeavour. Young men should not be interrupted by domestic concerns. They must not divert themselves with useless arts. Locke, the wily exponent of the interests of the new middle class, warned young men against music and poetry. Music should be left to women and acquired as an accomplishment for the recreation of their men folk . . . The confinement of women in the interior world of the family left bourgeois man 'free' to accumulate capital. (Rowbotham, 1973, p. 3)

Despite the predominance of this European ideology, the leisured middle-class woman did not exist in the American West. She was – quite apart from all sorts of ideological constraints – simply not practical. Instead, a particularly American notion about women developed from the 1830s until it matured and became firmly and gloriously established in the 1860s, namely 'the cult of true womanhood'. The rise of this 'cult' shows a determined effort to stabilise the 'domestic sphere' by instilling feminine ideals such as 'piety, purity, submissiveness, and domesticity', through sermons, etiquette books, women's novels, child-rearing books, and ladies' magazines which, for the first time, were widely available to the general public (Cott, 1972, p. 11). One feminist historian describes the prevalent view of women living in the mid-nineteenth century:

> She was the guardian of the home fires, nestled by the hearth, while the great common man conquered the West, built railways, and championed American democracy. The American democrat, however, was loath to call the female sex unequal or designate her sphere as inferior, subordinate, or servile. Woman's place was only different, as she was. Hers, in fact, was a far better place than the rough and tumble world of work, war and politics, and woman's superior nature – pure, pious, and gentle – entitled her to reign there. (Ryan, 1975, p. 139)

However, in the reality of frontier life women pioneered their way west on an equal footing with the men, often, out of sheer necessity, discarding any pretence of 'femininity'.[1] One of many examples is that of Kate White, who left a refined middle-class existence in Virginia to travel west, riding a horse, using a six-shooter and winning a reputation for being 'as big and broad and capable as a strong man' (Ryan, 1975, p. 140). Such pioneer women of repute who broke with conventional 'femininity' to travel west and establish a home life could not be ignored; but, rather than acknowledging their autonomy and self-possession, commentators located their achievements entirely in family life. In an unpredictable wilderness, they became not only mothers of the family, but 'mothers of civilization' (Ryan, p. 145). Only in this realm of motherhood could women wield any power and influence. Here, confined to a household, the 'true woman', the mother, reigned supreme as long as she fulfilled social expectations of warmth, cheer, nourishment, emotional support and glowing purity in the home.

The mythical elevation of the 'true woman' blunted the recognition of the potential power of the pioneer women and subsumed their active presence in the history-making of the West; once again Pygmalion's pedestal placed women in ideological perfection as the keepers of civilisation. The number of pamphlets, books and journals dedicated to this ideology was prodigious. Henry C. Wright's 1870 tract *The Empire of the Mother over the Character and Destiny of the Race* demonstrates such moralising principles:

> The influence of woman is not circumscribed by the narrow limits of the domestic circle. She controls the destiny of every community. The

character of society depends as much on the fiat of woman as the temperature of the country on the influence of the sun. (quoted in Ryan, 1975, p. 14)

Ideas such as these elevate woman to a certain tempting centrality; like the radiating sun she keeps the family warm, she guards and protects the community, and she safeguards the social order.

Against this comfortable, domestic background the theatrical form of American democracy enacts an encore: melodrama, developed from the ideas and cultural upheaval of the French Revolution, establishes itself as the dominant theatrical genre of this young, raw country. As we saw in Chapter 6, the violent transitions of the social order were dramatised in melodrama as an illusory villainy which temporarily triumphs over innocent virtue. The climax, however, reaffirms the pieties of a cosmos in which order is ultimately restored and 'good' vanquishes evil. Daniel Gerould, in his essay 'The Americanization of Melodrama', sees this theatrical genre as particularly democratic:

> Social background, genes, wealth, talent are not major determinants in melodrama. All empathy goes to long-shots who come from behind, to triumphant underdogs, to lucky lottery ticket holders. If not *every one* can win, *each* human being has the chance in a society unfettered by Old World hierarchies of class and profession. (Gerould, 1983, p. 9)

'Old World' theatrical imports, however, dominated the nineteenth-century American stage until 1852, when Harriet Beecher Stowe's *Uncle Tom's Cabin* broke this European strangle-hold on New World creativity with its international success. As theatrical versions of Beecher Stowe's novel proliferated, so too did indigenous American melodrama. The nascent American stage took the opportunity to steep itself in the characters, events and historical moments of its immediate past and its contemporary western frontier. The turbulent Gold Rush of 1848 often served as a backdrop to melodramatic scenarios, as in, for example, Alonzo Delano's *A Live Woman in the Mines; or, Pike County Ahead!* (1857).

Despite the American desire to break from the confines of European culture and to establish its own theatrical imagery, the portrayal of its indigenous women characters as innocent, helpless, righteous, saintly victims remained in keeping with their European counterparts: the virtuous woman. For example, in *Uncle Tom's Cabin* the power and warmth of 'mother love' made possible Eliza's miraculous escape across the ice from her enemies. And Delano's *A Live Woman in the Mines* articulates the need that dirty, wrangling, gold-hungry miners have for the civilizing presence of a virtuous woman.

Belasco's girl and the forces of civilising femininity

The most famous melodrama set in the American West is David Belasco's *The Girl of the Golden West*, which he wrote and produced in 1905 – admittedly a late point in the history of the melodrama, with silent cinema already gaining ground, not to mention the establishment of realism and naturalism in live theatre itself. But precisely because of this late intervention in a dying, old-fashioned genre, the play merits consideration.

Belasco's significant formal innovation is a particularly and specifically American female image: energetic, cheerful, apparently independent, vivacious, and 'natural' – an image I shall call the 'golden girl'. This image developed from a combination of the reality of the pioneer women with the ideologically promoted myth of the 'cult of true womanhood'. In some sense, the 'golden girl', arriving at the end of one dramatic era and the beginning of another, has perfect theatrical timing. She is an image that was to have a warm commercial welcome in the film industry and the musical theatre; she became Annie in *Annie Get Your Gun*, the ingenue hoofer in *42nd Street*, the awkward, androgynous and innocent Calamity in *Calamity Jane*. As the original heroine of Belasco's play she became heroine of the libretto for Puccini's opera *La Faniciulla del West*, produced in New York in 1910 as the first opera to receive its world premiere in America. Subsequently the play became a film starring Nelson Eddy and Jeannette MacDonald in 1938, and most recently the American Conservatory Theatre in San Francisco produced the original script in 1980 as a tribute to the author, their native son.

The plot is straightforward: the Girl – Belasco's bald and highly significant name for his heroine – lives in the Sierra Mountains in a small cabin with her companion and servant, Wowkle, an Indian squaw. The play is set at the height of the 'gold fever' in a mining camp in California where the Girl runs the Polka Saloon, inhabited by miners with characteristically colourful names of the American West: Sonora Slim, Trinidad Joe, Happy Halliday, Handsome Charlie. Jack Rance, the sheriff of the camp, wants to marry the Girl; he calls a toast in her absence at the beginning of the play: 'Gentlemen, the Girl! The only girl in the Camp – the girl I mean to make Mrs Jack Rance!' (Belasco, p. 194). Belasco establishes the male-dominated tone of the camp through several short scenes in which men gamble, sing with the local banjo player, fight, argue and finally provoke Sheriff Rance to pull his gun –violence that is only prevented by the bartender's warning that the Girl approaches. This ends the quarrel and the men drink to each other in apparent friendship. Belasco gives time and descriptive detail to the Girl's first appearance:

> The character of the Girl is rather complex. Her utter frankness takes away all suggestion of vice – showing her to be unsmirched, happy, careless, untouched by the life about her. Yet she has a thorough knowledge of what the men of her world generally want. She is used to flattery – knows exactly how to deal with men – is very shrewd – but quite capable of being a good friend to the camp boys. (p. 194)

Belasco's description astutely and deliberately qualifies the moral position of the Girl: the stereotype of the Western woman who worked in a saloon was that she was a 'bad woman', possibly a 'good-hearted prostitute' but a 'bad woman' nevertheless. Belasco is clearly aware that by placing his independent heroine in an all-male camp as proprietor of the Polka Saloon, he must dispel the conventional assumptions about such a woman. He immediately specifies, therefore, that she is free from 'vice'. However, he creates in her an odd mixture of apparent contradictions: 'untouched by life about her', at the same time she possesses a 'thorough knowledge' of what these tough, Western miners want. How is it that in creating his heroine Belasco wants to have his moral cake and eat it? Perhaps more importantly, how does he succeed? The answer lies in her name: she is the *Girl*. On the one hand she potentially has control over her own life, she is strong, she talks back to the men in the bar. When Rance continues to pester her about marriage she says:

> Look here, Jack: let's have it right now. I run this Polka alone because I

like it. My father taught me the business, and – well, don't worry about me – I can look after myself. I carry my little wepping [weapon] – (*Touching her pocket to show that she has a pistol.*) I'm independent – I'm happy – the Polka's paying an' – ha! – it's all bully! Say, what the devil do you mean proposin' to me with a wife in Noo Orleans? Now, this is a respectable saloon – an' I don't want no more of that talk. (p. 198)

Despite this display of control, her status as 'the Girl' in the midst of the miners continually undermines any autonomy she might have, and with the entry of Dick Johnson, a fashionable gentleman from Sacremento, the Girl is smitten. They dance together, she invites him to her cabin for a midnight supper. But in reality Johnson is the road-agent and bandit Ramerrez, hunted by Sheriff Rance and the Wells Fargo posse with a $5000 reward on his head. Johnson, who knows that his fellow road-agents are awaiting his signal to rob the Polka Saloon, agrees against his better judgement to the Girl's rendezvous; and when he discovers that the Girl runs the Polka he decides not to rob it.

During their meeting they talk intimately, slowly revealing their love for one another, interrupted by the sound of distant gun shots which the distracted Girl takes to mean that the Sheriff has tracked down Ramerrez. When Sheriff Rance knocks on the Girl's cabin, she hides Johnson (at his insistence) so her late night assignation with him will not compromise her. Sheriff Rance innocently reveals to her that Johnson is Ramerrez, and after the Sheriff's departure, the Girl angrily accuses Johnson/Ramerrez of deception. He replies:

I'm not going to say anything in defense of myself. It's all true – everything is true, except that I would have stolen from you. I am called Ramerrez – I have robbed – I am a vagabond – a vagabond by birth – a cheat and a swindler by profession. I'm all that – and my father was all that before me . . . it was in me – in the blood . . . I took to the road . . . And that's the man I am – the blackguard I am. (*With feeling.*) But, so help me God, from that moment I kissed you to-night, I meant to change, I meant to change. (p. 225)

As the changed Johnson/Ramerrez leaves the Girl's cabin Sheriff Rance shoots and wounds him. The Girl hides him in her attic but his blood dripping through the attic floor from his wound reveals his hide-out. Rance prepares to hand over the wounded, unconscious road-agent to the Wells Fargo posse for 'shooting or the tree'. But the Girl, always at the ready to redeem her man, pulls her pistol on Rance, and says to him:

> I live on chance money – drink money – card money – saloon money. We're gamblers – we're all gamblers . . . You asked me to-night if my answer to you was final. Now's your chance. I'll play you a game – straight poker . . . If you're lucky, you git him an' me; but if you lose, this man setting' between us is mine – mine to do with as I please – an' you shut up and lose like a gentleman.

In the amazing archetypal gambling scene that follows the Girl deftly plays poker for Johnson/Ramerrez. Belasco exploits her pure virgin-siren image – she feigns fainting in order to pull cards from her stocking and so saves the unconscious Johnson from Sheriff Rance by cheating, only to see him caught again on his recovery: this time the men of the camp, loyal to the Girl's wishes and fully sympathetic to the Girl's great love, decide to trick the Wells Fargo agent and free the road bandit. As the bartender of the saloon says after Ramerrez's escape, 'The Polka won't never be the same, boys – the Girl's gone. (p. 245).

The final act of the play creates a scenic panorama which displays 'The boundless prairies of the West', against which the Girl and Johnson return east to begin their new life. As they view the sunrise the Girl closes the play with these final lines.

> A new life. (*Putting her hands in his.*) Oh, my mountains – I'm leaving you – Oh, my California, I'm leaving you – Oh, my lovely West – my Sierras! – I'm leaving you! – Oh my – (*Turning to Johnson, going to him and resting in his arms.*) – my home. (p. 247)

With this sentimental coda Belasco returns his original and emancipated Girl to a conventional ending where his heroine finds fulfilment entirely in the man she loves. Formerly the Polka Saloon, bequeathed by her father, had been her 'home' but her comments made earlier in the play signal a change towards this conventional attitude:

> I can see mother now . . . Fussin' over father an' pettin' him, an' father dealin' faro – . . . Talk about married life! That was a little heaven. I guess everybody's got some remembrance of their mother tucked away. I always see mine at the faro table with her foot snuggled up to Dad's an' the light of lovin' in her eyes. Ah, she was a lady! (p. 199)

The Girl's romanticisation of her mother clearly reflects the moralising sentiment of the pamphlet propaganda which helped to create the 'cult of true womanhood'.

Belasco claimed that he created 'a new and unique type' of American heroine when he wrote *The Girl from the Golden West*. In a novelised version of the play, he describes his lively, independent creation as 'a child of nature, spontaneous and untrammelled by the dictates of society, and normally and healthily at home in the company of the opposite sex' (Gerould, 1983, p. 25). But in fact this unique character grafted together two established images: the innocent girl-child of traditional melodrama and the strong, self-reliant pioneer woman of reality. One might easily have predicted that such a combination of seemingly opposing characteristics might have proved inconsistent and dramatically ineffective, but the historical currency and popularity of this character indicates otherwise. What has proved effective is a female character, the Girl, who specifically promotes the conventional pieties of the good, pure woman under the superficial guise of personal strength and power; who advances the clear message that even strong-minded women will choose the home, hearth and husband. Indeed, they will not be truly 'home' until they do so.

Another of the Girl's qualities, which Belasco drew from popular images of women and the West, is her ability to change the male society around her for the better. Her mere presence civilises the all-male camp: the brawling stops on her first entrance; she runs a weekly 'Academy' at which she teaches the men of the camp – shown as rowdy, unruly boys who raise their hands and call out 'Teacher!' – how to read, constantly maintaining benevolent dominance over them. Here her character reflects another aspect of the transitioning image of women in the West, namely the link between teaching and mothering. As we have noted, the movement towards a 'cult of true womanhood' prompted the mythical elevation of the woman's domestic role. One important defender of this position was Catherine Beecher, who began her rise to prominence in the 1830s and stressed the important link between teaching and mothering:

> Beecher was their [women's] staunch defender (of monogamous marriage and the private household) and placed domesticity at the very center of her strategy for American women. She believed that woman's

influence must be different from man's and should rest on her ability to inculcate the 'spirit of benevolence' into the American character through children that she raised. Beecher's major innovation was to argue that teaching was a function similar to mothering, and was therefore an appropriate activity for women. (DuBois, 1981, p. 5)

But above her role as mother/teacher, the ultimate example of the Girl's civilising power lies in her relation to Johnson/Ramerrez. A most unusual innovation in Belasco's melodrama is its absence of a traditional villain. Sheriff Jack Rance hovers on the edge of evil, but proves himself a self-sacrificing and honest man when he re-linquishes the Girl and lets Ramerrez escape. Unusually, it is the doubly significant figure Johnson/Ramerrez who functions as both villain and hero. As Gerould (1983, p. 25) says, 'A divided hero with a dual name and identity assumes the functions of villain and generates the conflict. As Johnson, he is the suave gentlemanly suitor of the Girl, as Ramerrez, he is the bandit come to rob her.' The potency of the Girl's love transforms the lawless, wild, Spanish Ramerrez into the civilised Anglo Saxon Johnson and recreates him as the hero of the text.

Importantly this theatrical image of the Girl ends on the golden threshold to a new, married life. Her sexual innocence is about to vanish: we never see her after it has – or, perhaps more significantly, after she has been integrated into an Eastern society where her Western independence and self-reliance will not be valued. For Belasco finds it essential to freeze her in our dramatic memory as forever 'the Girl', a heroine who has the capacity to make choices, to control her own fate, but whose girlish lack of maturity ultimately undermines and trivialises her sense of autonomy. Thus Belasco transforms the reality of the pioneer women into the innocent girl, a 'child of nature', and in so doing makes her enjoyably safe to the male mining camp. For in the end, despite her openness, spontaneity and self-reliance, it is the Girl's unworldliness, her 'girlishness', that wins the support and enthusiasm of the miners. As Gerould observes, 'the Girl's innocence and belief in the power of self-transformation are the motive forces behind the struggle. For if melodrama can dispense with the villain, it cannot do without innocence, no matter how disguised this absence of sin and cynicism may be under a tough-talking, gun-toting exterior' (p. 25).

Belasco's 'creation' of this 'golden girl' has informed decades of film-making in America. A desexualised gamine appeal interwoven with innocent warmth and vitality is central to many filmic roles for women, from the early silent films of Charlie Chaplin – whose 'girl', often played by Paulette Goddard, acts as a tender-hearted, vibrant foil to Chaplin's tramp – to Mary Pickford, Lillian Gish and their later reincarnations Doris Day, Debbie Reynolds and Sandra Dee. Indeed, Mary Pickford, known as 'The Girl with the Curl', was the pioneer of American female film stars. The titles alone of some of her films indicate the nature of the filmic character she created: *Little Red Riding Hood*, *A Little Princess*, *Pollyana*, *Little Annie Rooney*, *The Foundling*, and *A Poor Little Rich Girl*. Despite the repetitive and formulaic nature of these 'girl' characters, directed and produced by D. W. Griffith, Mary Pickford was enduringly popular. Marjorie Rosen, in her book on women and American film, describes Pickford's attraction:

> *Rebecca of Sunnybrook Farm* (1917) . . . forever branded her child-woman image on the public consciousness. It is strikingly in keeping with the times that as she developed her curly-haired orphan into an independent little virago, she could exercise directness and make silly, outrageous demands which, coming from a real woman, would have been too aggressive and threatening. Which is perhaps another reason why her female fans adored her. Her unladylike spontaneity was an outlet for all their repressed energies and fantasies. (Rosen, 1975, p. 40)

The film critic Alexander Walker sees the popularity of the eternal little girl at the very beginning of the film industry's rise to power and influence as a continuation of late nineteenth-century obsessions with such stereotypical preconceptions:

> Mary Pickford was certainly assisted to stardom by the same idolizing of prepubertal girlhood which is so persistent, and at times sinister, a strain in Victorian popular sentiment. Her first director (Griffith) was a Tennysonian romantic. Her first fans were still nineteenth-century working-class folk. (quoted in Rosen, p. 37)

Never growing old in the American West: Lotta Crabtree's theatrical career

Throughout the nineteenth century child stars were a popular phenomenon. But perhaps nowhere did they receive a more riotous, ecstatic welcome than in the mining camps of California, where, if they performed well, their male audience not uncommonly showered them with gold nuggets. One child performer in particular embodies all the aspects of the 'golden girl', and we may consider her, if not the initiator, then certainly a primary inspirational source of the image; Lotta Crabtree.

The life and career of Lotta Crabtree deserve a detailed consideration in their own right for the way in which, first, she affected the fortunes of American theatre in the late nineteenth century, and, secondly, the way in which the narrative of her life dramatises the contradictions and paradoxes faced by women actresses in her time.[2]

Charlotte Crabtree was born in 1847 in New York. At the age of six she went with her mother to search for a wayward father who had temporarily vacated family life for the lure of California gold; by the age of eight she was touring the mining camps and performing solo song-and-dance numbers to a pleasure-starved, rowdy male audience. Her mother, Mary Ann, was a dominant woman who, faced with impending poverty and an unpredictable husband, quickly realised the potential of her daughter's stage career; when Mary Ann and Lotta arrived in San Francisco they would have opportunely noticed the popularity of Kate and Ellen Bateman, aged eleven and nine years old, who toured the West coast with their miniaturised renditions of *Hamlet, Richard III*, and *The Merchant of Venice*.

Already child performers had flooded the West like gold-diggers: El Dorado Country boasted its chorus of tiny girls known as the 'Fairy Minstrels', tiny infants rode bareback around the rings of touring circuses, and Miss Anna Maria Quin was proclaimed an acting prodigy for her precocious Hamlet.

The American West at this time was dramatically alive with a variety of makeshift theatrical events, and it was here that the child star phenomenon culminated. When Mary Ann Crabtree settled in the mining camp of Grass Valley it already boasted a playhouse, a troupe of child performers, a theatre company and a number of saloons with stages offering evening entertainment. The mining camps experienced a shortage of women, and the popular female performer in a sense solved the demand for women by allowing a collection of males to share one woman. One biographer of Lotta Crabtree has observed:

The prizes were going to women. In this new world composed preponderantly of men, women were rising to a singular eminence. For months all the drift of interest on stage had been toward women, Caroline Chapman, Lola Montez, Matilda Heron, Laura Keene, Catherine Sinclair . . . If the stage in California was still a gusty affair, full of dangerous, sudden changes, it offered an unparalleled opportunity for feminine initiative. (Rourke, 1928, p. 81)

Lotta's theatrical apprenticeship took her on extensive tours of the mining camps, and both her and her mother's perseverance in such a harsh, rigorous, often dangerous environment led to eventual star billing in the legitimate theatres in San Francisco, where between 1859 and 1864 she became a popular, successful performer known as 'Miss Lotta, the San Francisco Favorite' (Comer, 1979, p.7). Lotta's speciality did not lie in the serious Shakespearian drama of so many of her competitors, but rather comedy that included music, dance, burlesques of serious plays, farce, and minstrel-show routines. This Shirley Temple of the mining camps danced and sang her way into the hearts of these brutalised, childless miners and made the image of orphandom into a personal triumph. Young boy rascals and saucy, gamin-like waifs figured among her popular characters. One of her most famous achievements was in John Brougham's adaptation of Dickens's *The Old Curiosity Shop*, entitled *Little Nell and the Marchioness*, in which she played both the leading roles. When the production appeared in London, one critic delighted in her comic talent:

Lotta's Marchioness is a performance *sui generis*. It is the quaintest, oddest conception in the world . . . her breakdown is the funniest thing ever done in comic dancing . . . Lotta's face as she sits on the kitchen table, eyeing the dreadful mutton-bone, haunts me. No words can describe the fantastic tricks of this actress. (quoted in Rourke, 1928, p. 326)

Even before Lotta took the essential road to national fame in New York City, she had inspired numerous imitators, and once well-established in the East she became all the rage: her fans, now from coast to coast, danced the 'Lotta Polka' and the 'Lotta Gallop' (Dempsey, 1968, p. 170).

Lotta was forty-five when in 1891 an injury during performance forced her to retire from a career in which, one could say, her entire fame and fortune derived from playing versions of her eight-year-old self over nearly forty years. It is difficult not to recognise her as

Belasco's unacknowledged source for 'The Girl'.

Belasco knew Charlotte Crabtree well. A native son of San Francisco, Belasco had served as secretary to Tom Maguire, the city's leading theatre entrepreneur whose 1700 seat opera house featured the performances of Lotta, the city's ascendant star. Belasco actually performed with Lotta in the role of Foxy Joe in one of her productions of *Little Nell and the Marchioness* during the 1870s. In 1887, she commissioned him to write her a script entitled *Pawn Ticket 210*. The central character Belasco created for Lotta was a diminutive girl, Mag, whom her poverty stricken mother had pawned in a desperate need for ready money. While locked in the pawn shop Mag takes dramatic advantage of all the pawned musical instruments to play the banjo, sing and dance. So Belasco had first-hand knowledge of the golden advantage in the public enthusiasm for this theatrical image of 'the girl'.

Furthermore, Lotta's own private life ominously echoed her stage persona. Mary Ann Crabtree had sheltered her daughter from the possible taint of immorality which so persistently haunted other women performers, allowing her no friends among the theatrical circle and, whenever possible, accompanying her daughter backstage. Members of their acting company were carefully screened before being hired, and Lotta's mother maintained complete autocratic control over her fortune. Although Lotta had numerous admirers, she had no real suitors, and appears to have had no sexual life. Once when Mary Ann parted briefly from Lotta, then in middle age, a female member of staff was ordered to accompany her whenever she left her rooms. Mary Ann's own triumphant comment on this reveals the depth of her daughter's cloistered life:

> Lotta is a veritable child who never has done things like older women. She has been sheltered, cared for and has no idea of the value of money nor what it will buy. I have kept her that way and never consult her in regard to business outside the theater. (Johnson, 1984, p. 167)

The dramatic image of Belasco's 'Girl' exited against the golden tones of a scenic sunrise to a new married life, with her innocence and girlishness still intact. Charlotte Crabtree, however, lived the reality of the de-sexualised, innocent female in which autonomy and personal choice seem to have been the trade-offs in return for success in a theatrical world where comic women must remain essentially *girls*.

10

Women acting men

It is forbidden in the Bible
That a woman be so bold,
On pain of terrible torment,
To commit the idolatry
Of wearing on a single day of her life
The dress that belongs to a man.
    (Anonymous, *Le Miroir aux Dames*, fifteenth century)

              Hence lewd impudent
I know not what to term thee, man or woman,
For nature shaming to acknowledge thee
For either, hath produced thee to the world
Without a sex; some say thou art a woman,
Others a man, and many thou art both
Woman and man, but I think rather neither
Or man and horse, as the old centaurs were feigned.
(Nathan Field, *Amends for Ladies*, 1612)

The panting Breasts, white Hands and little Feet
No more shall your pall'd thoughts with pleasure meet.
The Woman in Boys Cloaths all Boy shall be,
And never raise your thoughts above the Knee.
    (Nathaniel Lee, *The Rival Queens*; *or the Death of Alexander*
                (Nathan Field, *Amends for Ladies*, 1612)

This final chapter differs radically from the previous four chapters.
Until now I have explored images of various kinds of femaleness, to
show that male playwrights throughout history have continually
defined women by their dress and by a variety of constructed
archetypes of Penitent Whore, Wilful Woman, Speechless Heroine

and Golden Girl. In several of these images – most notably the wilful woman and the golden girl – women are criticised and condemned for daring to appropriate aspects of masculinity. In this chapter, by wearing male clothing, they actually *do* appropriate an aspect of masculinity. This practice of women dressing as men clearly gives the lie to the old maxim 'we are what we look', at the same time it exposes gender as socially constructed and not innate, eternal or biologically 'natural'.

Monstrous contradictions: a woman of the masculine gender

Both paralleling and at times riding tandem to this theatrical practice of gender disguise is the subversive social practice of women dressing as men in daily life. Such social disguise prefigured the theatrical practice because women were banned from the public stage. We have seen in Chapter 1 how Mary Frith, or Moll Cutpurse, roamed the Elizabethan streets dressed as a man; and I have speculated how Middleton's play about her, *The Roaring Girl*, created a frisson of theatrical gender-play when the London audience could witness a young boy actor playing the female Moll dressed as a man on the stage, while at the same time being aware that outside the theatre Moll herself swaggered in masculine gear.

These off-stage transvestite heroines created a theatrically charged moment which temporarily eradicated any culturally held notions of art mimicking life; indeed, they inverted the traditional medieval associations of masculinity with the intellect and femininity with the body. Other such male-garbed heroines frequent our Western historical landscape: Joan of Arc, transvestite saints of the fifth century,[1] such as Saint Margaret of Antioch[2], Long Meg of Westminster, and George Sand, among many others. Though there is often a commonality of purpose behind this male disguise, the specific individual reasons vary.

Sara Maitland's intriguing account of Vesta Tilley, a famous male-impersonator in the music halls of the late nineteenth century, offers clear distinctions between the theatrical aims of disguise and 'performance drag':

A woman assumes male clothes (in performance) in order to play with – at whatever level of consciousness – ideas about gender in relationship with an 'audience'. This is radically different from the concept of disguise, since it is a primary necessity of all 'impersonation' that the audience should be aware that it *is* an impersonation. (Maitland, 1986, p. 88)

Late nineteenth-century music hall, characterised by its appeal to the working classes, undoubtedly elicits such an explicit dichotomy. Tilley, whose off-stage dress was the epitome of wealthy and stylish Victorian femininity, clearly separates her stage persona from her personal life, adding to the theatrical excitement of her male impersonations: one minute a respectable upper-class woman, on stage a clever, funny working class man.[3]

What I propose suggests a greater ambiguity between 'disguise' and 'performance drag' than indicated here by Maitland's classifications. Many of the transvestite heroines previously mentioned, such as Joan of Arc, relied on the open knowledge that she was a young girl in male dress. Her 'audience' was fully aware that she 'impersonated' a king's soldier; her 'disguise' was clearly transparent, yet she was not 'performing'. In contrast, the transvestite saints of the fifth century, such as Saint Euphrosyne who lived for thirty-eight years disguised as a monk, expected their true sexuality to remain rigorously hidden, but its eventual disclosure either after or just prior to death was essential to the construction of their martyrdom.

Keeping the ambiguous nature of 'disguise' and 'performance drag' in mind, this chapter assesses a variety of historical moments when women dressed as men, both for theatrical as well as social purposes both literally by wearing male costume and metaphorically by assuming roles of cultural creativity previously only socially sanctioned as 'male'. The early eighteenth century in particular provides a heady version of this phenomenon of women playing at being men or having cultural power normally attributed to men. The result was that moral criticism, much like the Swetnam pamphleteers of the Jacobean period, rose up to articulate its fear: the century was deviant, promiscuous, a world-turned-upside-down, a feminocracy.

In previous chapters we saw how contemporary critics considered the first actresses, both in Italian *commedia dell'arte* and the English Restoration, as merely *playing themselves* when they took the stage. Subsequently, the actresses of the Restoration immediately became viewed as objects in the sexual market of Charles II's court. Now, in the eighteenth century, commoditised female sexuality combines with the notion of 'playing the self' to merge in the promotion and celebration of the actress's personality. The extensively used device of a spoken prologue or epilogue en-couraged the development of this theatrical synthesis. Not only did the prologue/epilogue allow the actress to address the audience with the intimacy of the first person, but it even further conflated the idea of actress-as-self through self-referentiality in the text. In 1671 the actress Elizabeth Boutel, dressed in a page's costume, delivered this bargaining epilogue to Corye's play *The Generous Enemies*:

> As Woman let me with the men prevail,
> And with the Ladies as I look like Male.
> 'Tis worth your Money that such legs appear;
> These are not to be seen so cheap elsewhere:
> In short, commend this play, or by this light,
> We will not sup with one of you tonight.
>   (Wilson, 1958, p. 76)

Boutel's lines at the end of the play clearly link her role as an actress to her life beyond the stage: she will 'sup' with selected members of the audience after the show as long as they recommend the performance to others. The plays themselves luxuriate in nudging references to the actresses' real or supposed sexual exploits. Nell Gwynne and the actor Charles Hart, known as lovers offstage, often played a flirtatious, amorous couple on stage. After a failed rape attempt in her personal life, Anne Bracegirdle became famous for her public roles of virginal, chaste women in distress.

A remarkably forthright example of this kind of reference is found in the following epilogue spoken in 1696 by the new young actress, Maria Allison:

> I, who must make my Fortune o' the Stage,
> Will ne'er expose the Vices of the Age:
> Which I expect to find my chief Support;
> And thrive by them, as Flatterers do at Court.
> 'Tis not for me to ridicule a Beau;
> I may get Good of him, for aught I know.
> Why should I call that Damme Spark a Bully,
> Or the good natur'd keeping Fool a Cully?
> When I as well as others, soon may hope

To be maintain'd by some conceited Fop.
(Gildon, *The Roman Bride's Revenge*, quoted in Wilson, 1958, p. 17)

The twentieth century historian J. H. Wilson provides the 'obvious' explanation for Maria Allison's words: she 'set[s] forth without shame the ambition of the young actress' (p.17). Here Wilson merely reiterates the standard position of criticism taken by the majority of twentieth-century theatre historians: that the introduction of actresses damaged theatrical standards and that some of the most sexually explicit, and therefore debasing, theatre came as a result of the arrival of women on stage. Instead, the epilogue's significant feature is that it exposes the relationship between women and the stage – namely, that Maria Allison's acting on stage is merely an extension and exposure of her 'acting' offstage, where economic necessity requires that she must not reveal what she really thinks of her male admirers, the 'fop', the 'bully' or the 'fool'.

With the advent of the Restoration stage – where women not only performed but boldly spoke directly to the audience – the early Christian hatred of theatre and of women merge into what seems an exemplary instance of self-fulfilling prophecy. Jonas Barish, in a critical discussion of Tertullian's attack on theatre called *De spectaculis*, discusses this church father's view of the correlation between women and the theatre:

> one finds in it an early instance of a long-lasting motif: prejudice against the theater coupled with prejudice against women, especially beautiful, ornamental, and seductive women . . . As the theater is suspected of ill designs for its attractiveness, so are women. As the theater debases by its counterfeiting, so do women who affect a beauty not theirs by nature. God has given them one face, and they make themselves another, just as he has given men one identity and they arrogate to themselves another when they pretend to be what they are not in a play. (Barish, 1985, p. 50)

Centuries of Christian attack on the theatre had seemingly come to fruition. All the critics' worst imaginings had come true: the duplicitous nature of theatre and women had found a happy, thriving co-existence on the Restoration stage. The perceived hypocrisies of the female sex had found a home in the theatre which made counterfeit reality out of illusion and celebrated pretence and disguise. What better place to witness the apocalypse than from a box seat in a Restoration theatre?

The variety and type of disguise in the plays of this period was prodigious. Men still dressed in their Shakespearean women's weeds, as was the custom just twenty years earlier, but now only occasionally for comic purposes. The fashion for actresses playing male roles, however, ran rampant, as a great number of actresses became known for their roles in 'breeches parts'. Nearly every actress performed at least once in her career dressed as a man or boy, usually in a disguise necessary to the plot. From the re-opening of the theatres in 1660 until 1700, nearly 90 plays were staged (from among the total of 375 which included both new plays and re-worked pre-Restoration pieces) which contained one or more roles for an actress in boy's or man's clothes. In addition, at least fourteen more plays during this time had women playing male roles that were written specifically for men. In a celebrated example Peg Woffington originated the role of Sir Harry Wildair in George Farquhar's *The Constant Couple*. An additional endorsement of the popularity of breeches roles occurred in several other productions whose women played all roles, both male and female.

The masquerade ticket: voluptuous panic and feminine utopias

The popularity of theatrical disguise extended beyond the confines of the proscenium arch. The masquerade, both public and private, became one of the great social events of the eighteenth century. The public occasions began as an entrepreneurial exercise in making money for failed nobility; for example, Count Heidigger promoted and sold tickets to fashionable public masques at the Haymarket Theatre on evenings when operas were not performed. The 'Midnight Masque', as it became known, drew its participants from a wide social spectrum, thus popularising this participatory cultural entertainment. Terry Castle's scholarship on the eighteenth-century masquerade in England provides a sharp analysis of the centrality of disguise:

> The masquerade had its undeniably provocative elements: one took one's pleasure, above all, in seeing and being seen. With universal privileges granted to voyeurism and self-display, the masquerade was from the start ideally suited to the satisfaction of scopophilic and exhibitionist urges. Bodies were highlighted; other personal features

were subsumed. The event put a premium on the sensuality of the visual.
(Castle, 1986, p. 38)

The diversity of disguise displayed a spectrum of the incongruous
and the dissimilar: Iphiginia, Harlequin, Ruben's wife, Pierrot,
bears, monkeys, owls, nuns, priests, devils, a walking corpse, folk
figures such as Merry Andrew and Mad Tom, Falstaff, Don
Quixote, Liberty, Temperance, Justice; also present were two-in-
one costumes promoting the notion of motley unnatural unions.
Evidence of two such disguises describe a 'double Man', half
chimney-sweep, half miller; the other two-in-one figure depicts a
woman, one side old and decrepit, the other half young and vibrant
(Castle, 1987, p. 66). Homogeneous transvestite costume remained
very popular throughout the century; in one account of this
particular kind of masquerade, Elizabeth Inchbald, a well-known
actress famous for her breeches parts, attended a masquerade in
1781 dressed as a man, and so successful was her disguise that
several female masqueraders were openly affectionate and capti-
vated by her 'masculine' wiles (Castle, p. 48).

The masquerade, even more than the playhouse, became a place
for sexual assignations and promiscuity, resulting in yet more
endless criticism and puritanical moralising. But, as Castle makes
clear, sexual liberty was only one condition of 'the masquerade's
implicit utopianism', which revelled in the breaking loose from
mundane, ordinary experience. Costume provided the disguise
crucial to any escape, a visible exemption from the limitations of the
self. The masquerade of the eighteenth century proclaimed an
'overriding impulse . . . toward freedom' (Castle, p. 51)

For women in particular this sense of freedom must have been
exquisitely exhilarating. Although the critics of the masquerade
were quick to link masquing and female degeneracy with much talk
of an Amazonian race running amok, other readings of its
popularity stress the excitement it generated. In a period when
opportunities for paid work for women were shrinking, social
impositions created a strict moral code for 'respectable' women
which included the total repression of any physical or erotic
pleasure. The women of the middle class were expected to show no
signs of sexual desire, neither within marriage and certainly not
without; sexual pleasure for men, however, was socially institution-
alised through prostitution and brothels for all classes. The mas-

querade, therefore, provided women with an immunity, albeit a temporary one, from the social and cultural restrictions of the age, an opportunity to play-act their fantasies and imaginings. For women who spent their entire existence negotiating the multiple masks of female gender, the masquerade seemed to sanction as well as celebrate their female plurality. In some sense, it must have seemed as if the age-old Platonic obsession with the masculine vision of a single, autonomous 'essential self' was being gloriously repudiated. The masquerade invited women to a social event in which their individual identity became submerged in a crowd, an 'anonymous collectivity of masks'. The event itself was a visual phantasmagoria, an end-product created not by the individual vision of some essential self, but a *mélange* of multiple visions, a panoramic manifestation of chaos which relied on a 'personal abdication from the responsibilities of identity' (Castle, p. 73). In her memoir of 1825, Harriette Wilson describes her enthusiasm for the masquerades of her youth:

> I love a masquerade because a female can never enjoy the same liberty anywhere else . . . It is delightful to me to be able to wander about in a crowd making my observations, and conversing with whomever I please, without being liable to be stared at or remarked upon, and to speak to whom I please, and run away from them the moment I have discovered their stupidity. (quoted in Castle, 1986, p. 44)

In the previous ages of James I and Charles I, the authority of the state promulgated conspicuous display, and thus the court masques of that time involved elaborate, intricate costumes. But such theatrical trappings were never meant to obliterate or even obscure the identity of the royal personage underneath. Instead costume was used imaginatively to reinforce the monarch's power through visual imagery and ostentation. But with the Restoration came a shift from the notion of costume as display to that of costume as camouflage. For example, Charles II attended the theatre and masquerades in a disguise which deliberately obscured his royal personage. As one critic explains, Charles II's 'disguise was not expressive or revelatory; it hid his unique status so that he might exploit the liberating possibilities of ordinariness' (Maus, 1979, p. 610). Thus the common citizen sought freedom away from 'ordinariness', and Charles II sought freedom within it, but both

factions used the common denominator of costume to achieve a
sense of liberty.

This transformation in apparel from display to disguise was a
visual and social manifestation of a larger deviation in eighteenth
century consciousness: the shift away from the Renaissance vision
of a hierarchical universe towards a world view based on polarities
or oppositions. The masquerade epitomised the anti-hierarchical
frenzy of the times: a participant in a midnight masque could
embrace a kind of otherness, could celebrate the unfamiliar by
mixing one foreignness with another. The appeal of two-in-one
costumes, like sartorial microcosms of the masquerade itself,
blatantly signified internal opposition. In 1773 a man appeared at a
masquerade with one half of his face painted black and the word
'Plaintiff' written on it, and with the other half of his face white with
the word 'Defendant'. In Griffin's play *The Masquerade* one of the
female characters diguises herself as 'a kind of Hermaphroditical
Mixture; half Man, half Woman' (Castle, 1986, p. 66).

Indeed, vociferous critics, like some moral police force, focused
on the hermaphrodite as a monstrous emblem for the incongruity,
unreason, and anti-natural chaos of the age. In 1715 Alexander
Pope paid a visit to the popular 'curiosity' of the year, a hermaphrodite. He records his reactions to the event in a letter subsequently included in the 1735 publication of his work:

> it appears to be a most even disposition, partaking of good qualities of
> both sexes . . . Of how obliging and complaisant a turn appears by this,
> that he tells the Ladies he has the Inclinations of a Gentleman, and that
> she tells the Gentleman she has the *Tendre* of a Lady. (Pope, 1956, pp.
> 277–9)

Pope appears magnanimously to regard the hermaphrodite as
enjoying the best aspects of both sexes, but, as Penelope Wilson has
pointed out, Pope's letter professes a 'bawdily-tinged' voyeurism in
which 'thin partitions divide the good contradiction from the vile
antithesis' (Wilson, 1986, p.80). Pope found the hermaphrodite
'upon the whole . . . a woman' whose freakish physiciality – a
man's penis – he interprets as the outcome of female degeneracy:
where the mother's excessive, unbridled lust for the phallus results
in a child which embodies the baseness of her desire (Pope,
pp. 277–9).

The 'wonders' of staging female friendship

The hermaphrodite of Pope's London inspired literary discourse on the purity of 'nature' as well as inflamed prurient gossip on the deviancy of unrepressed women. At the beginning of the eighteenth century the theatre itself must have exacerbated male fears about a feminocracy of deviant women: here on the public stage women abrogated a cultural activity previously the property of men. Women acted, managed theatres, wrote plays, and within the narratives of those plays centred women protagonists. A recent study has shown the importance and success of women playwrights from 1695 until 1714, a period named, after the reigning monarch, as the Queen Anne era. In fact Kathryn Kendall's (1986) research brings to light that from 1695 to 1706, of all new plays produced for the London stage, between one-third and one-half were written by a group of six women – Mary Pix, Catharine Trotter, Delariviere Manley, Susanna Centlivre, Jane Wiseman, and Mary Davys. Kendall's absorbing account of the work of these six women shows their conscious awareness of following Aphra Behn, a dramatist who had challenged the supremacy of male playwrights in the previous generation.

The theatre was a commercial venture at this time, and such an output by these women writers would not have been conceivable without audience support. These dramatists received strong support largely from women in the audience, whose attendance steadily increased late in the seventeenth century – an audience grown tired of the old standing joke about women's adultery, the staple diet of so many male-written plays. Indeed, discontent with this diet had engendered resistance from female audience members who, in 1681, banded together to voice protest against yet another comedy about women's adultery, Ravenscroft's *The London Cuckolds* (Kendall, 1986, p. 64). Fifteen years later women playwrights were referring to the importance to their plays of the female section of their audience, overtly articulating a desire for their 'praise'. Kendall cites this prologue of Mary Pix's *Ibrahim* as an example of the influential link between the success of women dramatists and the patronage of female theatre-goers:

The Pit our Author dreads as too severe,
The ablest Writers scarce find Mercy there;

Her only hopes in yonder brightness lies,
If we read praise in those Commanding Eyes:
What rude Blustering Critique then will dare
To find a fault, or Contradict the Fair?
Th' humble Offering at your Feet she lays,
Nor wishes she to live without your Praise:
Strict Rules of Honour still she kept in view,
And always when she wrote, she thought on you.
Then Ladies own it, let not Detractors say,
You'll not protect one harmless, modest Play.
                                        (Kendall, 1986, p. 130)

These 'humble Offerings' did address issues similar to those of their male counterparts, but their placing of women in the forefront of the narrative action made them dramatically different. The theme of marriage remained popular for both male and female dramatists (they all took for granted that marriage for women was compulsory), but women writers tended to articulate the inevitable event from a more complicated, frustrated viewpoint, as Kendall points out:

> What galls the women playwrights is not the loss of sexual freedom lamented by male playwrights, so much as the loss of mobility, youth, health, and the dream of freedom, independence, and education. Once a woman married, her fate was sealed. She would begin the cycle of pregnancy, childbirth, and recovery, followed by pregnancy again; and she was unlikely to have any further opportunities to prove her worth in the world, to do service to her country except by propagation, or to imagine that she might achieve or accomplish what she had dreamed of in her youth. (Kendall, 1986, pp. 266–7)

Breeches parts also received a different treatment from the women playwrights. Women acting as men in their plays forced the narrative forward instead of serving the more conventional and gratuitous function of flagrantly exhibiting actresses' legs. In Catherine Trotter's *The Revolution of Sweden* (1706), for example, the central female character, dressed in men's clothes throughout the action, joins the army and saves the hero's life.

Perhaps even more than the fresh articulation of the marriage theme or the active, energetic use of breeches parts, these plays by women emphasise the relationships between female characters. Narratives focusing on women's friendships take centre stage in a majority of the plays by women in this period. In more than seven scripts, there is a startling break from traditional stereotyping; women either prefer or ultimately choose women's company over that of the limited possibilities with men. (Kendall, p. 163). One of the most popular plays in its decade, Centlivre's *The Wonder: A Woman Keeps a Secret* (1714) comically plays on the Jonsonian prejudice that women cannot be silent or discreet, while simultaneously proving otherwise by focusing on the priorities and obligations of female friendship. Here one woman's promise to protect another by keeping a secret gravely jeopardises the first woman's betrothal to a man she loves, culminating in an essential decision: divulge the friend's secret or lose her fiancé. Centlivre's 'wonder' rides rough-shod over patriarchal expectations: the woman, in an act of selfless constancy, safeguards her friend's secret.

These portrayals of friendships between women of equal rank have no theatrical precedent; until then (male) writers had always represented comradeship between men as the ultimate nourishing intimacy. Depicting women as faithful and steadfast rather than antagonistic or jealous breaks with conventional image-making and radically offers a different vision of the possibilities of female autonomy. With women so evidently encroaching upon territory which had, in a previous century, clearly been defined as 'male', the social and cultural hierarchy which had rested on the assumption that men had more intrinsic worth than women, that they belonged to a higher order which justified their historical dominance, began to crumble. With a well-liked, intelligent, reigning queen, and female dramatists so actively creating in the arena of the public stage, the patriarchal fiction of the inherent frailties, incompetence and ignorance of women began to appear blatantly false. The men who witnessed the narrational centring of women's friendship in the playhouses and observed the female faction of the audience clap enthusiastically could no longer assume that affectionate and intellectual loyalties existed solely man-to-man. So they took their masculine allegiances and defended them within the male-only confines of the eighteenth century coffee houses.

It can be no historical accident that coffee houses, the precursor to the men's club, began to proliferate and become the centre of male social life at exactly the same time that women started to recognise and enact their own affinity and mutuality. During the reign of Queen Anne there were some five hundred coffee houses catering to every variety of male companionship:

> The *beau monde* assembled at White's Chocolate House in St. James's
> Street . . . Tories went to the Cocoa Tree Chocolate House, Whigs to St.
> James's Coffee House, Will's near Covent Garden, was the resort of
> poets, critics and their patrons; Truby's served the clergy, and the
> Grecian the world of scholarship; nor were there lacking houses for
> Dissenters, for Quakers, for Papists and for Jacobites. (Trevelyan, 1963,
> p. 30)

The coffee house, less exclusive and pretentious than the later
men's club, provided an informal atmosphere, cheap non-alcoholic
drinking, and political, military and general interest news with
additional access to important business transactions.[4] It sustained
and elevated the stale and smokey exclusivity of male friendship
while rescuing the potency of masculine identity under such threat
elsewhere.

Fielding's dilemma: the vagaries of cross-dressing

After the death of Queen Anne the prominence of women
playwrights declined rapidly, and with them the short-lived public
focus on the importance of women's friendship.[5] Nevertheless this
aspect of early eighteenth-century history was surely well-known to
Henry Fielding when in 1746 he published an anonymous pamphlet
entitled *The Female Husband*. The pamphlet, as one historian says,
records '13 per cent fact, with the rest of the work factual pretence'
(Baker, 1978, p. 224). The scant truth of the pamphlet concerns the
trial on 7 October 1746 of Mary Hamilton, who disguised herself as
a man from the age of fourteen, married a woman in July of 1746,
and travelled with her for two months until the 'wife' had Hamilton
arrested for deception. The law having no precedent for such a
'crime', Hamilton was convicted on a trumped-up clause in the
vagrancy act. After details of her sentence – a series of public
whippings and six months in prison – she disappears from the
historical records.

The pamphlet exudes a prurient, scopophilic tone which delights
in the reality of these public whippings while adding sensational
details that Fielding has clearly manufactured:

> These whippings she has accordingly undergone, and very severely have
> they been inflicted, insomuch, that those persons who have more regard

to beauty than to justice, could not refrain from exerting some pity toward her, when they saw so lovely a skin scarified with rods, in such a manner that her back was almost flead; yet so little effect had the smart or shame of this punishment on the person who underwent it, that the very evening she had suffered the first whipping, she offered the gaoler money, to procure her a young girl to satisfy her most monstrous and unnatural desires. (Fielding, 1960, pp. 50–1)

Fielding's pamphlet (immediately sold out and reprinted) launches a grotesque attack on Hamilton, mixing the mock heroic with the near pornographic. Terry Castle, in his essay 'Matters Not Fit to be Mentioned: Fielding's *The Female Husband*', describes the pamphlet as a piece of 'anti-feminist propaganda' (1982, p. 611). However, Fielding, as Castle points out, displays an ultimate ambivalence about Mary Hamilton's sexual charade. Whatever the bitter satire of his qualms, he admires her ability to take theatrical illusion out into the streets and, for a brief time, to triumph in her disguise:

She is a successful perpetrator of illusion, an expert at creative escapism. She embodies theatrical values in her own person – the hallucinatory primacy of costume over 'identity', the suspension of so-called 'natural' categories, sexual release, the notion that anything is possible. (Castle, 1982, pp. 617–18)

These qualities which celebrate 'the primacy of costume over "identity"', feared similarly in the masquerade, appear to terrify some aspect of Fielding's assertive, stable, masculine self. Mary Hamilton disguised as a man poses a threat to the patriarchal confederacy, because through her theatrical charade, her daring and flamboyant use of costume, she reveals gender to be social construction. She has subverted that seemingly most natural of binary categories, the masculine/feminine, by exposing its false immutability. On the one hand Fielding shows his mock-heroic horror at the implications of her 'playhouse' act, while on the other her success mesmerises him: (her) art has triumphed over (his) nature.

Mary Hamilton was not alone in her subversive action. Lillian Faderman, in her book *Surpassing the Love of Men* (1981), cites numerous examples not merely of women disguising as men but of socially forbidden 'marriages' between women. In 1721 in Germany, Catherine Linck, who dressed as a soldier and served in several armies, faced execution for marrying a woman. As Faderman explains, such women's crimes were serious because they usurped male privilege:

> The women did something which their societies seemed to regard as being far more serious than simply having sex with other women: they impersonated men. They claimed for themselves a variety of privileges ordinarily reserved for men – self-sufficiency, freedom to wander unmolested, freedom to explore occupations more varied than those open to women. (Faderman, 1981, p. 52)

In 1755 a well-known actress published her memoirs: *A Narrative of the Life of Mrs Charlotte Charke*. A popular performer during the 1730s, Charke specialised in breeches roles. In the 1736–7 season at Henry Fielding's Little Theatre, Fielding cast Charke in male roles in three of his own plays, and she also played MacHeath in John Gay's *The Beggar's Opera* as well as the tragic character of George Barnwell in Lillo's *The London Merchant*. Charke, the disowned daughter of the playwright and actor Colley Cibber, was notorious for wearing male dress beyond the safety of the sanctioned playhouse, and not only had a variety of relationships with other women but created a dramatic scandal when she received a proposal of marriage from a fashionable lady (Castle, 1982, p. 617). Although Charke, unlike Mary Hamilton, was never persecuted for her behaviour, there is evidence of numerous prosecutions between 1761 and 1815 against women who dressed as men. Faderman suggests that Charke escaped such censure because of her notoriety as an actress (p. 58).

Nineteenth-century cross-dressing: Safety in classical costume

In 1846 the American actress Charlotte Cushman journeyed to London to play one of the roles which had already made her famous at home. Lisa Merrill, in her study of Cushman, explains the popularity of her Romeo:

> She did not win critical acclaim as the love-stricken young hero *despite the fact* that she was a woman, but *because of it*. Given the extreme sex-role stratification common during the Victorian age, the passion and eroticism Cushman manifested as Romeo was acceptable only *because*

she was a woman acting opposite another woman, and, therefore, considered incapable of truly feeling the sexual passion she depicted. (Merrill, 1984, p. 174)

Merrill cites several London critics who witnessed Cushman's Romeo and heartily praised it as a 'triumph', one of the great successes of the theatre season. The critic of the *Britannia* (3 January 1846) priggishly expressed his support of a woman playing Romeo thus:

> It is open to question whether Romeo may not best be personated by a woman, for it is thus only that in actual representation can we view the passionate love of this play made real and palpable . . . females may together give us an image of the desire of the lovers of Verona, without suggesting a thought of vice. (Merrill, 1984, p. 111)

This critic's view of a woman playing the male Romeo is a mirror inversion of Goethe's perception a century earlier when he witnessed a Roman actor play the female role of Mirandolina. For Goethe, the man-as-woman convention provides greater aesthetic pleasure for the spectator because it avoids the 'unmitigated truthfulness' that an actress would bring to the role, offering instead 'self-conscious illusion', 'skilful imitation', art. For the *Britannia* critic, steeped in Victorian sexual inhibitions, Cushman's woman-as-man Romeo is better than a male Romeo as it avoids the spectator's discomfort of having to think of sexual passion between men and women.

Yvonne Shafer, in her essay on Cushman (1981), points out how commonplace the practice was for actresses to include male roles as an essential part of their varied repertoire. Cushman, known for her large, portly presence, did not conform to the nineteenth-century image of delicate, acquiescent femininity.

Such Victorian sexual polarisation based on physicality determined the appropriateness of male roles for actresses. In their choice from the Shakespearean repertoire the women are limited to the young and boy-like male roles such as Romeo, Hamlet and Orlando, or the fantastical fairy such as Oberon. Rarely, if ever, did women perform the roles of Henry IV, King Lear, or Coriolanus, although Cushman is something of an exception in that she played Cardinal Wolsey (but tellingly not the title role) in *Henry VIII*. She also played Lady Macbeth, but never Macbeth – a fact which again highlights the century's implicit dichotomy of sexual roles: Lady Macbeth, that role of unsexed female evil, requires an actress whose physicality externalises such 'unnatural' femaleness. Cushman's ample size and reputation as a performer of strength and power did not signify 'femininity' for the image-making Victorians.

From unfeminine heroines back to playing feminine heroes, Eva Le Gallienne, the celebrated American actress, supported her decision to play Hamlet in 1936 by emphasising Hamlet's boyishness:

> If one thinks of Hamlet as a man in this thirties, the idea of a woman's attempting to play the part is of course ridiculous. But Hamlet's whole psychology has always seemed to me that of a youth rather than of a mature man . . . It is possible for an actress at the height of her powers to give the impression of being a boy, while having at her command all the craft, range, force, and subtlety which such great roles require. This has always been true of Rostand's *L'Aiglon*, which, with a few insignificant exceptions, has always been played by women; also DeMusset's Lorenzaccio, and – in a very different mood – Barrie's Peter Pan. (Le Gallienne, 1983, p. 51)

Despite the advent of dramatic realism at the end of the nineteenth century, which stopped the majority of actresses playing men's roles, a trickle of these roles remained in the twentieth century largely as vehicles for the accomplished actress. But as Le Gallienne's account informs us, the male roles retained in an actress's repertoire displayed a lack of traditional male virtues, such as strength and willpower, and in some cases were almost deemed unsuitable for actors. Erika Munk, in a recent article on women in male roles, provides an analysis of the female Hamlet syndrome this way:

> Female Hamlets are usually undertaken to extend and show off the actress's range, not to look newly at revenge, princeliness, or misogynistic priggishness. Hamlet, stereotyped as a waffling neurotic prone to violent fits, is considered proper for women to enact, unlike Lear, Henry V, Caesar, Coriolanus, or Falstaff . . . Basically such casting comes from producers' gimmickry and actresses' frustration, from the fact that most playwrights and most big roles are male; as long as men aren't clamoring to play Mother Courage or Juliet or Amanda Wingfield, Hamlet as a woman reemphasizes the universalist pretensions of maleness, the specific limitations of femaleness, in our culture. (Munk, 1985b, p. 80)

But other, more soundly pressing considerations were working against women playing male roles. In the early twentieth century, views of women's sexuality radically altered – a change which, in effect, led to the eradication of Cushman's dramatic accomplishments from the theatre history books. Havelock Ellis, for example, significantly broke through the hide-bound Victorian conscience which denied the idea that women could and did have sexual feelings, just as men. A woman capable of a sexual emotional life was equally capable of directing her feelings towards another woman:

> Suddenly behavior that had been totally acceptable in an earlier era came to be considered abnormal, although the behavior itself had not changed, only its interpretation. A woman like Cushman could no longer be considered a paragon of chaste virtue merely because she abstained from relationships with men. In fact, Ellis depicted loving relationships between women as abnormal, or 'inverted'. (Merrill, 1984, p. 177)

In this context the memory of Cushman as an impassioned Romeo in the embraces of a small, delicate female Juliet no longer exemplified a 'proper' way to stage the play but instead appeared as a gross abnormality charged with a disturbing subtext of women loving women – of 'inverts' who had turned their emotional world upside down and dared to place women first in their lives. Echoes of Fielding's 'matters not fit to be mentioned' haunt the memories of Cushman's accomplished staged performances; Cushman's career veers from a Romeo that does not suggest 'a thought of vice' to a Romeo who explodes with 'monstrous and unnatural acts'.

Women dancing men

A dance counterpart to women taking men's roles in the nineteenth-century theatre occurs in the Romantic ballet. We have already seen in Chapter 7 how the role of the female dancer became elevated to an aesthetic view of the feminine ideal – a willowy, vulnerable and silent creature who floated on stage. The principal ballerina achieved such acclaim and prominence that ballet, which once had celebrated the muscularity and male physicality of King Louis XIV and his court, became defined in relation to the idealised female dancer, and men who danced were scorned as 'umanly'.

Finally, these 'feminised' male roles, similar to the theatre's boyish, indecisive Hamlet or lovestruck, emotional Romeo, became the domain of women dancers dressed as men, the *danseuse en travesti*.

In an essay on these travesty dancers Lynn Garafola points out that from 1830, when the Paris Opera became a private enterprise no longer funded by the aristocracy, entrepreneurial success became essential to the survival of balletic art. Pandering, therefore, to wealthy male audience members became standard practice. Before private management took over in 1830, the Foyer de la Danse, a large warm-up room behind the stage, was defiantly off-limits to the audience. From 1830 the new director of the Opera, Dr Veron, transformed the straightforward, practical rehearsal space into a fashionable room that voyeuristically showcased his female dancers. The pre-performance warm-ups, displaying the once private and intimate limbering exercises, became an exclusive form of male entertainment which popularised the ballet overnight (Guest, 1966, p. 28).

Having virtually exiled the male dancer from ballet (with the occasional exception of character roles) the Foyer de la Danse bcame a kind of conspicuous spectacle, a cattle-market displaying the idealised female ballerina and the travesty dancer who, as a result of her male costume, could exhibit the female body in a variety of physical moves which differed dramatically from her tutued sister. As Garafola explains:

> The masquerade of transvestism fooled no one, nor was it meant to. The *danseuse en travesti* was always a woman and a highly desirable one (a splendid figure was one of the role's prerequisites). She may have aped the steps and motions of the male performer, but she never impersonated his nature. (Garafola, 1985–6, p. 37)

This description of the travesty dancer – as one that 'fools no one' – returns us to the realm of the fetishised female image. Just as earlier we saw how Gautam, the 'gotipua' dancer, impersonated female seductiveness for the male spectator, so from the opposite direction the travesty dancer addresses the male spectator by displaying her body in men's clothes. But in fact these two cross-dressed performances underscore the asymmetry of the disguises. The whole notion of men-playing-women is embedded in male artistic creation with its Pygmalion-like vision of perfecting and defining an image that exists outside the male self as 'feminine'. Recall Goethe's delight at witnessing a male actor play the role of Mirandolina better than any actress:

> the enjoyment of seeing not the thing itself but its imitation, to be entertained not through nature but through art, *to contemplate not an individuality but a result.* (Goethe, 1984, p. 100, my italics)

But with the fetish functioning as a phallic substitute, a projection of male narcissistic fantasy which reassures the male spectator, an additional layering occurs: beyond the sexualised underpinning of the fetish lies a simpler narcissism – one that straightforwardly congratulates the male fraternity for its inventiveness, its creativity, its 'results'.

In Chapter 5 we saw how actresses could step into their own fetishised images and still in effect be absent. The travesty dancer offers another example of females absented in this way:

> The fantasy of females at play for the male eye is a staple of erotic literature, a kind of travesty performance enacted in the privacy of the imagination. Ballet's travesty *pas de deux* gave public form to this private fantasy, whetting audience desire, while keeping safely within the bounds of audience decorum. (Garafola, 1985–6, p. 39)

Looking back over the many examples of women-acting-men in this chapter, one sees that provided the impersonation of men by women fools no one – as with the travesty dancer or the actress in breeches role – then patriarchal permission for the disguise is granted – indeed, encouraged. When the disguise does fool, does convince and disturb – as with the Midnight Masquers or Mary Hamilton, for example – then the wrath of the patriarchy descends to punish the offenders.

At the beginning of this book I proposed theatre as *the* exemplary art form to explore both gender relations and the representation of women – a representation which was exclusively male-generated and from which women were absent. If we move to this phenomenon of cross-dressing as it occurs in contemporary society, we find that such performance is almost exclusively male and, importantly, has shifted ground: camp performance, viewed as radical fifteen years ago, has now become mainstream, with Harvey Fierstein's *La Cage aux Folles* and David Henry Hwang's award-winning *M.*

Butterfly. Significantly, as Erika Munk has argued, men do not impersonate women by putting on jeans and tennis shoes; instead drag performances often depict grotesque caricatures or degrading stereotypes. Attending such events can be like witnessing a performance version of an eighteenth-century coffee-house – all male smugness and bonhommie. Munk continues her analysis of the contemporary popularity of men-as-women and the mainstream role of drag performance:

> At the moment, most men in drag are no more subversive than whites in blackface were when minstrel shows were America's most popular form of entertainment. Before the abolitionist movement grew strong, blackface minstrels scattered bits of anti-slavery sentiment in their portrayals; during the Civil War they became more actively hostile to blacks though remaining pro-Union; but from Reconstruction on they were thoroughly and vehemently racist. There is an instructive parallel here, however inexact: first the women's movement showed us that this particular imitation wasn't the sincerest form of flattery, then Reaganism gave drag performers an embattled interest in defending an image of femininity which had become a weapon of reaction. (Munk, 1985a, p. 93)

In this context the much vaunted freedom of Western women to wear trousers, suit jackets, shirts and ties becomes no more than window-dressing for another wave of reaction – one that marches backwards under the glib and treacherous misnomer of 'post-feminism'.

Epilogue

The same fearful prediction, that women would be turned into men, has
been made before each successive step of the equal rights movement.
(Alice Stone Blackwell, suffragette, 1893)

My only problem is finding a way to play my fortieth fallen female in a
different way from my thirty-ninth.
(Barbara Stanwyck, Hollywood actress, 1953)

In a book such as this it is impossible to reach a definitive
conclusion. There is no conventional ending, final result, or
declamatory resolution. Like a Restoration actress returning to the
stage for her parting words to the audience, I return briefly in post-
modern costume to address significant aspects of recent theatrical
work, aware that as soon as I itemise and delineate new plays by
women my list immediately becomes out of date. Nevertheless, the
following discussion locates within contemporary theatre productions and plays by women the theatrical images treated within the
body of this book. In no way does this attempt to be comprehensive,
but in a book that has focused entirely on the importance of
historical material it is essential to leave you, the reader, aware that
women in theatre today are active, productive, questioning.

For at least the last fifteen years women playwrights have
continually challenged archetypal images of women and questioned
patriarchal narratives in their work. The image of the 'woman as
man' has provided various views which highlight the fact that
gender is a social construct. In Pam Gems' *Queen Christina*, the
Swedish monarch Gustaf Adolpho has only one heir to his throne: a
daughter. He decides to raise her as his royal son and heir. Forced
by monarchial duties to marry and produce a male heir to the
throne, Christina rebels. Unable suddenly to become 'feminine'

and fulfil her biological destiny, Christina abdicates her father's throne and wanders around Europe trying with desperation throughout the narrative to reconcile, like Miss Julie, her male and female selves. In Eve Merriam's *The Club*, set in an exclusive Edwardian men's club, the male characters thrive on their masculine camaraderie while disparaging the women in their lives. But Merriam twists and exposes the inherent misogyny in such an establishment by having all the male roles played by women in drag. In Simone Benmussa's *The Singular Life of Albert Nobbs*, set in a Dublin hotel in the mid-nineteenth century, Albert, the perfect waiter, is a woman who dresses as a man in order to obtain steady employment and cathartically finds herself trapped in her subservient male role. In *Little Victories*, the playwright Lavonne Mueller juxtaposes Joan of Arc with Susan B. Anthony, the American suffragette; despite Joan of Arc's victorious military battles she faces condemnation for wearing soldier's clothes. In the Joint Stock production of Caryl Churchill and David Lan's *Mouthful of Birds*, gender underscores the unresolved question of the play, which reworks Euripides' *The Bacchae*, where Agave tears her son's head from his body when he commits the hubris of dressing as a woman. Juxtaposed with this narrative is the story of the nineteenth-century hermaphrodite, Herculine Barbin, who was born female and raised in a convent, but who later in her life developed male sexual organs. Herculine Barbin became Abel Barbin, and in the pain and confusion of this readjustment (in which French law intervenes to redefine her as 'male') commits suicide. The play seems to suggest that after centuries of acquiescing to social gender definition – what it means to be 'masculine', what it means to be 'feminine' – any attempt to change or question the definition will tear the individual apart.

Pam Gems's *Camille* revises the narrative of the 'penitent whore' by presenting prostitution explicitly as a business transaction with women as the commodity of transaction. By making Marguerite Gautier the mother of a young son, Gems further de-romanticises the story, for Marguerite sacrifices herself not for Armand, but for the economic future of her son. Here Marguerite's death depicts consumption as a horrific, blood-spattered demise with much physical suffering and fear of death, not the romantic fading away of Dumas fils's heroine collapsing majestically *sans* raspy cough in her lover's arms. In another revision of this story, also entitled *Camille*,

Nancy Sweet parallels the life of the 'real' courtesan on whom Dumas based his story with that of his fictional *demi-mondaine*. In both narratives, the story traps the heroine by forbidding her autonomous choice.

The 'speechless heroine' has been re-presented in a variety of illuminating ways. Helene Cixous's *Portrait of Dora*, based on Freud's first case study where he began his exploration of the interpretation of dreams, recounts the story from Dora's point of view. As Dora tells Freud her story she gradually realises that he is appropriating her speech, her language and using them against her to create a psychoanalytic view which re-interprets her actions by colluding with her father's version of their relationship. At the end of the play Dora chooses not to speak to Freud, and Cixous shows this action as a heroic, self-defining gesture, a fracturing rebellion against the domineering patriarchal discourse of psychoanalysis.

Another significant examination of this 'speechless heroine' theme is found in *The Daughters Cycle Trilogy – Daughters, Sister/Sister*, and *Electra Speaks* – co-authored by Clare Coss, Sondra Segal and Roberta Sklar, all artistic directors of The Women's Experimental Theater in New York City. The three plays of the trilogy use the format of classical Greek theatre, with an emphasis on ritual and the chorus, to examine women's lives within the patriarchal family. The final play (revised as a solo performance for video and television) is a powerfully articulated monolgue which documents Electra's attempt to speak for herself and in so doing to break out of the patriarchal narrative which has trapped her for centuries. The monologue mixes first person declaration and third person observation, brilliantly highlighting the subject/object division within women while simultaneously exploring the ways in which society renders women mute.

The male-conventional treatment of the 'wilful woman' is perhaps most thoroughly explored in Martha Boesing's script *Antigone Too*: *Rites of Love and Defiance*, created in a series of workshops by seventeen women sponsored by the At The Foot Of The Mountain theatre collective in Minneapolis. Boesing uses Sophocles' script *Antigone* as the source for her archetypal woman who chooses to contravene the laws of men. Against the original Greek myth are ranged the stories of numerous women from North America who have dared to defy male authority and have therefore faced imprisonment or death.

A 'wilful woman' of a different kind is Marlene in Caryl Churchill's *Top Girls*, who has had to fight against her working-class background in order to gain a high management position in an employment agency. Her 'imprisonment', unlike that of the wilful women in *Antigone Too*, is the metaphorical chain of the patriarchy she has internalised and accepted. By celebrating the new morality and economic vision of Thatcher and Reagan, Marlene isolates herself from her family and loses any sense of compassion and humanity.

Megan Terry and Joanne Metcalf re-work the image of the American 'golden girl' in their play *Mollie Bailey's Traveling Circus*. Mollie Bailey's life story is dramatically structured by the circus ring; she takes control of the narrative just as she controls the circus itself as a kind of energetic, benevolent ringmaster; while Mother Jones, the fiery labour organiser who travelled through the States during the nineteenth century, presents another aspect of the importance of working women in the history of America. The Western legend of Calamity Jane has provided another opportunity for a 'golden girl' re-vision in Martha Boesing's play *Dora Du Fran's Wild West Extravaganza, or, The Real Lowdown on Calamity Jane*. Enduringly trivialised by the Hollywood film-machine, Doris Day played the role as a naive, childish, girlish cutie. Boesing retrieves Calamity Jane's story by presenting her as a woman with complex personal needs and desires which conflict with her harsh reality: surviving as a woman alone in the pioneer West.

Another aspect of women's recent theatre work retrieves an aspect of theatre in the Queen Anne era, when women's relation-ships with women took centre stage in the dramatic narratives. In Joan Shenkar's moving, surreal play *Signs of Life*, the loving relationship of Alice James and her companion, Katherine Peabody, parallels the isolated, painful existence of the fictional character of the Elephant Woman. The Elephant Woman, caged and exhibited by P. T. Barnum, metaphorically represents male fears of women's 'elephantine' sexuality.

Two other plays stressing women's relationship with other women include Maria Irene Fornes's *Fefu and her Friends* and Kathleen Collins's *The Brothers*. In Fornes's play eight affluent middle-class women discuss plans for some unnamed academic conference. Their discussion reveals how much their personal esteem and daily existence depend on men and how their chronic inability to trust other women hinders their sense of autonomy. In Collins's play five black women review their lives by examining their relationships to four brothers (husbands, sons or brothers to the women). Their discussion reveals the aching emptiness of their lives as middle-class black women who exist as a peripheral audience to their people's struggle for freedom and civil rights.

In her play *For Colored Girls Who Have Considered Suicide When the Rainbow is Enuf*, Ntozake Shange stresses the political frustrations and ebullient hopes of contemporary black women, while simultaneously celebrating female sexuality through poetry and song.

Relationships between women figure prominently in a variety of women's plays where the role of the mother underpins the narrative. In Catherine Hayes's *Skirmishes* one daughter dutifully but resentfully tends her infantile, senile mother while another daughter makes short, ineffectual visits which reveal her revulsion for her mother's old age. The sisters' estranged relationship reveals both their sense of loss and the way in which their existence is marginalised by a world where caring and nurturing receive no rewards. Marsha Norman's play *'night, Mother* explores a mother/daughter alliance shattered by the daughter's revelation of her intended suicide. The American kitchen/breakfast room sets the claustrophobic atmosphere which isolates and contains the battle between the mother and daughter, exposing a new dimension to the 'joys' of family life. *Together Against Him* by Philomena Muinzer parallels the disintegrating hold a mother has on her children with the spiralling violence in Belfast. In an extended metaphor the father images the patriarchal state, setting up a destructive system and then absenting himself from the chaos and ensuing turmoil, thereby forcing the mother to destroy her compassion in order to keep the family together.

The sheer amount of contemporary theatre which explores issues of gender indicates that there is no conclusion to the playing out of these issues. We stand firmly on our transitional stage: at the beginning of a new meaning to the term 'acting women' – a changed meaning which recognises, at last, the impact of history which is still with us today. As Di Trevis, the first women director to have her own season at the National Theatre of Great Britain says: 'Being an actress was like being a woman twice.'

Notes

Prologue

1. Phyllis Rackin succinctly summarises many of the arguments, and it is useful to quote her in full (pp. 31–2). All references referred to in her article can be found in the bibliography.

> The issue of the changing positions of women in Renaissance England has been much debated in recent years. Was humanist education a force for women's liberation (Dusinberre, p. 2), or did it inculcate 'docility and obedience' (Jardine, p. 53)? Was the presence of a powerful female ruler 'a spur to feminism' (Dusinberre, p. 303), or was Elizabeth the proverbial 'token' woman who reinforces patriarchal restraints on the rest of her sex (Jardine, p. 195)? Does the *hic-mulier* controversy of the early seventeenth century point to a widespread female practice of transvestism and a growing assertiveness among women (Woodbridge, pp. 156–7, 265–6); does it betoken an intensified enforcement of patriarchal restrictions; or is it simply an expression of a general uneasiness about increased social mobility and disorder (Jardine, pp. 159–62)? Did the rising middle class elevate the status of women (Dusinberre, p. 7), or did feminism do better in an aristocratic society with 'a solid royalist regime' (Woodbridge, p. 328; cf. Kelly)? Did Protestantism and Puritanism, with their new conceptions of marriage, undermine 'the old Pauline orthodoxies about women' and provide for significant advance in women's status during the late sixteenth and early seventeenth centuries (Dusinberre, p. 5, Stone, *Crisis*, pp. 269–302)? Or did 'the Reformation actually [remove] some of the possibilities for women's independent thought and action' (Jardine, p. 49) and the Puritan conception of marriage actually lead to 'greater patriarchy in husband-wife relations', a 'decline' in the status and legal rights of wives, and the increasingly sanctified and nuclear family structure (Stone, *Family*, pp. 136–7)?

172

Chapter 1   The power of women on stage: the gender enigma in Renaissance England

1. For a more thorough discussion of these documents see Woodbridge (1984) pp. 87–103. In order to read the pamphlets themselves see Shepherd (1985) in which they are reprinted in full.
2. The anonymous author of *Swetnam the Woman-Hater* has been the source of much discussion. Woodbridge briefly surveys the possible authors (pp. 320–1) and puts forward her own candidate, John Webster: 'His fondness of "women in court" scenes . . . and the motif of one family member seeking the death or ruin of another . . . is one of Webster's most persistent themes, occurring in *The Duchess of Malfi*, *The White Devil*, and *The Devil's Law-Case*.' After reading the play I was reminded of the title of Mirra Bank's book which is described as a celebration of the women artists of traditional American art: *Anonymous Was A Woman* (New York: St. Martin's Press, 1979).

Chapter 2   Cross-dressing, the Greeks, and the wily phallus

1. For a fuller discussion of the complex associations surrounding Euripides as the 'old procuress' see Zeitlin, 1981, p. 193. Zeitlin also explains the details behind Mnesilochus' attempt to free himself from the women: he parodies the roles of Helen and Andromeda, the eponymous heroines of two plays presented by Euripides at the City Dionysia in the previous year (pp. 186–190).
2. The conspiring, wily phallus with a life and will of its own is not confined to the Greeks. Georges Duby points out in his book on marriage in Medieval France that the great Christian scholar Johannes Scotus Erigena (John the Scot) advanced this idea in his treatise *De divisione naturae*:

    Scotus . . . maintained that Adam could use his sexual organs, like all the others in his body, by mere willpower and without excitement or ardor. 'In tranquility of body and soul, without corrupting virginity, the husband was able, or rather may have been able, to render his wife's womb fruitful.' (p.50)

Chapter 3   Historical precedents: women unmasked

1. Richard Rastall in his article on 'Female Roles in All-Male Casts' provides a variety of evidence for voice changes in pubescent boys occurring much later than today. One of his sources is S. F. Daw's statistical analysis and investigation into the boys' choirs under Bach, entitled 'Age of Boys' Puberty in Leipzig 1727–49, as Indicated by

Voice Breaking in J. S. Bach's Choir Members', *Human Biology*, 42 (1970).

2. Lynette R. Muir (1985) describes how in the Passion Play at Oberammergau (which had been celebrated once nearly every decade since 1634) the Virgin Mary is played by an adolescent boy younger than the actor playing Christ, and that still no married women perform in these productions (p. 110).

3. Meg Bogin (1976, p. 22) describes how the Emperor Justinian was influenced by his wife, Theodora, in compiling the Code of Justinian. Theodora had been an actress and the Emperor had to change the law to marry her.

4. For more discussion on the position of women among the Cathars see Marina Warner's (1978) book on the Virgin Mary (pp. 143–4); and for an account on the secular literary movement of the troubadours see Meg Bogin's chapter entitled 'Courtly Love: A New Interpretation' (1976, pp. 37–61).

5. Carol Neuls-Bates (1982, p. xii) points out the effect that the ban against women performers had on both male and female singers: the number of *castrati* increased and singing roles for women in opera were virtually unavailable until the late eighteenth century.

Chapter 6   The penitent whore

1. Marina Warner, in her book on the Virgin Mary, discusses Mary Magdalene at length in her chapter entitled 'The Penitent Whore', which I gratefully acknowledge here (pp. 224–35). She analyses the historic misconception of Mary Magdalene's 'sin' (assumed to be prostitution) which has no literal reference in the New Testament:

> Luke tells the story of Jesus' supper with a pharisee called Simon . . . While he is dining, an unnamed woman enters and, kneeling at Christ's feet, washes them with precious ointment. The pharisee is appalled that Jesus should allow such a woman to touch him . . . Jesus sternly reminds his host that he did not wash his guest's feet, or kiss him, or anoint him with oil. But the woman did, so 'her sins which are many, are forgiven, for she loved much . . . ' (Luke 7:47) . . . It has always been assumed, without inquiry, that the sins of the woman are worldly, and specifically carnal . . . The implication that Jesus would be polluted by her touch has never led Christians to think of her as a murderess, a thief, a liar, but only as a whore. Christ's explanation, 'for she loved much . . . which manifestly describes the generosity of her gesture towards him, has even been misread as a reference to her sins. This aptly reflects Christian ideas about sexual love, but misunderstands altogether Christ's use of the verb *diligere* to love, or *agapo* in the Greek, which has no erotic connotation whatsoever. (Warner, 1978, p. 226)

2. David Coward, in his introduction to his new translation of *La Dame aux Camelias*, points out that in addition to the numerous stage productions ('Edwige Feuillère played Marguerite over a thousand times between 1939 and 1952'), there have been over twenty screen adaptations, the first made in 1909. (see Dumas, p. viii).

3. E. Ann Kaplan describes Puccini as an 'Italian version of the Bohemian artist'. He used his own life as source material for his operas. In *La Bohème* his heroine Mimi is based on his maid, Doria, who committed suicide after he had seduced her. Kaplan explains how he 'used' this death to further his artistic invention:

    > [Puccini] thought of the death solely in terms of the hero, not in terms of the heroine as herself. It is as if she did not exist for him as anything more than a function of his hero's emotions, a catalyst. He writes [in letters to his librettist] that he wants her death at once to invoke 'proud and gentle emotions' and 'to pierce the heart like a knife'. 'When this girl, for whom I have worked so hard, dies, I should like her to leave the world less for herself and a little more for him who loved her.' (Kaplan, 1983, pp. 154–5)

    Kaplan discusses Puccini in her analysis of Sally Potter's film *Thriller!*, which is a feminist deconstruction of Puccini's opera.

4. Despite the fact that the myth of the Bohemian male artist arrived much later in Great Britain, it became happily situated with the pre-Raphaelite painters, who celebrated its premise through their art and their lifestyles.

Chapter 8   The wilful woman

1. It is important to note here that the existence of a double standard of sexuality – pervasive and undeclared – is one of the first issues tackled by Christine de Pizan (1363–1429), who initiated the *querelle des femmes* in France when she wrote a response to Jean de Meung's misogynistic treatise *Roman de la Rose*. Importantly, Christine uses her own language to dissect that of Meung's and to expose his rhetoric as a vehicle for simple woman-hatred.

    In one part of the *Roman de la Rose* Meung has a discussion between his allegorical figures Reason and Love. Christine responds to his perverse definition of 'reason':

    > And I still cannot remain silent about . . . the lofty personage of Reason, whom [Meung] calls the daughter of God . . . wherein [Reason] says to the Lover that 'in the battle of love . . . it is better to deceive than be deceived' . . . For if one were better than the other, it would follow that both were worthy: which cannot be. I thus hold to the contrary that, to tell the truth, it is less bad to be deceived than to deceive. (de Pizan, p. 1986, p. 342)

Not only does Christine de Pizan query Meung's 'male' logic, but she also questions his claim to make a hierarchy of such distinctions. In another part of his treatise Meung refers to female sinners as meretricious, deceptive, cheap, insincere. In response to this Pizan states: 'I confess to you that it is not the name which makes a thing dishonest, but the reason that makes a name dishonest' (p. 342). She thus reverses the relation that Webster's Cardinal takes for granted. For Pizan it is not male language that has the power to name and create reality, it is reality that gives the lie to male naming.

2. Kathleen McCluskie questions the tendency of modern directors to cast a beautiful actress in the role of the Duchess. Such casting was the case of the 1981 production at the Manchester Royal Exchange, which stressed the Duchess's sexuality above all other aspects of her persona. She continues:

> It is, after all, hardly radical to suggest that sexual torture and murder of women is wrong – and by placing the action in a costume drama world of the past the production blots out the more complex sexism involved in the casting of the play and the relations this creates with the audience. The mere evocation of sympathy for suppressed individuals short circuits the true recognition of oppression . . . The potential radicalism of Webster's theatrical strategies, his calling into question of the clichés of sexism, were suppressed in favour of that mixture of sympathy and consolation called tragedy. (McCluskie, 1985, p. 90)

Chapter 9   The golden girl

1. Not only were women significantly involved in pioneering the American West, but the American suffragette movement became vocally active when in 1848 Elizabeth Cady Stanton and Lucretia Mott organised the Seneca Falls Convention for women's rights.

2. Very little has been written about Lotta Crabtree which assesses her contribution to the history of American theatre, and I feel she has been unfairly consigned to one of the footnotes of theatre history. A recent piece of research (Comer, 1979) begins to consider Lotta's artistic vision as an important source of American musicals. Johnson (1984) looks at her considerable talents as a female comedian. But no one, to my knowledge, has examined her relationship to one of the great American theatre entrepreneurs, David Belasco.

Chapter 10   Women acting men

1. Marina Warner, in her book on Joan of Arc (1983) discusses the popular image of female saints who had disguised themselves as men. These stories are numerous, and many of them are found in the

thirteenth-century compilation of stories of saints called *The Golden Legend*. The majority of these transvestite saints seem to have lived 'at the acme of the fifth century's passion for world-denying rigours . . . There is, unfortunately, little evidence for the incidence of holy transvestism in the realm of real women (Warner, p. 157). Despite the popularity of their stories, the Church vociferously condemns them. Often their male dress is used to prevent any sexual encounters, as if in order to protect their virginity, they had to eradicate their gender.

2. Significantly one of Joan of Arc's saintly voices is Margaret of Antioch who, in one of the many stories about her, cropped her hair in a masculine style and ran away from home on the eve of her arranged marriage. Her vow of chastity is only possible to maintain in male clothing when she disguises herself as a monk. (See Warner, 1983, p. 157)

3. Elaine Aston offers another perspective on Tilley's theatrical career in her article 'Male Impersonation in the Music Hall: the Case of Vesta Tilley' (1988).

4. Trevelyan offers Ned Ward's *Wealthy Shopkeeper* (1706) as an example of the importance of the coffee house in the lives of middle-class men:

> rise at 5; counting-house till 8; then breakfast on toast and Cheshire cheese; in his shop for two hours then a neighboring coffee house for news; shop again, till dinner at home (over the shop) at 12 on a 'thundering joint'; 1 o'clock on Change; 3, Lloyd's Coffee House for business; shop again for an hour; then another coffee house (not Lloyd's) for recreation, followed by 'sack shop' to drink with acquaintants, till home for a 'light supper' and so to bed. (Trevelyan, 1963, p. 30)

5. Queen Anne herself was influenced and supported by strong, emotionally charged relationships with two women at different times during her reign. Her monarchy impinged significantly on the women writers of her age, as Kendall articulates:

> Her example of intelligence, ability, and virtue is mentioned in numerous commendatory poems, prologues, and prefaces published with women's plays; and it is clear that Anne served as a model for women of her age who aspired to greatness in any field . . . The Queen's intimacy with another woman also served, apparently, as a model of chaste and virtuous noble behavior. (Kendall, 1986, p. 156–7)

Bibliography

Ackroyd, Peter (1979) *Dressing Up* (London: Thames and Hudson).

Altick, Richard D. (1978) *The Shows of London* (Cambridge: Mass.: Belknap).

Aston, Elaine (1988) 'Male Impersonation in the Music Hall: the Case of Vesta Tilley', *New Theatre Quarterly*, no. 15, August, 247–57.

Baker, Michael, (1978) *The Rise of the Victorian Actor* (London: Croom Helm).

Barish, Jonas (1985) *The Anti-theatrical Prejudice* (Berkeley: University of California).

Barish, Jonas (1956) 'Ovid, Juvenal, and *The Silent Woman*' *PMLA*, no. 71, 213–24.

Barras, M. (1933) *The Stage Controversy in France from Corneille to Rousseau* (New York: Publications of the Institute of French Studies).

Basnett, Susan (1987) 'Perceptions of the Female Role: the ISTA Congress', *The New Theatre Quarterly*, no. 11, August, 234–6.

Baudelaire, Charles (1986) *My Heart Laid Bare and Other Prose Writings*, trans. Norman Cameron (London: Soho).

Beauvoir, Simone de (1974) *The Second Sex*, trans. H. M. Parshley (New York: Vintage Books).

Bentley, G. E. (1956) *The Jacobean and Caroline Stage*, vols. I-VII (Oxford: Clarendon).

Berger, John (1972) *Ways of Seeing* (London: BBC/Penguin).

Berggren, Paula S. (1980) 'The Woman's Part: Female Sexuality as Power in Shakespeare's Plays', in C. R. S. Lenz (ed.) *The Woman's Part: Feminist Criticism of Shakespeare* (Urbana: University of Illinois).

Blewitt, David (1986) 'Drama in Tudor Education: Education in Tudor Drama', University of Brisol PhD dissertation.

Bogin, Meg (1976) *The Women Troubadours* (New York: W. W. Norton).

Brooks, Peter (1985) *The Melodramatic Imagination: Balzac, Henry James, Melodrama and the Mode of Excess* (New York: Columbia University).

Brunner, Cornelia (1980) 'Roberta Sklar: Toward Creating a Women's Theatre', *The Drama Review*, vol 24, no. 2, June, 23–40.

Cantarella, Eva (1987) *Pandora's Daughters: The Role and Status of*

Women in Greek and Roman Antiquity, trans. Maureen B. Fant (Baltimore: John Hopkins University).

Case, Sue-Ellen (1985) 'Classic Drag: The Greek Creation of Female Parts', *Theatre Journal*, October, 317–27.

Castle, Terry (1986) *Masquerade and Civilization: The Carnivalesque in 18th Century English Culture and Fiction* (Stanford: Stanford University Press).

Castle, Terry (1982) 'Matters Not Fit to be Mentioned: Fielding's *The Female Husband*', *English Literary History*, vol. 49, 602–22.

Chambers, E. K. (1954) *The Mediaeval Stage* (London: Oxford University).

Chaudhuri, Una (1983) 'Pamela's Aunt: The Ideal Woman in Early Eighteenth Century Drama', paper presented at the Northeast Modern Language Association Convention, Erie Pennsylvania, April.

Chesler, Phyllis (1986) *Mothers on Trial: The Battle of Children and Custody* (New York: McGraw Hill).

Chinoy, Helen Krich and Jenkins, Linda Walsh (eds) (1981) *Women in American Theater* (New York: Crown).

Clark, Alice (1919) *Working Life of Women in the Seventeenth Century* (London: Cass).

Comer, Irene Forsyth (1979) '*Little Nell and the Marchioness*: Milestone in the Development of American Musical Comedy', Tufts University PhD dissertation.

Coss, Clare, Roberta Sklar, Sandra Segal (1983) 'Notes on the Women's Experimental Theatre' in Karen Malpede (ed.) *Women in Theatre: Compassion and Hope* (New York: Drama Books).

Cott, Nancy F. (1972) *Root of Bitterness: Documents of the Social History of American Women* (New York: F. P. Dutton).

Cotton, Nancy (1980) *Women Playwrights in England c. 1363–1750* (Lewisburg: Bucknell University).

Crow, Duncan (1978) *The Edwardian Woman* (New York: St. Martin's Press).

Dash, Irene G. (1980) 'A Penchant for Perdita on the Eighteenth-Century English Stage', in C. R. S. Lenz (ed.) *The Woman's Part: Feminist Criticism of Shakespeare* (Urbana: University of Illinois).

Davis, Natalie Zemon (1978) 'Women on Top: Symbolic Sexual Inversion and Political Disorder in Early Modern Europe', in Barbara A. Babcock (ed.) *The Reversible World: Symbolic Inversion in Art and Society* (Ithaca: Cornell University Press).

Dempsey, David (1968) *The Triumphs and Trials of Lotta Crabtree* (New York: William Morrow).

Dolan, Jill (1985) 'Gender Impersonation Onstage: Destroying or Maintaining the Mirror of Gender Roles', *Women and Performance: A Journal of Feminist Theory*, no. 4, 3–11.

Dubois, Ellen Carol (ed.) (1981) *Elizabeth Cady Stanton, Susan B. Anthony: Correspondence Writings, Speeches* (New York: Schocken Books).

Duby, Georges (1985) *The Knight, The Lady and the Priest*, trans. Barbara Bray (Harmondsworth: Penguin).

Duchartre, Pierre Louis (1966) *The Italian Comedy*, trans. Randolph T. Weaver (New York: Dover).

Dumas, Alexandre fils (1986) *La Dame Aux Camélias*, trans. David Coward (Oxford: Oxford University Press).

Durham, Carolyn A. (1984) 'Medea: Hero or Heroine?' *Frontiers*, vol. VIII, no. 1, 54–9.

Dusinberre, Juliet (1975) *Shakespeare and the Nature of Women*, (London: Macmillan).

Faderman, Lillian (1981) *Surpassing the Love of Men: Romantic Friendship and Love Between Women from the Renaissance to the Present* (New York: Morrow).

Fielding, Henry (1960) *The Female Husband and Other Writings*, ed. Claude E. Jones (Liverpool: Liverpool University Press).

Foley, Helene P. (1981) 'The Conception of Women in Athenian Drama', in Helene P. Foley (ed.) *Reflections of Women in Antiquity* (New York: Gordon & Breach Science).

Foucault, Michel (1973) *The Order of Things: An Archaeology of the Human Sciences* (New York: Vintage Books).

Fraser, Antonia (1984) *The Weaker Vessel: Woman's Lot in Seventeenth Century England* (London: Weidenfeld and Nicolson).

Freeburg, Victor Oscar (1965) *Disguise Plots in Elizabethan Drama: A Study in Stage Tradition* (New York: Blom).

French, Marilyn (1982) *Shakespeare's Division of Experience* (London: Abacus).

Gagen, Jean Elizabeth (1954) *The New Woman: English Drama 1600–1730*, (New York: Twayne).

Garafola, Lynn (1985–6) 'The Travesty Dancer in Nineteenth Century Ballet', *Dance Research Journal*, vol. 17, no. 2 and vol. 18, no. 1.

Garner, Shirley Nelson (1983) 'Male Bonding and the Myth of Women's Deception in Shakespeare's Play', paper delivered at the American Theatre Association Annual Convention, Minneapolis, August.

Gerould, Daniel C. (1983) 'The Americanization of Melodrama', in D. C. Gerould (ed.) *American Melodrama* (New York: P. A. J.).

Gilbert, Sandra M. (1982) 'Costumes of the Mind: Transvestism as Metaphor in Modern Literature', in Elizabeth Abel (ed.) *Writing and Sexual Difference* (Chicago: University of Chicago).

Gilder, Rosamond (1960) *Enter the Actress: The First Women in the Theater* (New York: Theatre Arts Books).

Goethe, Johann Wolfgang (1984) 'Women's Parts Played by Men in the Roman Theatre', trans. Isa Ragusa *Medieval English Theatre*, vol. 6, no. 2, December, 96–100.

Grimsted, David (1968) *Melodrama Unveiled: American Theater and Culture 1800–1850* (Chicago: Unverisity of Chicago Press).

Gubar, Susan (1981) 'Blessings in Disguise: Cross-Dressing as Re-Dressing for Female Modernists', *The Massachusetts Review*, vol. XXII, no. 3, Autumn, 477–508.

Guest Ivor (1966) *The Romantic Ballet in Paris* (London: Sir Isaac Pitman and Sons).

Hanna, Judith Lynne (1988) *Dance, Sex and Gender: Signs of Identity, Dominance, Defiance, and Desire* (Chicago and London: University of Chicago Press).

Hartnoll, Phyllis (ed.) (1967) *The Oxford Companion to the Theatre* (London: Oxford University Press).

Haskell, Molly (1973) *From Reverence to Rape: The Treatment of Women in the Movies* (New York: Holt, Rinehart & Winston).

Hawkins, Harriet (1975) 'The Victim's Side: Chaucer's *Clerk's Tale* and Webster's *Duchess of Malfi*', *Sign: Journal of Women in Culture and Society* vol. I, no. 2, 339–61.

Heinemann, Margot (1980), *Puritanism and Theatre* (Cambridge: Cambridge University Press).

Heinemann, Margot (1973) 'The Reactions of Women', in Brian Manning (ed.) *Politics, Religion and the English Civil War* (London: Edward Arnold).

Holledge, Julie (1981) *Innocent Flowers: Women in the Edwardian Theatre* (London: Virago).

Hunter, G. K. and S. K. (eds) *John Webster, A Critical Anthology* (London: Penguin).

James, Henry (1984) *The Tragic Muse* (Harmondsworth: Penguin).

Jameson, Elizabeth (1984) 'Women as Workers, Women as Civilizers: True Womanhood in the American West', *Frontiers* vol. VII, no. 3, 1–8.

Jardine, Lisa (1983) *Still Harping on Daughters: Women and Drama in the Age of Shakespeare* (Sussex: Harvester).

Johnson, Claudia D. (1984) *American Actress: Perspective on the Nineteenth Century* (Chicago: Nelson Hall).

Juvenal (1985) *The Sixteen Satires*, trans. Peter Green (Harmondsworth: Penguin).

Kaplan, E. Ann (1983) *Women and Film: Both Sides of the Camera* (New York: Methuen).

Kelly, Joan (1977) 'Did Women Have a Renaissance?', In Renate Bridenthal and Claudia Koonz (eds.) *Becoming Visible: Women in European History* (Boston: Houghton).

Kendall, Kathryn McQueen (1986) 'Theatre, Society and Women Playwrights in London from 1695 through the Queen Anne Era', University of Texas PhD dissertation.

Kent, Christopher (1977) 'Image and Reality: The Actress and Society', in Martha Vicinus (ed.) *A Widening Sphere: Changing Roles of Victorian Women* (Bloomington: Indiana University Press).

Keuls, Eva C. (1985) *The Reign of the Phallus: Sexual Politics in Ancient Athens* (New York: Harper and Row).

Keyssar, Helene (1984) *Feminist Theatre* (London: Macmillan).

Le Gallienne, Eva (1983) 'Acting Hamlet', in Karen Malpede (ed.) *Women in Theatre*: Compassion and Hope (New York: Drama Books).

Levinson, Leonard Louis (ed.) (1962) *The Memoirs of Jacques Casanova* (New York: Collier).

Lucas, R. Valerie (1988) '*Hic Mulier*: The Female Transvestite in Early Modern England', *Renaissance and Reformation*, vol. XXIV, no. 1, 65–84.

MacLean, Ian, (1977) *Woman Triumphant; Feminism in French Literature 1610–1652* (Oxford: Clarendon).

Maitland, Sara (1986) *Vesta Tilley* (London: Virago).

Maurier, George de (1895) *Trilby* (London: Osgoods, McIlvaine).

Maus,Katherine Eisaman (1978) ' "Playhouse Flesh and Blood": Sexual Ideology and the Restoration Actress', *English Literary History*, no. 46, 595–617.

McCluskie, Kathleen (1985) 'Drama and Sexual Politics: The Case of Webster's Duchess', in James Redmond (ed.) *Themes in Drama: Drama, Sex and Politics* (Cambridge: Cambridge University Press).

Merrill, Lisa (1984) 'Charlotte Cushman: American Actress on the Vanguard of New Roles for Women', New York University PhD dissertation.

Moore, Don D. (1966) *John Webster and His Critics 1617–1964* (Baton Rouge: Louisiana State University Press).

Muir, Lynette R. (1985) 'Women on the Medieval Stage: The Evidence from France', *Medieval English Theatre*, vol. 7, no. 2, December, 107–19.

Munk, Erika (1985a) 'Cross Left – Drag: 1. Men', *The Village Voice*, 5 February, 89–90.

Munk, Erika (1985b) "Cross Left – Drag: 2. Women", *The Village Voice*, 12 March, 79–80.

Munk, Erika (1986) 'The Rites of Women', *Performing Arts Journal*, vol. X, no. 2, 29, 35–42.

Natalle, Elizabeth J. (1985) *Feminist Theatre: A Study in Persuasion* (Metuchen, N J: Scarecrow).

Neuls-Bates, Carol (ed.) (1982) *Women in Music* (New York: Harper & Row).

Newton, Esther (1979) *Mother Camp: Female Impersonators in America* (Chicago: University of Chicago Press).

Nicoll, Allardyce (1928) *The History of Restoration Drama 1660–1700* (Cambridge: Cambridge University Press).

Nicoll, Allardyce (1963) *The World of Harlequin* (Cambridge: Cambridge University Press).

Nietzsche, Friedrich (1974) *The Gay Science*, trans. Walter Kaufman (New York: Vintage Books).

Ovid (1986) *Metamorphoses*, trans. Mary Innes (Harmondsworth: Penguin).

Phelan, Peggy (1988) 'Feminist Theory, Poststructuralism, and Perform-ance', *The Drama Review*, T117, Spring, 107–27.

Phillips, Henry (1980) *The Theatre and Its Critics in Seventeenth Century France* (Oxford: Oxford University Press).

Pisan, Christine de (1986) 'Christine's Response to the Treatise on the *Romance of the Rose* by John of Montreuil, June-July 1401: The First Extant Combative Document in the Debate', trans. Nadia Margolos, in Elizabeth A. Petroff (ed.) *Medieval Women's Visionary Literature* (Oxford: Oxford University Press).

Pope, Alexander (1956) *Correspondence*, (ed.) George Sherburn (Oxford: Oxford University Press).

Prosperi, Mario (1982) 'The Masks of Lipari', *The Drama Review*, vol. 26, no. 4, Winter, 25–36.

Rackin, Phyllis (1987) 'Androgny, Mimesis, and the Marriage of the Boy Heroine on the English Renaissance Stage', *PMLA*, January, 29–41.

Rastall, Richard (1985) 'Female Roles in All-Males Casts', *Medieval English Theatre* vol. 7, no. 1, July, 25–51.

Rendall, Jane (1985) *The Origins of Modern Feminism* (London: Macmillan).

Rosen, Marjorie (1975) *Popcorn Venus: Women, Movies and the American Dream* (London: Peter Owen).

Roth, Martha (1983) 'Notes Toward a Feminist Performance Aesthetic' *Women and Performance*: *A Journal of Feminist Theory*, vol. 1, no. 1, Spring/Summer, 5–14.

Rotman, Brian (1987) *Signifying Nothing*: *The Semiotics of Zero* (London: Macmillan).

Rourke, Constance (1928) *Troupers of the Gold Coast or the Rise of Lotta Crabtree* (New York: Harcourt, Brace, Javonovich).

Rowbotham, Sheila (1973) *Hidden from History* (London: Pluto Press).

Russo, Mary (1988) 'Female Grotesques: Carnival and Theory', in Teresa de Lauretis (ed.) *Feminist Studies/Critical Studies* (London: Macmillan).

Ryan, Mary P. (1975) *Womanhood in America*: *From Colonial Times to the Present* (New York: New Viewpoints).

Sedgwick, Eve Kosofsky (1985) *Between Men: English Literature and Male Homosocial Desire* (New York: Columbia University Press).

Shafer, Yvonne (1981) 'Women in Male Roles: Charlotte Cushman and Others', in Helen Krich Chinoy and Linda Walsh Jenkins (eds) *Women in American Theater* (New York: Crown).

Shelling, Felix E. (1971) *Foreign Influences in Elizabethan Plays* (New York: AMS Press).

Shepherd, Simon (1981) *Amazons and Warrior Women* (Sussex: Harvester).

Shepherd Simon, (1985) (ed.) *The Women's Sharp Revenge: Five Women's Pamphlets from the Renaissance* (London: Fourth Estate).

Stedman, Jane W. (1972) 'From Dame to Woman: W. S. Gilbert and Theatrical Transvestism', in Martha Vicinus (ed.) *Suffer and Be Still: Women in the Victorian Age* (Bloomington: Indiana University Press).

Stone, Lawrence (1965) *The Crisis of the Aristocracy, 1558–1641* (Oxford: Clarendon).

Stone, Lawrence (1977) *The Family, Sex and Marriage: In England 1500–1800* (New York: Harper).

Todd, Janet (1986) *Sensibility* (London: Methuen).

Trevelyan, G. M. (1963) *Illustrated British Social History: Vol. Three, The Eighteenth Century* (London: Reprint Society).

Twycross, Meg (1983) ' "Transvestism" in the Mystery Plays', *Medieval English Theatre*, vol. 5, no. 2, December, 123–80.

Ure, Peter (1974) 'The Widow of Ephesus: Some Reflections on an International Comic Theme', in J. C. Maxwell (ed.) *Elizabethan and Jacobean Drama Critical Essays* (Liverpool: Liverpool University Press).

184   *Bibliography*

Ward, Mrs Humphrey (1884) *Miss Bretherton* (London: Macmillan).
Warner, Marina (1978) *Alone of All Her Sex: The Myth and the Cult of the Virgin Mary* (London: Quartet).
Warner, Marina (1983) *Joan of Arc: The Image of Female Heroism* (Harmondsworth: Penguin).
Warner, Marina (1985) *Monuments and Maidens: The Allegory of the Female Form* (London: Weidenfeld and Nicolson).
Welter, Barbara (1973) 'The Cult of True Womanhood: 1820–1860', in Michael Gordon (ed.) *The American Family in Social-Historical Perspective* (New York: St. Martin's).
Wickham, Glynne (1980) *Early English Stages 1300–1660* (London: Routledge & Kegan Paul).
Williamson, Judith (1986) *Consuming Passions: The Dynamics of Popular Culture* (London: Marion Boyars).
Williman, Daniel (1986) *Legal Terminology: An Historical Guide to Technical Language of Law* (Canada: Broadview Press).
Wilson, John Harold (1958) *All the Kings Ladies: Actresses of the Restoration* (Chicago: University of Chicago Press).
Wilson, Penelope (1986) 'Feminism and the Augustans: Some Readings and Problems', *Critical Quarterly*, vol. 28, nos. 1 & 2, Spring/Summer, 80–92.
Wind, Edgar (1963) *Art and Anarchy* (London: J. M. Dent).
Woodbridge, Linda (1984) *Women and the English Renaissance: Literature and the Nature of Womankind, 1540–1620* (Urbana: University of Illionois Press).
Woolf, Virginia (1985) *A Room of One's Own* (London: Grafton).
Zeitlin, Froma I. (1978) 'The Dynamics of Misogyny: Myth and Myth-making in the *Oresteia*', *Aresthusa*, vol. II, 149–84.
Zeitlin, Froma I. (1981) 'Travesties of Gender and Genre in Aristophanes' *Thesmophoriazousae*' in Helene P. Foley (ed.) *Reflections of Women in Antiquity* (New York: Gordon and Breach Science).

Playscripts

Aeschylus (1983) *The Oresteian Trilogy* trans. Philip Vellacott (Harmondsworth: Penguin).
Anonymous (1969) *Swetman, the Woman-Hater, Arraigned By Women*, ed. Coryl Crandall (Purdue: Purdue University Studies).
Aristophanes (1979) *The Assemblywomen*, trans. David Barrett (Harmondsworth: Penguin).
Aristophanes (1975) *The Poet and the Women (Thesmophoriazusae)*, trans. David Barrett (Harmondsworth: penguin).
Beaumont, Francis, and Fletcher, John (1976) *Love's Cure, or, The Martial Maid*, ed. George Walton Williams, in *The Dramatic Works in The Beaumont and Fletcher Canon* (Cambridge: Cambridge University Press).
Belasco, David (1983) *The Girl of the Golden West*, in Daniel C. Gerould (ed.) *American Melodrama* (New York: PAJ).

Benmussa, Simone (1979) *The Singular Life of Albert Nobbs*, trans. Barbara Wright (London: John Calder).

Boesing, Martha (1979) *Dora Du Fran's Wild West Extravaganza, or, the Real Lowdown on Calamity Jane* (Minneapolis: unpublished manuscript).

Boesing, Martha (1985) *Antigone Too: Rites of Love and Defiance* (Minneapolis: unpublished manuscript).

Churchill, Caryl and Lan, David (1986) *A Mouthful of Birds* (London: Methuen).

Churchill, Caryl (1982) *Top Girls* (London: Methuen).

Cibber, Colley (1966) *The Careless Husband*, ed. William W. Appleton (Lincoln: University of Nebraska Press).

Cixous, Hélène (1979) *Portrait of Dora* (London: John Calder).

Collins, Kathleen (1986) *The Brothers*, in Margaret B. Wilkerson (ed.) *Nine Plays by Black Women* (New York: Mentor Books).

Coss, Clare, Segal, Sandra, Sklar Roberta (1983) *Electra Speaks*, video screening at American Theatre Association, Minneapolis, August 1983.

Davenant, William (1967) *Salmacida Spolia*, in *A Book of Masques* (Cambridge: Cambridge University Press).

Delano, Alonzo (1983) *A Live Woman In the Mines*, in Glenn Loney (ed.) *California Gold-Rush Plays* (New York: PAJ).

Dumas, Alexander fils (1976) *The Lady of the Camellias*, in James L. Smith (ed.) *Victorian Melodramas* (London: Dent).

Euripides (1980) *Orestes*, trans. Philip Vellacott, in *Orestes and Other Plays* (Harmondsworth: Penguin).

Euripides (1985) *Medea*, trans. Moses Hadas and John McLean, in Moses Hadas (ed.) *Ten Plays by Eurpides* (New York: Bantam Books).

Fornes, Maria Irene (1978) *Fefu and her Friends*, in *Performing Arts Journal*, Winter.

Gems, Pam (1985) *Three Plays*: *Piaf, Camille, Loving Women* (Harmondsworth: Penguin)

Gems, Pam (1982) *Queen Christina* (London: St Luke's Press).

Goldoni, Carlo (1982) *Mirandolina* (*La Locandiera*) trans, and ed. Frederick Davies, *Goldoni: Four Comedies* (Harmondsworth: Penguin).

Hayes, Catherine (1984) *Skirmishes* (London: Methuen).

Heywood, John (1962) *The Four PP.*, in Vincent F. Hopper (ed.) *Medieval Mysteries, Moralities and Interludes* (New York: Barron's Educational Series).

Hrotsvit [Roswitha] (1966) *Paphnutius*, trans Christopher St John in *The Plays of Roswitha* (New York: Benjamin Blom).

Jonson, Ben (1971) *Epicoene*, ed. Edward Partridge (New Haven: Yale University Press).

Merriam, Eve (1976) *The Club* (New York: Samuel French).

Middleton, Thomas and Dekker, Thomas (1976) *The Roaring Girl*, ed. Andor Gomme (London:Ernest Benn).

Mueller, Lavonne (1984) *Little Victories*, in Julia Miles (ed.) *The Women's Project 2* (New York: PAJ).

Muinzer, Philomena (1983) *Together Against Him* (London: unpublishd manuscript).

186   *Bibliography*

Norman, Marsha (1983) *'night, Mother* (New York: Hill and Wang).
Orgel, Stephen (ed.) *The Complete Masques of Ben Jonson* (New Haven: Yale University Press).
Shakespeare, William (1959) *The Complete Works of William Shakespeare*, ed. W. J. Craig (London: Oxford University Press).
Shange, Ntozake (1976) *For Colored Girls Who Have Considered Suicide/ When the Rainbow is Enuf* (New York: Macmillan).
Shenkar, Joan (1980) *Signs of Life*, in Julia Miles (ed.) *The Women's Project Anthology* (New York: PAJ).
Sklar, Roberta (1983) "Sisters" or Never Trust Anyone Outside the Family" *Women and Performance: A Journal of Feminist Theory* vol. I, no. 1, Spring/Summer, 58–70.
Strindberg, August (1983) *Miss Julie*, trans. Peter Watts (Harmondsworth: Penguin).
Sweet, Nancy (1987) *Camille*, production seen at the Old Red Lion Theatre, Islington, London, November 1987.
Terry, Megan and Metcalf, JoAnne (1983) *Mollie Bailey's Traveling Family Circus featuring Scenes from the Life of Mother Jones* (New York; Broadway Play Publishing).
Webster, John (1953) *The Duchess of Malfi*, ed. Fred B. Millet (Illinois: AHM Publishing).
Wycherly, William (1953) *The Country Wife*, in *Restoration Plays* (London: J. M. Dent).

Index